China in Comparative Perspective

China in Comparative Perspective

Stephan Feuchtwang
Hans Steinmüller

London School of Economics, UK

World Scientific

NEW JERSEY • LONDON • SINGAPORE • BEIJING • SHANGHAI • HONG KONG • TAIPEI • CHENNAI • TOKYO

Published by

World Scientific Publishing Europe Ltd.
57 Shelton Street, Covent Garden, London WC2H 9HE
Head office: 5 Toh Tuck Link, Singapore 596224
USA office: 27 Warren Street, Suite 401-402, Hackensack, NJ 07601

Library of Congress Cataloging-in-Publication Data
Names: Feuchtwang, Stephan, author. | Steinmüller, Hans, author.
Title: China in comparative perspective / by Stephan Feuchtwang, London School of Economics, UK; Hans Steinmüller, London School of Economics, UK.
Description: New Jersey : World Scientific, 2017. | Includes index.
Identifiers: LCCN 2016041700| ISBN 9781786342386 (hc : alk. paper) | ISBN 9781786342393 (pbk : alk. paper)
Subjects: LCSH: China--History. | China--Politics and government. | China--Social conditions. | China--Economic conditions. | Comparative government. | Comparative economics. | Comparative civilization. | Social institutions--Cross-cultural studies.
Classification: LCC DS735 .F44 2017 | DDC 951--dc23
LC record available at https://lccn.loc.gov/2016041700

British Library Cataloguing-in-Publication Data
A catalogue record for this book is available from the British Library.

Desk Editors: Herbert Moses/Mary Simpson

Typeset by Stallion Press
Email: enquiries@stallionpress.com

Printed in Singapore by B & Jo Enterprise Pte Ltd

About the Authors

Stephan Feuchtwang is an Emeritus Professor in the Department of Anthropology, London School of Economics. His main area of research has been China, most recently on neighbourhood planning and governance in Chinese cities. Particular research interests include popular religious festivals and the state, charismatic leadership and followership and racism, its policing and administration, and in the formation of occupational ghettoes, reinforcing various ways of categorising populations, from skin to ethnicised religion.

Hans Steinmüller has conducted long-term fieldwork in the Enshi region of Hubei Province. The main object of his research is the ethics of everyday life in rural China. Both have also written about the nature of the Chinese state on topics such as gambling, rural development, and Chinese geomancy (*fengshui*). Hans is the convenor of the MSc programme 'China in Comparative Perspective'.

Acknowledgement

The course upon which this book is based demanded constant rethinking over the years. We hope that anyone using this book will also find that it asks questions and suggests ideas that demand constant rethinking of what is Chinese. We are particularly grateful to the rethinking and contributions made by our two teaching fellows, James Johnston and Andrea Pia. They are virtual co-authors of some of what we have written.

Over the decade of teaching, our students have stimulated us with their own questions and contributions, including their own different perspectives and their knowledge of China. They are of course too numerous to mention by name, but we thank them anonymously for their generous participation.

Contents

Chapter 1

Introduction

You may read the chapters of this book as a textbook. It is based on 10 years of teaching the core course of a Master's degree on China in comparative perspective. Each chapter expounds a topic in the study of China, with appropriate comparators, just as we taught it. The book and the course take up the challenge of asking whether there is anything unique or exceptional in the civilisation, cultures, politics, economies, social institutions, legal system, and states to be found in China. We hope it also challenges readers, as it has us and our students, to deepen and question their own ideas about China.

Every chapter introduces a number of different approaches to the topic; different general treatments and their particular applications to analyses of China and comparable countries. You will note that in most cases these are given some historical depth as well as dealing with contemporary China, chiefly the People's Republic of China.

You may also read this book simply as an in-depth introduction to the study of China, appropriate to a number of social science disciplines ranging through economic history, international history, political science, sociology, demography, religious studies, and anthropology. As anthropologists, we have stretched ourselves to include the best writing in the other disciplines on China and its contrasting or similar countries of comparison.

The studies that we introduce in each chapter are available in English. Only in one or two cases are they only in Chinese, not translated. This matches the perspective we offer: China seen both by insiders (Chinese) writing in English and outsiders who read and speak Chinese and making explicit what might be left implicit without comparison. Many of the students taking our course have in fact been of Chinese origin, bringing themselves out of their home context and more or less willingly taken even further out by this course to view their own histories and country as one among others. To those who have come or are coming to China from outside, the problems are not those of assuming familiarity but those of treating China as exotic. In both cases, China or the West would be a contrasting other. We can illustrate this briefly by two classical sociologists of China, one European, and the other Chinese: Max Weber and Fei Xiaotong.

Max Weber and Fei Xiaotong

Let us consider them in chronological order, Weber working in the 1910s and 1920s, Fei in the 1940s. Both are still relevant.

Weber's starting point was to explain the emergence of industrial capitalism in Europe and nowhere else. He asked what orientation was there to stimulate large-scale capitalist enterprise, uniquely in Europe and among Europeans in the USA of the seventeenth century. What was the orientation, which means an action-guiding worldview, bearing such an affinity with capitalist endeavour? This was the key enquiry of the new sociology of action, which he created in the same years. Before embarking on his comparison, he had already found his answer in his book *The Protestant Ethic and the Spirit of Capitalism* (1905). But to be sure that the Calvinist ethic and its affinity with the spirit of capitalist enterprise were uniquely seventeenth century European, he then proceeded to undertake a comparison in the sociology of religion. He confined himself to what he called the world religions, which were later called by his follower, the philosopher and psychologist Karl Jaspers, the 'axial' civilisations. These are religions conveying a sense of moral humanity that could be used in judgement of worldly action and reality. He found that none generated the abstract and anxiety-inducing drive that Calvinism did to test whether one had been saved in the results of worldly action. His reasoning will be further expounded in Chapter 3 where we reconsider the comparative project of the conditions for the existence of industrial capitalism.

Weber proposed a religious condition necessary for the existence of industrial capitalism. But he had already answered it before he conducted his comparison. That is one rather obvious methodological flaw in his endeavour. But his reading of sources, all in translation into European languages, was prodigious and many of his contrasts are still of great interest, including his contrast of Calvinist individualist innovation with Confucian perfection of self through a conservative adjustment to change in the world.

The other flaw in his method is that it is Eurocentric, as he makes quite clear in what he sought to confirm, namely that what is necessary for capitalism is a certain kind of individualism that was unique to Europe. That clarity is a virtue compared to the assumption that this individualism is universally human and the basis of all economics or in social psychology that compares individualism with collectivism — the latter being both pre-modern and also still to be found in contemporary cultures, particularly Asian.

Weber's sophisticated but still Eurocentric comparison can fruitfully be compared with an equally sophisticated but Sinocentric comparison, accomplished by Fei Xiaotong in the 1940s. Fei was a sociologist and anthropologist who had completed a PhD under the tuition of pioneering anthropologists Bronislaw Malinowski and Raymond Firth at the London School of Economics in 1938. He had direct experience of social life, not only in the city of London but also in small town and rural England and then in the USA. So, although these experiences were not prolonged nor were they undertaken as fieldwork, he had direct experience to add to his reading of English-language publications for comparison with his fieldwork in China and his extensive reading of Chinese philosophical classics and histories. In China in the late 1940s, he composed a series of essays on the essential character of Chinese society and what was needed to strengthen it after European military humiliation and Japanese military occupation and bring it into the industrial world. The book of these essays, originally published in 1947, was translated into English by Gary Hamilton and Wang Zheng and published in 1992 as *From the Soil: The Foundations of Chinese Society* (Fei, 1992). As the translators write in their introduction (p. 4), the essays were an 'effort to construct a non-Western theoretical foundation for a sociology of Chinese society'. This foundation is still a key reference point for anthropologists and sociologists of China, Chinese and non-Chinese. Fei contrasted two kinds of moral person, the Chinese and the Western Christian selves. The Chinese self is always in relationships that are asymmetrical, or hierarchical, by age, gender (male over female), reciprocal friendship and political authority and loyalty, as expounded in Confucian classical philosophy and also to be found in what was still mainly rural practice. Society is made from the networks, based on these relationships, created by individual Chinese selves always in a deferential or reciprocal dyad. In contrast, according to Fei, the Western Christian self is the same one autonomous conscience in a social world of organisations and institutions, of work and other roles, in which that individual is an active member and has joined with others in creating and reproducing the organisations in which the individual is a member.

Note how far his differentiated self and its created network is from the Western stereotype of collectivist Asians. Note too that his version of the Christian individual could be a less well-specified version of Weber's Calvinist individual. For Fei as well as Weber, with whose sociology Fei was familiar, characterisation of the essential Chinese social self is an ideal type. An ideal type is a sociological construct, empirically based and useful for the interpretation of observed social action and its results but with no claim to its existence in its pure form. Fei's ideal typical Western individual is useful as a contrast for what he is mainly after, which is a Chinese theoretical basis for the analysis of Chinese society. He is not interested in an equally searching analysis of society in the UK or the USA. His stereotype is a rejection of the relevance of the Western individual to the analysis of Chinese society and that is his one and only project.

After a visit to the USA in the 1940s, Fei wrote a short essay offering a further contrast, reprinted in 1989 (Fei, 1989). In it, he writes of his discomfort in US houses. What causes his discomfort is the absence of ghosts — by which he means the familiar ghosts of a long-settled family home, such as his own in Jiangnan, in the Yangtze delta region. The implications of this simple contrast are great, indicating two kinds of nations and their societies: in one, people stay in or know where to return as a home-place, having an ancestral sense of family history, linked to national history; in the other, people constantly move, settling anew, maintaining a nation that knows itself as a land of opportunity.

So, we have in these two master sociologists a self-confessed Eurocentric proposal of the reason for the emergence in Europe of industrial capitalism and a self-confessed Sinocentric basis for the eventual industrialisation of China in terms of its own moral selfhood, not conforming to the European. Each raises issues of the institutional basis for industrialisation and its economy that are still live. Similarly, each raises issues of the pre-requisites and effects of modernisation (industrialisation, labour migration to wage work, and urbanisation) on family formation and transformation. All these issues will be raised in detail in subsequent chapters. Each makes possibly valid claims about orientations, or ideologies of aspiration, in Europe and China.

Here, the point of introducing them is to start a methodological discussion of how to conduct comparison. The virtue of both these sociologists is that they make the comparison explicit instead of assuming the world to be like their own societies and judging the rest of the world by implication better or worse, more or less (developed, civilised, etc.). But both are 'centric' in assuming from the beginning their own starting point, conducting the comparison simply to elaborate that starting point and not opening it out to being questioned.

Orientalism and Occidentalism

Comparison is based upon a ground of similarity and a contrast of differences. But because the comparison is never the first, it comes laden with the results of previous comparisons and with generalising concepts and theories of the differences found. So, treating something in China as a case study of a more general topic, such as politics or religion, is by implication a comparative study because the concept or category 'politics' or 'religion' is meant to apply anywhere. Then the comparison can become a questioning of the very categories themselves.

There is also another more historical ground for comparison, where similarities are the result of long contact and mutual influence. So, for instance, there can be comparisons within a region of mutual influences or a region of the dominance of a civilisation. And now, the historical spread over four centuries from Europe of industrial capitalism, scientific knowledge and the modern state, and even more recently, the accelerated pace of the migration of capital, labour, consumer products and digital media have increased the grounds of historical similarity on which comparisons can be based.

We are used to thinking that what we can call 'the modern', its main economy (capitalism), its knowledge products (science and technology), and its chief political institution (the nation-state), spread to encompass the globe from Western Europe. This same habit of historical thinking from origins brings with it the overwhelming temptation to measure the world by Western European standards, justified by the very spread of European institutions with imperialism from Western Europe and later from its main ex-colony, the USA.

Even those who gave intellectual and inspirational leadership to anti-imperialist movements, like Gandhi in India, Mao in China, Franz Fanon in North Africa, and Nelson Mandela in South Africa, have taken up traditions stemming from the European Enlightenment — humanism, Marxism, the secular state, the sovereignty of peoples — and accused the imperial powers of betraying their own civilisation. But in this very fact we are brought short because they question some if not all the assumptions of the European Enlightenment even though they are bound by the spread of European knowledge and authority (political, military, and scientific).

The introductions to Breckenridge and van der Veer (eds.) (1993) and to Carrier (ed.) (1995) make a valid point that Western studies of others have been framed EITHER as the negative of their own idealised self-images, OR as romanticised images of their own dystopian (the opposite of utopian) view of modern Western materialistic civilisation. In other words, in the knowledge that accompanied Western imperialism, a double pairing occurred in social sciences and humanities, of Occidentalism and Orientalism. In one, the Capitalist (the progressive, the historical, the materialist, the rational and the secular) is contrasted with the pre-capitalist, the primitive, the good but childish, and the fixed and static East. In the other, the more spiritual East, the more in-touch with body and natural surroundings, a spirituality and oneness is contrasted with the materialism of progress.

Euro-American social sciences provide more analytic dichotomies of the advanced and the backward, the free and the despotic, organic division of labour and mechanical (segmentary) division of labour, society based on contract and law versus society based on status and hierarchy, abstract versus intuitive or pragmatic thinking; adversarial habits of discourse versus reference to authority. These dichotomies are like West/East, or like modern/traditional, or modern/primitive. They seem to refer to all societies and all histories in their scope. But do they when held up to the light of comparison? Is there not a huge scope for criticising them by findings of much that does not fit?

Both these introductions pick out one of the most worked-out anthropologies of such a dichotomy in the books of a French anthropologist Louis Dumont. His knowledge of European Enlightenment and post-Enlightenment thought was extensive and enabled him to produce a much more worked-out dichotomy than his predecessors, contrasting the egalitarian and individualist ideology of Western Europe with the Indian jajmani system of local castes ranked according to an ideology of purity and pollution.

Both introductions also take as their touchstone a book that has made one of the deepest impacts on cultural studies and anthropology, Said's (1978) *Orientalism*. Said's main idea is that the studies of the Orient confirm and elaborate the East as politically despotic, economically stagnant and dependent, and psychologically given to hedonism and patriarchy, treating it as the other of the European Enlightenment. His book is a warning: We must be careful not to reproduce these unthinking, uncritical dichotomies. This warning has become the touchstone or point of critical departure for subsequent writings.

Breckenridge and van der Veer, and Carrier take a further step and show how this idealised self-image of the West, which they call Occidentalism, is reversed in very interesting ways in the self-other dichotomies of the non-Western peoples that anthropologists have studied and which are the subjects of the chapters of the two books they edited. These chapters stress the agency of the colonised and show that what the colonised produced, their various nationalisms, were a response to and an alternate, non-European version of the European concepts of culture and civilisation. In response to European imperialism and its self-image, they produced their own self-images in their own versions of a (national) civilisation and culture, such as Hinduism, in which they took pride and which they posited as their own, eternal and universal humanity. These are counter assertions of the negative images of the other produced in the imperialist West, just like the counter assertion of Blackness in the USA or South Africa, or, in French-speaking Africa, Negritude. These counter assertions have usually accompanied a further doubling within their own countries, in India of tribals to be Hinduised or civilised, and within China intellectual romanticisation of peasants and the non-Han minorities on the one hand, and on the other, treating them as backward.

Another and equally important theme of the chapters of these two books is that not only do these counter assertions produce their own forms of Orientalism, they also produce positive and negative idealisations of the Occident — whether it be of technological and scientific achievement, of freedom and democracy, or of socialism, on the one hand, or on the other hand of gross materialism, individualism, and greed.

What lessons can we learn from all these Western and other dichotomies?

- That comparison should avoid dichotomies. For instance, we could establish quite a number of different ideologies of hierarchy, not just that exemplified by caste.
- That self/othering is a fact of life, worth studying in context and as context-dependent, but not as a fixing of identities.
- That one major phenomenon of the spread of capitalism and its nationalisms has been the self-consciousness of what was distinctive and taken for granted, turning it into 'culture', 'identity' or 'tradition'.

Occidentalism in China

Dai Jinhua of Peking University, in her foreword to Chen Xiaomei (1994) discusses the tendency of looking West, the Occidentalism, of Chinese political leaders. She says they exhibit a layered set of appropriations of the West that are at the same time misreadings. Lenin and then Stalin misread Marx in their different ways, insisting that a world anti-capitalist revolution could be launched in economically 'backward' countries where the industrial proletariat was tiny, even without the aid of proletarian movements in the industrialised countries. Then Mao misread Lenin and Stalin, producing an unyielding nationalism that was anti-imperialist and anti-capitalist while wanting to take part in global capitalism. Each misreading was given out as orthodoxy. Each orthodoxy disguised something glaring and crucial: on the one hand, divisions within the socialist international, on the other hand, devastations in China, such as the Cultural Revolution.

Each is at once a misreading, an appropriation, and a disguise. Currently in Chinese government, there is misreading and appropriation not of Marx, Lenin and Stalin, but of neo-liberal economics and political philosophy as a programme for the state's cultivation of corporate capital while continuing the former, Cold War stance of socialism and nationalism. Interestingly, this leaves people like Dai Jinhua and Chen Xiaomei, according to Dai herself, with the task "to self-consciously carry on the historical legacy of socialism, clearing the historical debt of the socialist era, and to directly combat the course of global capitalism while refusing to cede authority to the [Chinese] political regime" (p. xii). It also means exposing what the misread adulation of global capitalism and pride in China's economic growth performance disguises — growing disparities of income in China and the world.

An example of Occidentalism in China was the TV series twice broadcast in 1988, called River Elegy (*He Shang*), about which Chen Xiaomei writes in Chapter 2. It appears to be, but it is not simply a eulogy for turning away from the dead end of the yellow earth and toward the blue oceans of openness to the West, in particular the USA. She points out that it is also an ironic rewriting of eulogies of glorious and ancient China, stemming from the loess lands of the northern plain and the Yellow River, including the official nationalism of the black-haired race stemming from the Yellow Emperor. Its Occidentalism is not simply an advocacy of Eurocentric neo-liberalism, it is as much a plea for openness and internal criticism, another kind of patriotism, one that seeks spiritual rejuvenation.

Another example of Chinese Occidentalism is described in Chapter 7, where Chen Xiaomei discusses novels and stories about Chinese emigrants' successes in the USA, designed for readers in China, stories of sexual freedom and money-making. Chen Xiaomei reads these stories against the background of anti-colonialism and standing up against the humiliation of China by imperialist powers, saying they defy the racism and Eurocentrism of foreigners. She also points out their iconoclastic relation to Chinese official ideology, yet they show pride in being a Chinese success abroad as another kind of patriotism.

These are exemplary because they are studies of Occidentalism as a phenomenon, but not depending on it or reproducing it as a methodological assumption.

These then are some of the challenges of comparison that the following chapters of this book take up.

Summary of the Chapters

Chapter 2: Empire and Bureaucracy

This chapter discusses two central features of Chinese history: the Chinese empire and its bureaucracy. The continuity of both seems to mark a singularity in world history, but they can be usefully compared with other empires, particularly the Roman empire and its successors in Europe. The history of the dynasties presents serious questions about the Sinocentrism of imperial Chinese historians, both Chinese and non-Chinese, as well as a source for a contemporary doctrine of a Chinese world order.

Chapter 3: The Great Divergence: Industrial Revolution

Given that China was relatively advanced in terms of economic and scientific development for centuries, why did the industrial revolution first take place in Europe? This chapter outlines the main contours of this comparison, its scales and scopes, focusing on investment in production, scientific development and inventions, and asking whether we can specify particular institutions necessary and sufficient for industrialisation.

Chapter 4: Demographic Transition

This chapter outlines the eventual introduction of steam-based industry to the Chinese economy, in which the main comparators are Russia, Japan and India. It raises questions of the comparison and universality of 'modernity' in family form, individualism, and the demographic transition, in which the comparison is between China and Europe and North America.

Chapter 5: Religion and Civilisation

One central distinction that has been made in comparative religion is that between universal religions, such as Christianity, and folk religion, magic, and superstition. This distinction is contrasted with anthropological definitions of religion that focus on the importance of ritual. This leads to a discussion of Chinese religions focusing on the place of literacy and writing. It also relates the 'invention of Confucianism' to the modern category of religion and compares the role of spirituality in the development of secular governments in India and China.

Chapter 6: Statehood and National Independence

This chapter presents theories of the historical development of nationalism, which dwell on print capitalism, industrialisation, anti-feudalism and anti-colonialism. The merits of each are discussed for the case of China, specifically in comparison with India. Modern nationalism is also related to the formation of modern subjectivity, which is discussed in the context of cultural diversity, mass literacy, and the management of memory in state patriotism.

Chapter 7: Revolution and Maoism

The social history, sociology and political theories of the self-named revolutions are first considered. Then we turn to what might have been peculiar to the Chinese revolution and to Maoism in particular and the capacity of the Chinese Communist Party (CCP) to mobilise popular support. Maoism may be a prime example of partisan war.

Chapter 8: Socialism

This chapter introduces debates in the sociology and political science of socialism. Its main topics are the distinction between 'reds' and 'experts' in China, and the comparison between Stalinism in the Soviet Union and Maoism in China, focusing on the organisation and ideology of production and class identity.

Chapter 9: Post-Socialism

This chapter discusses the changes that the Chinese economy and politics underwent in the 1980s and 1990s. The main debates about the transition from socialism deal with China's relative economic success and the changes in the political regime, including questions of social pluralism and managed authoritarianism. The main comparator is Russia, but other post-socialist countries are also drawn upon.

Chapter 10: Property Relations and China's Contemporary Economy

Too often predictions of the collapse of the Chinese economy and its polity are based on comparison of (some) facts with an ideal of how a market economy (or an 'efficient') economy works. This chapter will counter these shallow and false comparisons with a comparison between the reform process in Russia and China, and focus in particular on institutions of ownership and managerial control, on how the Communist party has conducted economic policy and what means of governance in its implementation are at the disposal of local cadres and officials and their relations with businesses and entrepreneurs.

Chapter 11: The Countryside and Migration

Both in political ideology and in theory, the idea of the peasant brought about major changes in the traditions of agrarian China and in what its farmers might have in common with peasantry throughout the world. Then, turning peasants into collective farmers and keeping them at home during the decades of collectivisation in China created layers of new over older identifications, which became explicit in the course of decollectivisation. As the economy, industrialisation and urbanisation grew, another worldwide phenomenon occurred in China: massive rural-to-urban migration. In this chapter, we ask whether there are any Chinese characteristics of a peasant economy (a mixture of subsistence and marketing) and of rural–urban migration.

Chapter 12: The City

Capitalist industrialisation separates workspaces from home and work time from leisure. We note modifications to this generalisation in India as well as China. Then we bring the Soviet Union into the comparison of the partial unification of domestic residence and workspaces in the Soviet Union and complete unification in China of a command economy. But the greatest growth of industry and cities in China has taken place in the years of the re-separation of work and residence. Have Chinese cities, from their financial districts to their migrant workers' dormitories, become the same as every other city in the world?

Chapter 13: The Family and Gender

Familism and patriarchy are ways of characterising Chinese kinship and kinship-derived relations, including those of political rule. Studies of the practical realities of domestic and interpersonal relations qualify but do not contradict this characterisation. But this way of comparing Chinese kinship with other kinship systems is merely the background to our main question in this chapter, which is whether generalisations about modernisation (wage work and urban residence), in creating small families and an individualistic self, apply well to China. Has modernisation changed gender and generational relations in China and does the filial self persist?

Chapter 14: Schooling

Mass literacy through a schooling system is characteristic of most modern states. China is no exception, but it has its own history of civilisation. How that has fed into the teaching of China as a nation, particularly through the teaching of history is the main subject of comparison with other school systems in this chapter. Learning through non-curricular activities, both at home and at school, is also compared using theories of practice and of distinction. Schooling sets up a particularly steep hierarchy in China, of aspirations to social mobility entailing relations of mutual sacrifice between child and parents and grandparents. Is this a developmental stage?

Chapter 15: Civil Society and Political Society

Our main comparator and contrast, both in the development of theory and in political practice, is India. Chinese traditions of deference and expectations of morally trustworthy leadership are bases for mounting serious questions about the applicability of the ideals and theories of civil society to China. A different critique is mounted on the basis of Indian political practice, stemming from British rule and the struggles for independence. We put the two together. The idea of the public sphere and its translation into Chinese is another way of seeing how China differs from the Euro-North American political theoretical tradition. Observations of non-governmental organisations and grassroots public spaces are the main testing grounds of the questions raised.

Chapter 16: Rule of Law

Starting from the classic opposition between Confucian and Legalist schools of thought, this chapter deals with legal discourse and practice in China. The importance of the rule of law in the development of the modern nation-state is discussed with reference to and contrast with India. Contemporary legal practice is related to political rule in different ways in each country, in the ways it is socially embedded and subject to the exercise of moral sovereignty.

Chapter 17: Democracy

This chapter sets out liberal, republican and participatory models of democracy and different theories about the historical development of democracy. These are then applied to Chinese theories of democracy (including Maoist 'people's democracy') and the development of governance and political participation. The chapter also compares contemporary democratic practice in India, China, and elsewhere.

Chapter 18: Conclusion

The conclusion relates the contents of the book to a general outline of comparative social science. The benefits of this method are illustrated with key examples from the book.

Core Readings

Breckenridge, C. A., and van der veer P. (eds.) 1993. *Orientalism and the Postcolonial Predicament: Perspectives on South Asia*. Philadelphia: University of Pennsylvania Press.

Carrier, J. G. (ed.) 1995. *Occidentalism: Images of the West*. Oxford: Oxford University Press (Introduction, also read the chapter on Japan by Creighton).

Chen Xiaomei 1994. *Occidentalism: A Theory of Counter-Discourse in Post-Mao China*. Oxford: Oxford University Press (Foreword by Dai Jinhua, and Chapters 2 and 7).

Further Readings

Dubs, H. H. 1953. Review of the religion of China, confucianism and taoism by Max Weber. Translated and edited by Hans H. Gerth, *Philosophy,* **28**(105), pp. 187–189.

Fei Xiaotong 1992 [1948]. *From the Soil, the Foundations of Chinese Society: A Translation of Fei Xiaotong's Xiangtu Zhongguo, with an Introduction and Epilogue*. Berkeley: University of California Press, pp. 37–44 and 60–70 (Chapters 1 and 4).

Fei Xiaotong 1989. Land without ghosts. In R. D. Arkush and L. O. Lee (eds.), *Land Without Ghosts: Chinese Impressions of America from the Mid-nineteenth Century to the Present*. Berkeley: University of California Press.

Said, E. W. 1985 [1978]. *Orientalism*. London: Penguin.

Steinmüller, H. 2011. The reflective peephole method: Ruralism and awkwardness in the ethnography of rural China. *Australian Journal of Anthropology*, **22**(2), pp. 220–235.

van der Sprenkel, Otto B. 1964. Max Weber on China. *History and Theory,* **3**(3), pp. 348–370.

Yang, C. K. 1951. Introduction. In *The Religion of China: Confucianism and Taoism*, by Max Weber, Transl. Hans H. Gerth, New York: The Free Press, pp. xii–xliii.

Chapter 2

Empire and Bureaucracy

In 1793, the English King George III sent an ambassador, George Macartney, to meet with the Chinese emperor Qianlong. The task Macartney was entrusted with was to establish diplomatic and commercial relations. The encounter, however, ended in a series of 'misunderstandings' between the British delegation and the Chinese court: Macartney refused to kowtow in front of the Chinese emperor, and Qianlong refused to accept the presents of the British delegation.

Fundamental 'misunderstandings' in this encounter had to do with the meanings of 'ritual', 'ceremony' and 'business'. What Macartney understood to be 'presents' to a foreign dignitary, were supposed to be 'tributes' to the sovereign of the central realm from the Chinese perspective. Whereas the British wanted to 'talk business', with the aim of allowing British trade access to Chinese ports, the Chinese court saw them as 'barbarians' who were unable to adopt appropriate attitudes in the ceremonial realm. Ultimately, this famous encounter can be seen as a conflict between the Chinese world system of *Tianxia* (All Under Heaven) and an emerging European system of sovereign states that were connected through diplomatic relations (on the Macartney embassy, see Sahlins, 1994, 2005; Hevia, 1995).

This chapter deals with the long-term history of the Chinese state as an empire. It will focus on the comparative history of empires, on the bureaucracy that upheld the empire, and on the cosmological patterns that held it together. It will point towards some possible comparisons (especially with the Roman empire), and emphasise some particularities of the

Chinese imperial bureaucracy. The last sections deal with the legacies of empire and imperial bureaucracy in modern China.

The long-standing history of the empire and its bureaucracy are crucial features that set China apart from other countries and regions. In this chapter, the imperial bureaucracy will be presented in a rather unitary and general way, in particular focusing on its organisational form, the tribute system, and the accompanying worldview. But it should become clear that these are 'ideal-types', that is, models which in idealised form represent some core features, but which are never the same as (messy) reality.

Empire: China and Rome

There are numerous definitions of 'empire', but perhaps the central element of most definitions is that empires see themselves as the centre of the world and make claims to universal rule. Empires are states that encompass different groups, set off from the central ruling lines of descent.

The historian of Russia, Lieven (2000), suggests a helpful comparison between the Roman and the Chinese empires. In principle, empires can try to assimilate outsiders or exclude them. Both Rome and China mainly tried to assimilate outsiders by what he, in his comparative framework, calls 'culture' but which in those empires was thought to be the apex of humanity, a universal 'civilisation' defined in Roman or Chinese terms. In principle, anyone could become "Roman" or "Chinese", only by learning the culture; in turn, both empires shared a similar sense of cultural arrogance towards barbarians outside their realm. But there were also remarkable differences in the intellectual traditions and cosmologies that underpinned such a sense of superiority. Even in classical Rome and Han dynasty China, the difference between a focus on law and dogma, on the one hand, and appropriate behaviour and ritual, on the other, was already present. In China, a bureaucracy was ultimately unified in the figure of the emperor, who was both the highest priest and official. He was supported by a mandarin elite that was meant to guarantee moral order and cosmic harmony.

This was based on two doctrines. One was that the emperor act as 'Son of Heaven' — the chief mediator between humanity and the celestial forces and principles of the cosmos. Such a concept of the 'Son of Heaven' had existed since the Zhou dynasties (tenth century BCE). The second doctrine is that the ruler should be a sage (*sheng*) and that his main advisors, the literate elite, should have undergone self-cultivation and aspire to sagehood. Following from those two doctrines, events and conditions of imperial rule should indicate that the ruler is a sage and has the mandate of Heaven (*tianming*). If the subjects of the empire suffer abnormal hardship, and the imperial court and administrative bureaucracy are ridden with corrupt officials, and great natural, disruptive events are occurring, the emperor's sagehood and legitimacy can be questioned and he needs to heed the advice of his sage elite, in particular a civil institution called the Censorate (*dachayuan*) — otherwise, such doubts might lead to chaos and rebellion.

In contrast to the relative contempt for the military that the Chinese civilian elite exhibited, in Rome, the governing elite itself was a military aristocracy. While both empires always had to guard themselves against military revolt, a substantially weaker role of the military in China resulted in different dynamics of civilian–military relations.

Lieven (2000, 27ff.) goes on to discuss a number of reasons for the predominance of empire in East Asia after the fall of the Han dynasty, against the collapse of the empire in Europe. The relative continuity of the empire in China might be, after all, just based on a series of historical contingencies. Both empires were vulnerable to invasion by nomadic neighbours, yet in China the empire would be reunited by its Northern neighbours. But there are also a number of identifiable social and political differences that set both empires apart. Since the Qin (the first but brief unifying dynasty) reforms, China had a relatively unified script. Yet, Europe also had the Latin script, which continued to be used by intellectuals until modernity. Empires in East Asia and in Europe faced continuous external threats: the 'barbarians' of central Asia, and Islam in Spain. One core difference is perhaps the unifying ideologies of monotheism and Confucianism. It might be argued that the monotheistic universalist religious culture of Europe bred ideological explosions, whereas the Confucian political culture of East Asia emphasised correct behaviour and obedience. The ideals and interests of the Confucian scholar-official elite were closely linked to the empire, and reinforced through the centralised examination system. The focus on the 'Son of Heaven', who united political and spiritual authority contrasted with the emerging division between religious and political authority in Europe. The relative continuity of empire in China contrasted with an emerging competition between states, and a balance of power, in Europe.

Chinese Power Inside: The Imperial Bureaucracy

One central feature of the history of the Chinese empire was the relative success and continuity of the imperial bureaucracy. Yet, perhaps, the notions that have been developed on the basis of European historical experiences are not adequate for the study of the Chinese imperial bureaucracy.

We have to question the classical Weberian categories of bureaucratic rule before we can address the Chinese bureaucracy. Rather than starting from Weber's notion of formal rationality that he opposed to substantive rationality, and concepts such as patriarchy and patrimonialism, it will be helpful to question these notions before proceeding to a comparison. Hamilton (1984, 1989) suggests a useful comparative framework of Western and Chinese concepts of patriarchy, power and rule. He follows Weber's basic outline, but adds an explicit conceptualisation of 'Western' concepts of power and political organisation. This conceptualisation includes three basic features:

(1) a centrist conception of legitimate power,
(2) a top-down administrative conception of political organisation,
(3) a territorial unit in which the centre's authority has legitimate jurisdiction.

This concept of political organisation might be likened to a line and block chart, with delimited spheres of responsibility and authority, and defined chains of command. According to Hamilton, particular concepts of bureaucracy, patrimonialism, bureaucrat, official, ruler, emperor, empire and state come from this conception. And all of them are without foundation in the Chinese political organisation. He directly opposes the Chinese concepts of power and political organisation to this schematised description of Western power:

1. The concern with the definition and delimitation of power in the West is opposed to a Chinese concern with obedience.
2. Whereas in the West competing centres of power need to be delimited and exact borders drawn between different powers, in China, the responsibilities and authorities of different actors are modelled on higher levels without an exact delimitation of power and a drawing of boundaries.
3. Without a centrist legitimation for authority except that of moral propriety, and without defined jurisdictions, no Western style administrative command structure arose in China (and therefore the relative number of officials remained much lower, while a large 'sub-bureaucracy' operated informally and pragmatically).

Hamilton argues that ultimately these different forms of power and political organisation have their roots in the differences between Chinese and Western cosmologies: whereas the Christian good is absolutely transcendent and the foundation of truth, reason, and the origin of the cosmos, Chinese cosmologies emphasise the harmony of heaven, earth, and humankind. These two opposed cosmologies he related to two different senses of epistemology: a kind of 'billiard ball causation' in the West, where exact reasons and exact consequences are central, and 'associate thinking' in China, an epistemology of correlation and analogy. In terms of social and political organisation, this explains the focus on personal will in the West, and on fulfilling roles and being responsive in China.

According to Hamilton, these differences are ultimately based on the primacy of the concept of filial piety (*xiao*) in Chinese political philosophy. What is built up here, instead of a Western (modern?) bureaucracy is a 'status hierarchy' that is in some ways comparable to schools or universities in the West, as much as 'rule' and 'power' in such institutions are based on the fulfilment of obligations and the emulation of an ideal rule. Commoners, officials, emperor, and outsiders have different obligations.

The most fundamental obligation is filial piety, which to some extent applies to everyone. Towards the ruler, loyalty (*zhong*) is demanded. And the ruler himself has to mediate between the forces of the cosmos and human society. Between the different positions in this 'status structure', there is not a transmission of will (power), but instead only a correction of inappropriate behaviour — Hamilton cites the original etymologies of the Chinese word for 'politics', *zheng-zhi*, which are 'to follow' and 'to correct'.

The problem with such a presentation of Chinese political philosophy is that the main emphasis is on a unitary picture of the Chinese government that is always diametrically opposed to parallel features in the West. Additionally, military power and internal conflict in China are downplayed. A particularly interesting argument to counter these claims would be to say that China, actually, achieved many of the benchmarks of a modern bureaucracy much earlier than the West. That is what Alexander Woodside is arguing in his book *Lost Modernities* (see Woodside, 2006): there was a potential in the Chinese bureaucracy for rational governance, the construction of a welfare state, and most importantly, the Chinese bureaucracy already exhibited the core features and dilemmas of 'modern' rational bureaucracy (accountability, moral identification, and instability of impersonal relations) long before they appeared in Europe.

Chinese Power Outside: The Tribute System

As with the imperial bureaucracy inside China, the external relations of the Chinese empire need to be considered within a framework different to the modern system of nation-states. The 'Chinese world order', as it has been described by the sinologist and historian Fairbank (1968), was Sinocentric, hierarchical and non-egalitarian. Fairbank describes this order as a world governed by the same principles as Chinese society itself. Therefore, rather than an 'international' or 'interstate system', this was the order of an entire world. In the introduction to an influential collection of essays, Fairbank summarises the 'preliminary assumptions' about the 'Chinese World Order'. Based on thousands of years of agrarian culture, the 'Chinese World', according to Fairbank never lost a sense of cultural unity. At its apex stands the emperor, who as 'Son of Heaven' is the mediator between this world and heaven.

The emperor is the highest ruler and exemplar, as a filial son and as a writer. In his person, he rules over a system of education and indoctrination in which ideological orthodoxy is emphasised. The core assumption here is that correct teachings will lead to virtuous conduct, scholar-officials therefore should lead the way and others emulate them. Everyone has to participate in ceremonies (li 礼) that aim at the cultivation of the self and harmonious relations in society. Additionally, men of superior rank have to learn principles (li 理), while law is meted out on inferiors (fa 法). Fairbank does not mention the subordination of women and the young in the family, which is a direct extension of the hierarchical ordering of society and the state (the equivalence between relations in the family and relations in the polity is of central importance to ideological orthodoxy). Rule is rather superficial (as we have seen above), and combines personal and bureaucratic/impersonal relations. Outsiders are generally included through personal and 'feudal' relations, and have to show some ideological commitment to the empire. The system has a tendency to expand and make exterior relations into interior vassals. Its comprehensiveness is reflected in an official terminology in which many of the same terms apply for internal and external relations (such as, for instance, 'vassal', fan 藩 and 'tribute', gong 贡). Finally, and most importantly, non-Chinese rulers can participate in the 'Chinese World' by observing ritual (li 礼) and paying tribute to the 'Son of Heaven'. Fairbank's summary is often called, therefore, the 'tribute system'.

In principle, Fairbank's model suggested that the formalities of tribute and ritual would override military and economic necessities (and the Macartney embassy in 1793 might be quoted as an example when the imperial court indeed prioritised ritual tribute). Yet, in reality not everyone did become a tributary to the 'Son of Heaven'. Hence, the main problem becomes: how to "square theory with fact, the ideological claim with the actual practice" (p. 3). The actual practices, for instance, in the exchanges with Inner-Asian peoples, were often very complicated in nature, and economic and military necessities surely also played their roles. The mounted bowmen of inner Asia, including the Mongolians and the Manchus, were a crucial military power to be reckoned with. As Fairbank notes, they at various times became the rulers of China (principally in the Yuan and in the Qing Dynasty). And economic interactions with Chinese cultural and economic power (for instance, in numerous 'tea-horse routes', *cha ma dao*) also at various times turned into invasion and war.

The recurrent tensions between the (ideal) aims and the means that were available to Chinese rulers included adaptation to the necessities of military organisation and deployment and conflicts of interest over trade. Fairbank suggests that historians could research under which circumstances military weakness (and the relative neglect of military organisation) led to situations in which foreign rulers were accommodated. Similarly, for the case of trade relationships, the question of how far material interest stood behind tribute relationships also remained an empirical question. Finally, he also pointed out that the *tianxia* system also had a capacity for adjustment and toleration of cultural difference — the extent of which should also be empirically investigated.

Historians of later periods have raised more fundamental criticisms of Fairbank's model. Zhang Feng, for instance, points out that the system in itself was logically inconsistent, Sinocentric, and inaccurate as a description of what actually happened (Zhang, 2009).

It is also remarkable that Fairbank's tribute system seems to be more popular today with Chinese scholars than with international relations scholars elsewhere — why is that the case?

Regarding the Sinocentrism of the system, historians of a younger generation outside China have focused in particular on the history of the last dynasty, the Manchu Qing. The so-called 'New Qing history', represented by scholars such as Pamela Kyle Crossley, Evelyn Rawski, Mark Elliot, and James Millward, for instance, has criticised in particular the Sinocentrism of earlier understandings of the Chinese empire. Working with Manchu sources, these historians put particular emphasis on Manchu identity and Manchu traditions of rule in the Qing dynasty.

If previous studies would have seen a clearly delineated Manchu identity which gradually moved away to Chinese identity, these studies turn around the process: Manchu identity emerged gradually from various Tungusic peoples, in particular the Jurchen, and played an increasingly important role throughout the dynasty. In the summer palace in Chengde, outside the great wall, Manchu emperors and noblemen would practice bow-hunting in the traditional Manchu way. Even though many of them were accomplished literati versed in Chinese, the Northern Manchu identity was often opposed to the decadence of Chinese learning, as represented in particular by China's richest region at the Yangtze Delta, Jiangnan. These issues had a crucial impact on governance and, in particular on the relations between the Manchus and their non-Chinese neighbours. The relations with Mongolia, Xinjiang, Tibet, and the Northeast (that had been home to the Manchu) were often characterised by distinctly Inner-Asian modes of rule, and Manchu rulers would adopt different roles and titles *vis-à-vis* those peoples. The "New Qing History" sees the Qing dynasty as a multi-national and -cultural empire, similar to the Ottoman, Mughal, and Romanov empires elsewhere in Eurasia at the same time (for this reason, this group of scholars is sometimes said to have taken a 'Eurasian turn'). In this empire, the Chinese heartland was only one part, even though a very important one (see Millward *et al.*, 2004).

The Qing dynasty is also crucially important, because the foundations for the modern Chinese state were laid then, and the modern state inherited its basic geographical contours from the Qing expansion (Esherick, 2006). Beyond that, the notion of 'China' (*zhongguo*) itself, as the unity of geography, civilisation and polity, has arguably its roots in the Qing Dynasty. Even though *zhongguo* had been in use long before for the central plains, only in the Qing dynasty did the concept become a label for the empire itself (Zhao, 2006).

Tianxia Today?

The re-emergence of China as a global power in the last decades has led some observers (in particular — but not only — in China itself) to ask questions about the impact this will have on global politics. Could it be possible to conceive a new Chinese World Order? Or can we identify in the behaviour of the Chinese nation-state remnants of its imperial prehistory (one might think, in particular, of the relationships with former 'vassals', such as Korea, Laos or Burma).

The Chinese political philosopher Zhao Tingyang has argued for a renewal of the classical notion of 'All Under Heaven', *Tianxia* (Zhao, 2006). He explicitly juxtaposes the notion of 'All Under Heaven' to the modern (Western) notion of the nation-state. Instead of the Westphalian order of nation-states, Zhao puts an all-inclusive world order, in which 'nothing and no-one is foreign'. He explicitly calls for a 'world institution' that could realise these demands, and that would set harmony and 'worldness' against nation-states and their conflicts. The ideals of equality, universality, and harmony would have to be inculcated through families.

At the same time, one might wonder whether the revival of a Chinese concept of *tianxia* is not really a return to Chinese hegemony — or, what is more, a new blueprint for Chinese hegemony? It seems that the essential hierarchy of the model and its Sinocentrism could cover a new assertion of Chinese superiority. And ultimately, it seems clear that the model is largely utopian — Zhao Tingyang (2006, 2009) does not arrive at very concrete outlines of how a world institution, for instance, could be established. The final question here is whether a return to a 'Chinese World' of 'All Under Heaven' is possible without the Sinocentrism and the hierarchy, and often the contempt for others, that characterised it in imperial times, is possible today?

Conclusion

Lieven (2000) and Balazs (1964) saw their research into the history of the Russian and Chinese empires as directly relevant for their present and what was happening in 1990 and 1957 in both countries. Balazs felt that the Chinese empire was a precursor to the totalitarian regimes of his times. Lieven is convinced that Soviet Russia, including its end under Glasnost and Perestroika, should be understood in the context of Russian imperial history. The legacy of empire is still important for China today. In this chapter, we have presented two relatively unitary interpretations of the Chinese empire, Hamilton's analysis of the imperial bureaucracy and Fairbank's model of the tribute system. Both have been criticised, along similar lines: they present what might be seen as Eurocentric or Sinocentric; they focus on culture and downplay the importance of the military and the economy.

Seminar Question

Do Hamilton and Fairbank over-emphasise the unity of China?

Key Readings

Fairbank, J. K. 1968. A preliminary framework. In *The Chinese World Order: Traditional China's Foreign Relations*, J. K. Fairbank (ed.). Cambridge, MA: Harvard University Press, pp. 1–19.

Hamilton, G. G. 1989. Heaven is high and the emperor is far away. *Revue europeenne des sciences sociales* 27, pp. 141–167.

Lieven, D. 2000. *Empire: The Russian Empire and Its Rivals*. London: John Murray, Chapter 2, pp. 27–45.

Further Readings

Balazs, E. 1964. China as a permanently bureaucratic society. In *Chinese Civilization and Bureaucracy: Variations on a Theme*. New Haven: Yale University Press, pp. 13–27.

Burbank, J., and Cooper F. 2010. *Empires in World History: Power and the Politics of Difference*. Princeton, NJ: Princeton University Press.

Esherick, J. W., Kalayi, H. and Young, E. Van (eds) 2006. *Empire to Nation: Historical Perspectives on the Making of the Modern World*. Lanham, MD: Rowman & Littlefield.

Hamilton, G. G. 1984. Patriarchalism in Imperial China and Western Europe: A revision of Weber's sociology of domination. *Theory and Society*, **13**(3), pp. 393–425.

Hevia, J. L. 1995. *Cherishing Men from Afar: Qing Guest Ritual and the Macartney Embassy of 1793*. Durham, NC; London: Duke University Press.

Millward, J. A., Dunnell, R. W., Elliott, M. C., and Forêt, P. (eds.) 2004. *New Qing Imperial History: The Making of Inner Asian Empire at Qing Chengde*. London: Routledge.

Mutschler, F.-H., and Mittag, A. (eds.) 2008. *Conceiving the Empire: China and Rome Compared*. Oxford: Oxford University Press.

Sahlins, M. 1994. Cosmologies of capitalism: The trans-pacific sector of the "world system." In *Culture/Power/History. A Reader in Contemporary Social Theory*, N. Dirks, G. Eley, and S. Ortner (eds.), Princeton University Press, pp. 412–455.

Woodside, A. 2006. *Lost modernities: China, Vietnam, Korea, and the Hazards of World History*. Boston, MA: Harvard University Press.

Zhang, Feng 2009. Rethinking the "tribute system": Broadening the conceptual horizon of historical East Asian politics. *The Chinese Journal of International Politics*, **2**(4), pp. 545–574.

Zhang, Feng 2010. The Tianxia system: World order in a Chinese utopia, review essay, *Global Asia*, available online at http://www.globalasia.org/l.php?c=e252 [accessed 24 September 2011].

Zhao, Gang 2006. Reinventing China: Imperial qing ideology and the rise of modern Chinese national identity in the early twentieth century. *Modern China*, **32**(1), pp. 3–30.

Zhao, Tingyang 2009. A political world philosophy in terms of all-under-heaven (*Tian-xia*). *Diogenes*, **56**(1), pp. 5–18.

Zhao, Tingyang 2006. Rethinking empire from a Chinese concept "All-under-Heaven" (*Tian-xia*). *Social Identities*, **12**(1), pp. 29–41.

Chapter 3

The Great Divergence: Industrial Revolution

During the Tang dynasty (618–907 CE), a commercialised economy had developed in China to the extent that a system of legally authorised contracts and sufficient literacy prevailed for scribes to write for ordinary farmers and money lenders letters and agreements for rental, or for sale of land, for mortgages, and for purchase of slaves (Hansen, 2000, pp. 216–219). The Tang was a very open empire, open to Indian Buddhism, Turkish princesses and wives, and Persian luxuries and crafts as well as to foreign merchants.

The steady growth in the commoditisation of China's economy, the development of markets for every product, speeded up in the next dynasty of the unified empire: the Song dynasty in the eleventh century, for instance, recognised the first paper money in the world issued against the value of reserves of the money commodities of iron and bronze (Hansen, 2000, pp. 270–271). Later, the main money commodity was silver, the accumulation of which in China in the Ming and Qing dynasties (fourteenth–nineteenth centuries) gave China world economic influence. China was at the centre of a world system of trade, directly by Chinese traders themselves or indirectly through intermediaries, reaching western Europe and the East coast of Africa.

Can we describe this as capitalism? If so, what kind of capitalism was this? Certainly, it was not industrialised mass production of all commodities. The question that is often asked, then, is why industrialisation did not occur as an outcome of China's own commodity-producing growth. This is a major topic for economic historians. Inevitably, this becomes a comparison with Europe.

European Capitalism and its History

The economic historian Epstein (2000) concentrated on Europe, but kept an eye open for the possibility of comparison with China. In writing about capitalism and its pre-industrial growth in Europe, he distinguished three kinds of growth: Smithian, capitalist and large-scale industrial growth.

By *Smithian growth*, Epstein meant the increase of productivity per person through market competition and increase in demand, as first described by the Scottish political economist and moral philosopher, Adam Smith, in the eighteenth century. It includes reducing transaction costs by economies of scale in commercial services and from further division of labour. Growth in market size is both a function of and an effect of Smithian growth, so it would keep on growing if there were no constraints, or if constraints were removed and uniformity extended.

According to Epstein, the major constraints to market size were coordination failures, which raised the costs of trade (p. 7). These failures are institutional in two senses. One is that they exist due to monopolising institutions. The second is that their removal also depends on an institution, the sovereign state. They persist when the state lacks the *capacity* or *political will* to enforce a unified, non-discriminatory fiscal and legal regime (p. 8). Only states can establish uniform conditions for cooperation and competition. Corporate monopolies create problems of coordination among themselves. Feudal European markets were exclusive and unlinked to each other: most of the population was excluded from participation in them. Global trade by feudal empires was a tiny portion of the economies of the European city-state empires. Italian city-states had abolished serfdom by 1300, but did not unify conditions of trade. Instead, vested interests from various cities divided the market and so growth had ceased by 1500.

The large absolute sovereignties of sixteenth and seventeenth centuries European land empires did create large markets and instituted individual property rights and labour markets that were *capitalist*, in the sense that property owners hired wage labour for their enterprises. Then one of these states, England, also integrated markets in the late seventeenth century (p. 3, Fn 4). The ensuing growth was, Epstein argues, necessary for further Smithian growth. But, it was not a sufficient condition for industrialisation (p. 173). The additional necessary condition is technological innovation and its spread.

Now let us compare this to China over the same period. China was, of course, already a single empire with a supreme sovereign emperor who could through his bureaucracy act to integrate markets and so meet at least Epstein's conditions for Smithian growth. It had a customary if not a statutory body of law according to which land and other means of production were privately owned, sold and bought. China's Smithian growth into capitalism compared favourably with European. But what about the potential for industrial capitalism?

Epstein points out that world trading systems before the nineteenth century were marginal in European economies and that European and overseas markets were not integrated, and were therefore not capable of producing a world division of labour, until the introduction in the nineteenth century of rail and ship steam transport (p. 3). Only these new forms of transport enabled exchange in bulk enabling a deeper and broader division of labour. The issue here is how great must be the bulk of commodities traded between markets to induce a deeper division of labour across the globe or across lesser distances.

Aside from global market integration, large-scale industrial production-led growth also required further and constant technological changes, which assumes not just a technical invention, but also encouragement of *innovation*, which is the *use* of inventions. So, he specifies two conditions: (1) a sufficiently large integrated market for large-scale accumulation of capital to occur; (2) encouragement of innovation by capitalists.

That is as far as we can go with Epstein. We must turn to other comparative answers to the questions — why no industrial capitalism in China, and hence why not a technical revolution? As Joseph Needham's monumental work *Science and Civilisation in China* published in the second half of the twentieth century has demonstrated, China had considerable technological superiority over Europe until the seventeenth century. So the puzzle is why this and China's Smithian capitalist growth did not produce an industrial revolution?

Comparison with Europe: Weber

The question 'why did industrialisation and the scientific revolution that fuelled it with inventions begin in Europe?' was put by one of the founders of sociology, Max Weber, in the first decades of the twentieth century. He asked what was unique to Northern Europe and North America to have brought industrial capitalism out of mercantile capitalism. His answer was that it had to be something in what he called the 'orientation' of individual social actors. This led to his comparative studies of Confucianism, Daoism, Hinduism, Buddhism, Islam, Catholicism, and the Protestant ethic, in particular Calvinism. He concluded that the Calvinist belief in pre-destination of salvation and its proof in wealth had an elective affinity with the entrepreneurial spirit of capitalism and crucially with the abstract and unlimitable estimation of accumulated value. This was the spirit that would risk investment of capital in innovation.

Puritan prophets, such as Calvin, created and systematically oriented 'conduct to one internal measure of value' (Weber, 1951, p. 235), whose equivalent in the world is capital, an abstract accumulation of quantifiable value. Puritans internalised, as human creatures of God, a transcendental standard by which to conduct themselves and evaluate the world. In contrast, Weber claimed, Confucianism moulded a people of this material world, to which to adapt. Confucian propriety in the conduct of personal relations and the extension of the family, which he called 'the sib' — meaning kinship reaching beyond the domestic unit — contrasts with Puritan impersonal and vocational rationality. Confucian rationality was, Weber claimed, a barrier to the ethic of economic rationality (p. 236) and 'the pure business relation' (p. 241). This is, of course, highly disputable, not least by those who propagate 'Confucian' or 'Asian' values that include the ethic of hard work and extensive business relationships among contemporary Chinese entrepreneurs and cheap labour migrants. But we should remember that this comes after China's eventual industrialisation and extensive investment, first of all, from Overseas Chinese entrepreneurs. So, let us hear Weber out in his attribution of different kinds of spirit to Protestant Europe and Confucian China.

He presents a historically transmitted (Confucian) personality of patience, tolerance of repetition, of decorum covering over mistrust of others, that lacks fixed (market-determined) prices and instead inspires a bargaining relation and interpersonal transactions, and a trust that differed from that of brethren of a Puritan sect and the contractual relations they made with strangers. In China, trust did not spread beyond a merchant guild, which was like an extended family, because it was not from an internal autonomous source. Finally, he attributed to the Confucian character formed in China a great fear of innovation. Instead of Puritan and capitalist mastery of the world (nature) and of self by rational endeavour, he claims to have found in China a Confucian perfection of self through a moral and traditional adjustment in the world of kinship. Kin (ancestors and ancestral heroes — gods) were charismatic. Wealth was the result of their powers, whereas for Puritans wealth and their own modesty and asceticism was a sign of pre-destined grace and individual charisma.

Most important to Weber was the presence in Puritanism and the absence in Confucianism 'of an inward core, of a unified way of life flowing from some central and autonomous value position' (p. 232). Confucianism instead bred into the population an 'aesthetically cool temper' (p. 234) and adjustment to the externalities of the world.

Note that there is nothing pre-ordained about modern capitalism in Europe for Weber's history. Modern, industrial capitalism is the 'unintended consequence' (p. 238) of the Puritan turn in Christianity. Modern capitalism, for him, emerges from early forms of capital and economic rationality, which existed in both Europe and China along with money-mindedness and calculation, which was pre-eminent in China. For Weber, modern capitalism, which he describes (p. 242) as 'great and methodical business conceptions', stemmed from the compulsion to save, not to spend but instead to reinvest. It was thus a Western accident. According to Weber, the nearest thing to this in China, from the beginning of the empire onwards, was 'political capitalism', state monopolies and controls of mercantile activity, and wealth accumulated by extortion through holding an office of government. There were many technical inventions in China, but they 'were little used for economic purposes' and there was no 'genuine, technically valuable system of commercial correspondence, accounting or bookkeeping' (p. 243).

More empirical findings are needed on the scale of use of inventions and on the precise differences between European and Chinese forms of bookkeeping, such as their regulation by an impersonal rule of law. Nevertheless, note what for Weber are the key characteristics of what he called 'modern', which is to say industrialising capitalism:

- An abstract and universal measure of value that is infinite.
- Compulsion to accumulate but not hoard, to reinvest and so lead to great business enterprises.
- An impersonal system, trust in law, and accounting procedures.
- Individual autonomy and will to master the world and self.

He claims that these characteristics had what he called (in *The Protestant Ethic and the Spirit of Capitalism*) an elective affinity with the Puritan ethic, which created a personality who is a this-worldly ascetic seeking for signs of transcendental salvation.

All this amounts to answering the question, as Weber himself posed it, what sufficed to create modern capitalism in the West, when the conditions for capitalism existed in China even more than they did in feudal Europe? His answer does not mean that modern capitalism and its demands cannot be assimilated in China, since as he knew they already had been in Japan without the help of a Protestant ethic, but by the absorption of the results of European industrial capitalism (p. 248).

Some Questions of Method in Making the Comparison between Europe and China

Weber's comparison starts from a conclusion and then seeks to explain it. The conclusion is that industrial capitalism occurred endogenously only in Europe and nowhere else. Therefore, he proceeds to look for what was unique in Europe and lacking everywhere else for his comparison and finds it in a 'spirit'. This is essentially a negative comparison, finding a lack in Confucian (or Daoist) China. Weber is at least able to specify conditions and date them while others have gone further in such negative comparison, seeking the future — namely industrial capitalism — in the roots of European civilisation itself.

In such comparisons, the end result is positive; what is now called 'development', namely economic growth and increases in personal incomes, which were, eventually, faster in Europe than in China. They imply China's relative backwardness. This is before doubts set in about the desirability of growth for its own sake, before questions about quality of life and sustainability, including environmental destruction, are raised.

Even before such doubts about growth for its own sake there are still some serious questions of how to conduct comparison. Comparisons start from a basis of economic performance — or growth of Gross Domestic Product (GDP). The same rates of growth, measured in the same way between two different regions, can occur despite the fact that they were achieved in quite different cultural and institutional contexts. This raises the question of the importance of institutions, which institutions if any — in particular which state institutions — are critical for industrial capitalism to emerge and grow? Industrialised capitalism affords sustained growth, so the question is whether any one or more preconditions or institutions can be shown to have been necessary for the sustaining of growth and the huge increases of population and its livelihood that it in turn enabled.

It is poor comparison to assume that because industrial capitalism emerged in England for the first time that this must have been due to unspecified, or over-generalised, institutions unique to Europe, let alone to some longer history of European civilisation. It is wrong simply to concentrate on either England or just on China and then holistically explain their economic performances by reference to their civilisations and long-term histories.

If comparison is instead able to *specify* the crucial institutions and economic conditions for the transition to industrial capitalism on the one hand, and on the other hand, to *specify* institutions that prevented capital becoming the industrial capital in China, despite conditions and other institutions opening out that possibility, then comparisons cannot be faulted. Such economic history relies on performance figures but explains the results by specifying critical institutions.

The High-level Equilibrium Trap Theory

One historian of China's economy developed a theory of ceilings to development that could be applied to any economy and therefore could be used for comparison. Mark Elvin, in *The Pattern of the Chinese Past* (see Elvin, 1973), argued that China's development reached a ceiling, which he called a high-level equilibrium trap. This was a trap due to the growth in population that peace, particularly during the Qing dynasty, allowed, along with intensification of agriculture and maximum extension of land use. The growth in population matched increased productivity and innovation so that income per person did not increase and the surplus above subsistence did not increase. In other words, population growth was a break on the surplus that could be accumulated as capital for re-investment. Agrarian innovation occurred but the increasing production by agriculture was for the most part absorbed by the increase in population, so that the returns that could be expected from further investment in agriculture or transport were diminished. Nevertheless, some accumulation did occur. Some manufacturing enterprises were large, for instance, iron works in Sichuan could employ as many as three thousand workers (p. 286). Chinese invention of manufacturing technology was capable of the breakthrough into large-scale industrial machinery. But in the absence of 'the seventeenth-century European mania for tinkering and improving' it did not occur (pp. 297–298). Further, ownership of land and of manufacture was rarely large in scale. There was nothing equivalent to the English clearances of serfs and free farmers from land to create large private estates in the seventeenth century.

Elvin says that although in China products at the upper reaches of the hierarchy of commercial centres could be accumulated on a large scale, there were no incentives to invest in large-scale agriculture or manufacture. Resource allocation, market capacity, technological advancement and population density reached both equilibrium and maximum levels, beyond which they could not go without a breakthrough, which never came from within China.

To this we can add that, in contrast to China, European state violence and state-tolerated violence in trade and investment was the crucial institutional factor for creating large-sale agricultural and manufacturing industry in slave plantations and in land clearances, as argued by Graeber

(2011 *Debt, the first five thousand years*, Part IV 'So what is capitalism anyway?'). Graeber invaluably points out that all the financial institutions of modern capitalism had already been created, before the industrial revolution, to finance government debt that in turn was to finance military expenditure and that huge speculative bubbles thrived in them. Furthermore, most wage labour in the industrial revolution was indentured, debt or chattel slavery. The theorists of political economy such as Enlightenment French philosophers and in Scotland Adam Smith either predicted the imminent moral collapse of capitalism or put forward a utopian conception of it, what it should be as an ideal. Max Weber was writing in this idealising tradition.

Gates (1996) elaborates another theory of the limitation of growth based on the interaction of two economies joined intimately. One was the economy of the state, the Tributary Mode of Production (a concept first developed by the anthropologist Eric Wolf), and which includes or is the same as what other historians call 'feudal' except that in China it did not include serfdom (labour tied to the land owned by noble families), as it did in Europe.

The revenue base of the dynastic state in China consisted of the following elements: *taxes* (paid in grain or other commodities), principally an agricultural tax on land, a tax on commerce, and a labour tax, or labour conscription for large-scale projects of irrigation, transport (such as the digging of canals) and the building of city walls and the Great Wall; *tribute* from vassal kings and princes; and *monopolies of trade* in certain goods, such as salt, wine, silk, iron, and tea, though only at the uppermost levels of trade with tributary kings and with other empires. It also included grain storage for release to control the market price of grains and for emergency relief.

This was organised and managed through the nested hierarchy of imperial state administrative capitals, from county (*xian*), to prefecture (*fu*), to province (*sheng*), to the imperial capital (*jingcheng*) and through a hierarchy of military commands and their regions. The imperial state also controlled currency, chiefly bronze convertible to silver, according to official weights and measures. Provinces and regions produced their own currencies, so this was a set of currencies convertible between regional economies.

The state economy, she claims, acted as a constraint on the marketing economy, which Gates calls a Petty Commodity Mode of Production.

Gates stresses the same point that Mark Elvin had made, that all the units of production were small, even when they were concentrated in the streets of cities specialising in one product and accumulation for trade. Townships could specialise in the production of a commodity sold to many of the regions of China, such as paper in Sichuan, silk in Jiangsu, or the famous ceramics township of Jingdezhen in Zhejiang, which also produced goods for export. But these were concentrations of comparatively small units of production.

In the ranking of classes of occupation, as taught in imperial schools, scholars, bureaucrats and military commanders came top. Farmers were second, artisans third, and merchants last. This is a status ranking, which had its own economic significance, as we shall see. But it is misleading as a picture of economic classes, for two main reasons. One is that families combined aspiration to literacy not only with their wealth in land ownership but also with commercial wealth. The possibility of the accumulation of wealth and therefore social mobility was least of all through land owning and farming, due to partible inheritance, equal among all sons. The quickest was through trade or for the small minority that were appointed to civil service, using their positions to extort wealth. The other reason to question the reality of this ideological hierarchy is that production for the market and commercial activities flourished in China. Imperial officials themselves engaged in avoidance of commercial tax and in smuggling the goods of imperial monopolies. The economic significance of this status ranking is that it encouraged a constant turning of wealth into land ownership and into schooling for the imperial examinations and aspiration to move up the commercial hierarchy into the highest, imperially recognised merchant associations and bankers.

In Gates' theory, there is a strong implication that the Tributary state economy and its ideology of land and learning held Petty Commodity production back from becoming large-scale commodity production.

Exemplary Comparisons of Europe and China: The Great Divergence

The authors considered until this point are historians who focused on either Europe or on China. We now turn to historians who followed Weber in looking at both China and Europe, but with far better data and with far greater attention to methodology.

For these authors, the comparator is a core region, not a whole country. The highly developed Yangtze basin achieved rates of economic growth at least as great and sometimes greater than any European cores despite differences in the institutional context of property owning and the state until at least the nineteenth century.

Wong (1997), *China Transformed: Historical Change and the Limits of European Experience*, shows that there was in the core regions of both China and Europe an increasing population: land ratio relieved by an increasing division of labour, in which some households became increasingly dependent on small-scale artisan manufacture (proto-industry). But, he notes, diversification of income in Chinese households produced less migration to towns than in England. In England, the peasantry was forced off the land by landlords and their armed militia, supported by the state. This produced a rural proletariat that migrated to cities to find work. There was no equivalent in China. Historians have argued that this pool of untied labour was a key precondition for industrial production. But Wong points out against this argument that industrialisation proper occurred in England both where clearances and urban migration had *not* happened as well as in some but not all the places where it *had* happened. Both in feudal/tributary Europe and in China there was the same lack of formal law. But there were, according to Wong, two other critically important distinctions of institutional context: (a) the greater frequency of war in Europe and (b) the property rights of traders and manufacturers in European 'free' cities, independent of the feudal relations in the countryside. Maybe these were conducive to industrialisation.

But the most proximate answer to why the Yangtze basin was overtaken by the core regions of western Europe given by Wong is that an *energy revolution* took place in the north of England: coal, iron ore and water transport were by good chance close together and to centres for the invention of technology to make use of all three. Coal was vital because the use of timber for charcoal had been exhausted, hillsides denuded. The northwest of England produced the first large-scale ironworks and, soon after, the invention of steam power and the production of steam-powered machinery (such as pumps in mines) and transport (on canals, rivers, sea, then rail). All these elements, except the production of steam-powered machinery, existed in China, but not so conveniently together. The change was not a gradual one, but sudden and overwhelming, transforming the earlier industrialisation in European maritime empires of plantation production of tobacco, sugar and cotton with steam-powered mills and factories.

The importance of maritime empires is stressed by another theorist, Kenneth Pomeranz, author of the book *The Great Divergence* (Pomeranz, 2000). Everywhere, he argues, both in Europe and in China, the core regions reached *resource bottlenecks*, and ceilings of population density and so forth, as Elvin had already pointed out for China. There were also ecological constraints on land use, as Pomeranz points out, in Eurasia as a whole. The constraints were to some extent relieved by consensual trade (not enforced trade that was limited to the areas of enforcement), population movement, and primary production in less densely populated areas. In these conditions, the Yangtze region had a more developed market and the most productive agriculture in the world. Then, western European 'transatlantic relations' following the conquest of the New World, and enforced trade with Africa, principally the slave trade, relieved the European population pressure by the colonisation of the Americas. Migration from England and other European countries to the Americas, some of them becoming slave and plantation owners producing tobacco, cotton and sugar on a large scale 'made the flow of needed resources to Europe self-catalysing in ways that consensual trade between Old World regions was not; [conquest of the Americas] anticipated, even before industrialisation, the self-perpetuating division of labour between primary products exporters and manufacturing regions in the modern world' (pp. 24–25). A world division of labour not just for luxury products but for everyday commodities was established.

In other words, it was not a purely technical or an economic symbiosis, but a military and a state-organised economic 'event' — the taking of slaves and the conquest of the Americas enforcing the use of land for settlement and making it plentiful at the expense of its former inhabitants — that produced the ecological and economic windfall in Europe that was the catalyst for industrialisation. It also brought the windfall of gold and silver from the plunder of the central and south American empires and their mines. Gold and silver were the money commodities of Europe and this windfall therefore brought about great accumulations of money for investment.

Deng (2003) produces a theory that is similar economically to both Elvin and Pomeranz, but finds it necessary to modify their theories. He too argues there were *ceilings of development* in China. He agrees that there was a windfall for Europe with the conquest of the New World and the slave trade, but both China and Europe over the long term broke through a series of lower equilibriums or ceilings. Western Europe may, before the conquest of the Americas, have had a similar looking demographic and productivity growth curve, but it was already unlike China's economy because it reflected increasing returns from incipient industrialisation, including military related industry. Further, China had, several times, received similar windfalls by conquests of the western provinces of Sichuan and Yunnan, the provinces further south than the Yangtze basin, and in the last dynasty, equivalent to the New World, the absorption of Manchuria and conquest of the far west.

Critically, Deng points out that the Chinese imperial state's monopolies and their commercial agents traded only in goods that reached the top of the marketing hierarchy, in trade across the large economic regions of the empire and for export and import. This was a very small part of the total trade in China. Deng cites calculations that such inter-regional and export–import trade as late as 1840 was under 1% of China's total and around 10% of China's commercial GDP. In other words, there was little state control of trade and China's external trade was only a tiny part of its economy. We may add that, on Deng's analysis, what Hill Gates calls the tributary mode of production was not a significant economic factor, though it might well have been a significant ideological factor. There was great internal commerce but it was in commodities produced by small units. Deng does not think that the Chinese state held back Chinese commerce and its capitalist growth. Something else did.

His own theory is that China's ceilings were based on an originally militarily enforced formula with advantages over all neighbouring states, established 2200 years ago. The Qin (the unifying dynastic state power) formula for conquest and rule was an understood social contract between state and peasants in which the state extended its tax and recruitment base by allowing peasants private property in land and by the state conquering land for its peasants to settle when the pressure on land grew too great.

Deng provides substantial references to provide evidence that a large proportion of land was granted as freeholds to peasants recruited into the military in the form of frontier garrison settlements from the Qin dynasty onwards in every subsequent dynasty. It is very common in China for villagers to trace back their ancestors to the first settlers who came as part of a military garrison intermarrying with locals. He also provides evidence that the state at least partially opened up its civil service to those who could take the examinations in classical, Confucian knowledge and ideology, though it was not until the Song dynasty (eleventh century) that all civil service positions were filled in this way and not simply by personal recommendation and noble birth (Hansen, 2000, p. 267). In addition, as he points out, the most important revenue base for most dynasties from unification onward was land and agricultural tax. Finally, he shows that the free-holding peasantry would rebel when the tax was raised too high. This was the base of all the changes of dynasty, conquest always being enabled by peasant rebellion that had already weakened the forces of state.

China was an agrarian and market economy based on private property in land, in which *most* farmers were owners of their land either as long-term leaseholders or as freeholders. Compared to the feudal relations of European and Russian empires, which he calls patron-client relations, China was an economy and a polity of freeholds. Land was a commodity that could be bought and sold, but it was also the one great security to which farmers were attached, unwilling to risk it for other kinds of investment. Land was therefore transferred through male inheritance in preference over sale.

The ceiling beyond which the economy could not go was set by what Deng calls the 'customary-mercantile-state' symbiosis. Chinese capitalism never turned into industrial capitalism because state regulation and engagement in trade never turned into law-making that favours large-scale enterprises because the state relied on the peasant economy, and peasant entrepreneurs far outnumbered merchants. What he means by 'customary' is never defined, but from context it seems to mean (1) attachment to land and to ancestors from whom the land was inherited, (2) life-chances that led to reasonable expectations held by enough people to be a sustained hope that they could over generations accumulate land by purchase and could also reach into greater mercantile enterprise and wealth, and achieve literati status through education. The market in China was characterised by interpersonal relations and a high number of interfaces and agents, maintaining market fragmentation and high transaction costs.

Was this really a break on industrialising entrepreneurship, we may ask, when precisely this kind of mutual trust network was the basis for post-Mao industrialisation, as we shall see? Further, Deng stays with the equilibrium model and takes insufficient account of the importance of comparison with the militarism in Europe. Wong agrees with this implicit criticism.

In the most recent instalment of his argument, Rosenthal and Wong (2011) add two further refinements, which significantly do not refer to the fortunate symbiosis of coal and iron in northwest England, but instead return to the warring between European states and to a comparison, not of regions but of Europe as a whole with China as a whole, in the form of their states. His refinements concern the political and the pricing conditions that led to the divergence of Europe from China in the eighteenth and nineteenth centuries. They do not focus on what particular institutions were the necessary preconditions for large-scale capitalism and industrialisation. Different institutions could produce the same economic results. For instance, he and Rosenthal point out that the mix of informal, customary and formal laws and changing balances between the two were similar in both Western Europe and China, and that China's late twentieth-century industrialisation relied more on informal relations, whereas in Europe it had relied more on formal law. Instead, they point to the effects of a political condition in Europe that was a major constraint on Smithian growth, namely that no one European state was near as large as was China and so the size of their markets was a great deal smaller. Paradoxically, this same condition produced the conditions for large-scale capital and innovation. How did this paradox work itself out?

The divergence began when China began its sequence of dynasties over a unified territory with the Mongol dynasty of the Yuan, from 1271 to the twentieth century, having before that been fragmented more often than not just as Europe was from the end of the Roman Empire. In contrast, Europe did not unite again. Among inter state and imperial rivalries in Europe were religious wars that began after the Reformation, which was the formation of an anti-Papal protest by the various sects of Protestantism. The constant costs of preparation for and the waging of war required the raising of taxes and borrowing by the European states. This also set up increases in some and decreases in other factor prices, credit, and land. In particular, it meant raising wages, the price of labour. Note that high wages do not necessarily entail a high standard of living, given other factors. The highest wages may have been in late medieval European cities, where the great merchants, bankers and factories thrived, but their death rates were so high that they needed a constant influx of new migrants attracted by the high wages. High wages were incentives to save on labour and invest capital in labour-saving devices long before the industrial revolution. Warring and its costs reduced public goods, such as transport and irrigation and flood controls, which were therefore far fewer in Europe than in China. China's empire was a low tax regime in which public goods were locally financed by the organisational efforts of local elites, not by office-holders. But, in Europe, warring and its costs also stimulated great inventiveness in fiscal techniques, in particular the use of debt, namely bonds, and the greater efficiency of scale for financiers to lend (buy bonds). Warring and its walled defences created the cities, within which the commerce and the finance that European courts depended upon could flourish, so European rulers' courts allowed the cities to flourish, granting them freedoms to publish, innovate and accumulate capital. Large-scale capitalism and the incentive to devise labour-saving technologies were thus unintended consequences of warring European states and their fragmented markets. Finally, preparation for war was also preparation for conquest, in particular overseas and then the overseas possessions extended the size of the markets for European monarchies and produced Pomeranz's windfalls of relief from population pressure, plantation products for manufacture, and gold and silver.

We might add that high-taxing and oppressive, militarised states in conjunction with relatively free cities were also the preconditions for a bourgeois revolution in Europe and the rise of the doctrine of free trade and rationality, the utopian visions of an ideal for capitalism.

'Science' and the 'Needham Puzzle'

We are still left with the question of what were the conditions for a step-increase in the inventions, namely, a scientific revolution whose inventions could become innovations in industry. Joseph Needham, who directed the research and wrote much of the multi-volume *Science and Civilisation in China*, posed for himself and others what has become known as the 'Needham puzzle'. His history demonstrates that Chinese scientific discovery and technical invention was equal or superior to Europe's until the sixteenth century. The puzzle is why it did not produce the innovations that made the industrial revolution possible. The reason has to lie in the institutions both of scientific discovery and of economic organisation and enterprise that could stimulate and use inventions.

Economic historians have, as the foregoing sections discuss, dealt with the latter, but not with the former, the institutions of scientific discovery.

The key period in Chinese history for tremendous invention and innovation and for intensive economic growth is the southern Song dynasty, twelfth and thirteenth centuries, including iron works on the scale achieved in England only much later, in the late eighteenth and nineteenth centuries. One explanation for such a breakthrough, by Justin Lin (Lin Yifu) (1995), is that the Song was an anomalous dynasty, unlike subsequent dynasties, in which there were factors that inhibited large-scale commercial investment in innovation. The southern Song suffered a fiscal crisis brought about by promoting land and marketing security to peasants and opening to them the possibility of entering the imperial bureaucracy through civil service examinations, which gave them access to means of accumulating land and claiming tax privileges. On top of this, the Song, already defeated in the North by invaders, needed silver to pay off the continued threats from the North. To solve this crisis, the state needed to expand its tax base to non-agricultural production, so it did a number of unusual things for a Chinese court. It encouraged maritime trade. It increased the infrastructure for agricultural specialisation, the growing of cash crops, including grain. It took measures of economic integration, marketing and manufacturing specialisation linked by commerce, for instance in textiles and ceramics. But subsequent dynasties — particularly the mid- to late-Ming dynasty emperors — closed down maritime trade, restricted commerce in manufactures and concentrated on agriculture as their tax base even while the internal commercialisation of exchange accelerated along with improvements of infrastructural and administrative bases for food production and technical innovation to increase agricultural productivity.

As in England, much of Chinese technology was developed by artisans, trained in apprenticeship systems, not by higher-prestige intellectuals. So far, then, this line of argument gets us to the point of asking the question again: what institutions encouraged scientific invention for large-scale industrial innovation? Justin Lin's answer is that Chinese science and invention was based on experience, but not on experiment.

Historians of science try to specify what were the mindsets or disciplines that brought about a scientific revolution in Europe from the fifteenth century onwards. Alastair Crombie (as reported in Elvin, 2008, Fn. 44, p 103) isolated five cognitive foundations for modern science: postulation, experimental test, hypothetical modelling, taxonomic or typological differentiation and its history, and *formal (mathematical) calculation of probabilities*. Elvin points out, there were individual Chinese scientists 'who conducted investigations combining precise experiment, a mathematical formulation, a result that is still essentially correct, and publication of their findings.' (p. 103). According to Elvin, what was missing were, in mathematics, the calculation of probabilities and in general the growth of a movement of such scientists to communicate and work together. There was in China what he calls '*an insufficient density of interest* .... to sustain the socio-economic networks of cooperation, communication, criticism and transmission' (p. 103) such as those that developed in Europe through institutions like the Royal Society in London, and more generally what can be described as a scientific culture. In Europe, scientific culture grew out of an agnostic removal of 'natural law' from the theology of a creator God and into the search for *proof* of natural laws. The mastery of knowledge of these laws through inventions could harness and exploit energy resources (Gaukroger, 2006, Chapter 1).

This returns us to Weber, to whose 'spirit' of capitalism we must now add a spirit of shared experiment and proof. But why first in England and not in the other countries of Europe was the invention of the atmospheric engine put to use in steam-engines? Goldstone (2002) shows that in England, experimentation by engineers, such as blacksmiths, was combined with the work of scientists, who relied not only on mathematics and deduction but also as the development of machines called 'engines' of measurement and demonstration. They could flourish because the Anglican church preached the discoveries of Isaac Newton and his divine mechanics while on the continent, the churches, even in Holland the Calvinist church, proscribed and marginalised Newton's physics.

Conclusion

To explain why industrialisation did not occur endogenously in China despite its superiority to Europe in science, technology and economic productivity, we now have a quite elaborate economic history of Europe as well as of China, specifying key institutions and political conditions in the period of fifteenth–nineteenth centuries. China continued through many quite radical transformations in its long history of Smithian growth and its state-peasant compact, while European states' war economies needing and guaranteeing free city-states eventually conquered overseas territories, producing conditions that broke through population pressure ceilings and produced a capitalism of sustained growth. China's idealisation of male inheritance of land and aspiration to elite literate culture continued through several transformations and, in particular through the long period of unified empire, despite the terrible civil wars at the end of the Yuan and the Ming dynasties, while Europe's civil and other wars were in part spurred by the anti-papal Reformation that also produced a spirit with affinities to large-scale business enterprise and a scientific culture stemming from agnostic enquiry into natural law.

Goldstone (2002) gives us a thorough comparison of Europe and China over this whole period pulling his own and others' studies together in a masterful way. He does this in order to point out that in all periods of their history, but especially for China over the decades of 1670–1770, Europe and China had periods of growth in which both productivity, population and income grew accompanied by urbanisation and great building projects. But they were not sustained because the new and the old elites resting on these advances sought to preserve them and therefore established an equilibrium. This could of course occur more than once in each area, after political turmoil and readjustment or openings to global trade. He calls such periods 'efflorescences'. What was peculiar to the English efflorescence of the eighteenth century is that it became self-sustaining through the innovations of steam power.

Of course, China's economy did industrialise later, but as a result of European and Japanese imperial expansion. This will be the subject of the next chapter.

Seminar Questions

What are the main problems and key issues of comparison raised by the question of what brought about industrial revolution?

Are any of the specifics of what induced endogenous industrial revolution in Europe, or its blockage in China, instructive for understanding how industrialisation did eventually occur in China?

Required Readings

Deng, K. 2003. Development and its deadlock in imperial China. *Economic Development and Cultural Change*, **51**(2), pp. 479–522.

Goldstone, J. A. 2002. Efflorescences and economic growth in world history: Rethinking the "rise of the West" and the industrial revolution. *Journal of World History*, **13**(2), pp. 323–389.

Lin, Justin Yifu 1995. The needham puzzle: Why the industrial revolution did not originate in China. *Economic Development and Cultural Change*, **43**(2), pp. 269–292.

Pomeranz, K. 2000. *The Great Divergence: Europe, China and the Making of the Modern World Economy*. Princeton University Press (Introduction).

Further Readings

Atiyah, P. S. 1989. *An Introduction to the Law of Contract*. Oxford: Clarendon Press, pp. 15–34.

Cohen, M. 2005. *Kinship, Contract, Community, and State: Anthropological perspectives on China*. Stanford University Press (Chapters 8 and 9).

Elvin, M. 1973. *The Pattern of the Chinese Past*. Stanford: Stanford University Press.

Elvin, M. 2008. Historian as haruspex. *New Left Review* 52, pp. 83–110.

Epstein, S. R. 2000. *Freedom and Growth: The Rise of States and Markets in Europe,* London and New York: Routledge (Chapter 8, Conclusion).

Gates, H. 1996. *China's Motor: A Thousand Years of Petty Capitalism*. Ithaca: Cornell University Press. (Chapter 1) (Try to read more).

Gaukroger, S. 2006. *The Emergence of a Scientific Culture: Science and the Shaping of Modernity*, Oxford: Oxford University Press.

Graeber, D. 2011. *Debt: The First Five Thousand Years*. New York: Melville House Publishing.

Goody, J. 2004. *Capitalism and Modernity*. Cambridge: Polity (Chapters 5 and 6).

Hamashita, T., Selden M. and Grove L. (eds.) 2008. *China, East Asia and the Global Economy*. London: Routledge (Chapters 2, 6 and 9).

Hansen, V. 2000. *The Open Empire: A History of China to 1600*. New York: Norton.

Jones, E. 1981. *The European Miracle: Environments, Economies and Geopolitics in the History of Europe and Asia*. Cambridge: Cambridge University Press.

Mokyr, J. 1990. *The Lever of Riches: Technological Creativity and Economic Progress*. Oxford: Oxford University Press.

Perdue, P. 2005. *China Marches West: The Qing Conquest of Central Eurasia*. Cambridge, MA: Harvard University Press (Chapter 15).

Rosenthal, J.-L., and R. Bin Wong 2011. *Before and Beyond Divergence: The Politics of Economic Change in China and Europe*. Cambridge MA: Harvard University Press (Introduction).

Weber, M. 1951. Conclusions: Confucianism and Puritanism, from Weber, Max. *The Religion of China: Confucianism and Taoism*. Transl. Hans H. Gerth, pp. 226–249, New York: The Free Press.

Wong, Robin Bin 1997. *China Transformed: Historical Change and the Limits of the European Experience*. Ithaca: Cornell University Press.

Chapter 4

Demographic Transition

The 'demographic transition' is from couples with many children to couples with few in most of a country's population. Lower fertility rates are combined with lower rates of mortality, which means people live longer and more of their children survive. It is what economic historians argue occurred either prior to and as a precondition for, or at the same time as, the transition to a reasonably prosperous industrial capitalist economy. It is more than just the breaking out from the kind of demographic growth that produced what Mark Elvin called China's high-level equilibrium trap because its main condition is security of income for the relatively poor. So it is more than simply the relief of the population pressure on land.

It is an index related to those of 'development' such as income per person above the absolute poverty line and growth of Gross Domestic Product (GDP) per person providing that minimum, which is sufficiency of income and its security. But upper classes with high incomes do not necessarily, even with income security, have small families — they can afford many children. So all three indexes indicate lower fertility among the relatively poor. The precondition is the availability of waged work on a large scale with or without increased agricultural productivity. The long-standing resort to which peasant farmers have turned when their land is insufficient to feed the whole family is migration, which is either upland into as-yet uncultivated land or to work as landless labour for other, richer farmers, or to wage work or self-employed small-scale commerce in towns and cities, sending remittances home if possible. But none of these resorts and their availability are a sufficient condition for the demographic transition, as we will see.

Related questions about the demographic transition are when it occurred after industrialisation and under what additional conditions than simply urbanisation and industrialisation, and how unevenly, geographically, did the demographic transition come about within the territory of a state. They are related because they raise the same questions about the precondition being not just economic, but also cultural and to do with state policies. For instance, it can be argued that a policy encouraging women to be earners (as several micro-credit organisations do) and to pursue their own education are necessary to the demographic transition not just because of the additional income but because the women are free to have another aspiration outside the family and so take measures to reduce their child bearing.

The transition to smaller families refers to a transition beyond the need for children to guarantee two things: family labour (diversified as much as possible against the risk of crop or price failure or unemployment in any one occupation) and care for their parents if they survive to old age beyond the average low life expectancy. It is also the transition beyond the high chance that children will themselves not survive because of malnutrition and disease (high infant mortality). In other words, 'demographic transition' is a correlate of security of income beyond bare subsistence.

The transition seen in this way is from a population in which those below the age of say 15 years make up half or more of the total, to a profile in which those over the age of 60 make up almost as many as those in work, who have few children. So the transition is from a demographic profile that looks like a pyramid to one that looks more like a rectangle. And it is a movement toward an economy that no longer has at its disposal a great well of desperately poor and young cheap labour.

Social Consequences or Preconditions?

A concomitant of demographic transition, migrant labour and wage earning by the young, instead of shared labour on a farm, gives rise according to many theorists to greater individualism, replacing reliance on joint household income. Family structure, it is thought, also changes as the old rely less on children of the same family to care of them financially, relying instead on pension and insurance schemes.

In 1963, William J. Goode's *World Revolution and Family Patterns*, based on a survey of every statistical study of the family in the context of industrialisation that he could find, posited a number of crucial correlations (leaving aside what caused what) between family formation and industrialisation (see Goode, 1963). One was the formation of independent conjugal families. Another was that parents' authority over children was diminished. Greater autonomy of the individual went with reduction of extensive kinship obligations, such as dowries and bride-wealth.

These concomitants can be questioned. For instance, historians have argued that in England, nuclear families were the norm *before* industrialisation (Laslett, 1972, pp. 125–158). And the individualism that was supposed to have resulted from industrialisation *preceded* it in England (Macfarlane, 1978). In China, an extended family of more than three generations in depth may have been the ideal, but in fact such families were very rare because of great poverty. Most families were in fact nuclear, a couple and their children. Surveys during the 1930s (conducted by John Lossing Buck for farm families) had already shown that even in the countryside 60% of all families were nuclear and of these 80% had between 3 and 6 members only (Taeuber, 1970). They showed that extension beyond nuclear families and increasing sizes of household depended on the size of the land holding; the greater the wealth above subsistence, the larger the number of children. This applied also in cities. Nevertheless, there are powerful arguments and ethnography, such as Yan's (2003, pp. 108–110), that claim that economic prosperity and wage earning are now accompanied by changing gender relations, in which both young women and young men earn, resulting in families where the conjugal couple as parents becomes dominant and that romance, privacy and individualism go with this.

China's Industrialisation

Perhaps, the *generalisation* of these conditions including individualism and smaller more conjugal families does depend on industrialisation and urbanisation. If so, they hinge on the larger question of what are the necessary institutional conditions of the rise of large-scale industrial capitalism, the precondition for sustained growth of income.

We must therefore note what kind of state it was that managed the various phases of Chinese industrialisation in the face of imperialist powers' incursions. The first was the reforming period of the last decades of the Qing dynasty, in which local governors-general and the advice of reformers such as Kang Youwei and Liang Qichiao to the central state created a self-strengthening movement. This included the training of new kinds of armies, and the establishing of large-scale manufacturing of armaments, modelled on European examples, but it also included reforms in schooling and further education to include mathematics, science, and engineering. But unlike the success of the Meiji restoration of the Japanese imperial court and its similar reforms, these reforms were not able to prevent further incursions of European and US economic investment and commerce, probably because they were already greater in China than they were in Japan. The Republican revolution and its defeat of dynastic rule in 1911 at first locally, under reforming warlords and the areas of Nationalist (Guomindang) rule, installed a new system of compulsory schooling, the conversion of temples into schools, a policy of the redistribution of land whose implementation was largely prevented by the interests of absentee landlords, and eventual repeal of the unequal treaties with the European powers. In other words, industrialisation was managed in China by the state system usually named the nation-state, led by a single party, at first the Guomindang and after 1949 and a devastating civil war, occupation by imperial Japan and anti-imperial war, the Chinese Communist Party (CCP).

So, China's industrialisation occurred in four distinct phases:

(1) Opening of factories, mines, and railways by foreign, militarily-backed companies in areas protected by their own troops and police, while Chinese businessmen under the late Qing dynasty and then the Republican states tried to compete; reforms under the Qing abolished the civil service examination system in 1907, instituting a new system and curriculum of schooling, which was taken further by the Republican

governments, including mathematical and scientific subjects, and state-sponsored armaments manufacture and military training, modelled on what was learned from Germany and Japan.

(2) Nationalisation of Chinese private industries first by the Nationalist government in the 1930s, then by the Communist government, which also expelled foreign owners and nationalised their industries, and then in loan agreements with the Soviet Union, importing from the USSR, along with Soviet experts, whole large-scale industrial plants for steel, advanced weaponry, and other industries.

(3) After the rift with the USSR in 1959–1960 and paying off loans during the Great Leap Forward, development by collectives of rural industries as well as continued state development of large-scale industries, such as oil and petroleum, weapons (including nuclear), and steel.

Under the command economy years of 1953–1978, as Chinese heavy industrialisation was achieved by state management and collectivised agriculture, income was guaranteed. Large areas of the countryside were still absolutely poor, suffering malnutrition. Nevertheless, China achieved remarkably high average ages of life expectancy.

(4) After the death of Mao and the rise of Deng Xiaoping, over the years since 1978, foreign investment, state investment, and Chinese private investment industrialisation grew at a rate far faster than the previous growth, but to some extent relying on the basis of previous industrialisation (usually not acknowledged or measured). It is in this period that absolute poverty, meaning shorter lives and the permanent danger of malnutrition, was most extensively reduced.

What these governments eventually, particularly under the CCP, achieved were

- a higher degree of market integration,
- large-scale labour-intensive Chinese-owned industry,
- land redistribution to peasant farmers,
- some (subsequent) economies of scale in agriculture,

- a huge increase in state projects of the construction of infrastructure, principally in transport and irrigation, currency reform, control of inflation, and mass schooling, including education in maths and sciences.

Demographic Transition and its Regimes in China, Europe and India

According to Hussain, Cassen and Dyson (2006) the facts are that in China, as in India, demographic transition occurred not when industrial capitalism had been introduced by foreign powers, but after governments in both countries had established regimes that nationalised industries, protected the domestic market, and invested in large-scale manufacture, in both cases from the 1950s onwards.

In Europe, the demographic transition had occurred more than a century after the first steam-driven factories and mills came into operation. It occurred in Britain only in the later half of the nineteenth century when city governments instituted public preventative health measures and the building of infrastructures, of sewage disposal, the paving of roads, and the provision of drinking water to prevent cholera and other epidemics (Szreter, 2004). Or it occurred and was reinforced when central states, such as the Prussian state led by Bismarck, followed by the British state, in the late nineteenth century created institutions and laws to provide minimum social security. In both countries, a concern for the poor was linked with a concern to strengthen the recruits into the armed forces and with the conquest of territories in the continent and particularly against France for Germany, overseas and particularly in South Africa in the war against the Boers for Britain. In Britain, imperialism as a state policy flirted with eugenics at the turn of the nineteenth–twentieth centuries, namely the prevention of the unworthy poor from breeding and the encouragement of the educated to breed more in order to improve the 'quality' of the population. Policies of preventing the poor, the disabled, the inebriate and the mentally deficient from breeding were in fact implemented in some Scandinavian countries and some of the southern states of the USA but not in the UK.

So, we are alerted to the importance of local and central states' welfare policies in addition to their actions in creating the conditions for industrialisation. Let us therefore turn to the most obvious state action, namely that of counting population for taxation.

Demography and the State

Under the imperial dynasties, the population of China was addressed through the direct system of reward, instruction, census and tax, and also indirectly through the hierarchy of local elites. On the one hand, it was addressed as a tax and labour resource based in family units of residence. On the other hand, it was addressed as selves who are filial subjects of their seniors; on a greater scale, as the common people filially loyal to the rule of Heaven and its mediator, the Emperor. Whatever the imperial system's state of efficiency in keeping a record, in revenue collection, and the inculcation of moral conduct, we can distinguish it and its purposes from the censuses of the republican Chinese state, which in this respect is typical of all modern states.

Demography is the counting of individual members of a population and the registration of deaths, births and marriages, to know a population's size and health, with the implication that the population is treated as one of the resources of a modern state. The first successful census by a republican state in China, after an unsuccessful attempt by the Nationalists in the 1920s, was completed in the first year of the People Republic of China's (PRC's) First Five Year Plan, 1953. It was initially supposed to include questions on literacy and on class, the basic parameters of categorisation for the CCP at the time. But these proved too difficult — requiring more training of the huge number of enumerators needed than the time or their competence permitted (Orleans, 1972, pp. 14–17). So the basic data provided were number, age, sex, composition and place of household residence. Sorting into categories could go from there, e.g., rural/urban, male/female balances, and the age profile of the total population. Later, censuses included further categorisation such as levels of educational qualification. Planning population as a resource crucially included the formation of loyal subjects and their literacy, from the basic competence to read instructions and propaganda to the engineering skills needed to build or manage the machinery and other means of large-scale industrial production and its infrastructure.

The census was also linked to the policing of the population through a system of household registration (*hukou*) including the keeping of a register of births, marriages, and deaths, dividing the population between agricultural and non-agricultural, plus the keeping of personnel files on every adult at work, moving with them to whichever work unit they were allocated. Censuses were, until the census of 2013, taken in place of permanent registration, rather than temporary registration after migration. The system of registration had, until the 1990s, been reinforced as a deterrent on migration by a system of rationing, in which grain was available in cities at fixed low prices but only for those registered there.

Finally, everyone carried an identity card on which 'class' and nationality were registered. 'Class' was based on parental class, always in relation to the socialist revolution. In the design of the system, there was a distinction between class origin (*chusheng*) and class composition (*chengfen*) based on present ideological commitment, but the two were merged in practice (White, 1976).

The system of control of population movement under the PRC was much more thorough than during the dynasties of imperial rule. The economic object of counting the population was to plan it alongside other crucial resources of the economy. Note how different this is from simply focusing on tax revenue and the implicit compact of providing land and not taxing excessively. Note too that, as so much else in the PRC's policies and their implementation, population counting and control is part of state scientific knowledge, legitimising policy. The most recent changes in knowledge for rule can be seen through population policy, which is the planning of demographic transition, without naming it as such.

Population Fertility Control

Population fertility control was first implemented in 1971 with a campaign in the countryside to give birth later, fewer times and more widely spaced, ideally limited to two children. Before that, the means of contraception had been made more widely available at no cost. The policy was accompanied by some coercive measures, enforcing sterilisation and the use of intra-uterine devices and by women in neighbourhoods and teams monitoring their fertile women's menstruation (Whyte, 2015). Urban living and its smaller space per person was already an inhibition to having more children.

In the late 1970s, intent on becoming part of the international system, the PRC took as its responsibility the reduction of the world's largest population under a single state. This was part of its objective to become a global power. The PRC government was aiming for great increases in productivity and did not want population to expand with them, which would have diluted household prosperity. It was also goaded by the alarmist reports by US demographers warning of a global population bomb (Whyte, 2015).

As pointed out by Harrell *et al.* (2011), in some rural areas there were the same incentives as in urban work units to have fewer children; the converse of the same incentives is that the value of more children as household labour was reduced or minimised. These incentives were secure and sufficient income per person and pay according to a scale of wages or work-points according to hours and skill, though both were skewed in favour of males. But in other rural areas, probably most, the distribution of money or grain was per person, so it was an opposite incentive to have more children. The campaign to reduce fertility was anyway very unevenly implemented.

From 1978 onwards, fertility control was much more severely implemented as a single-child family policy, as part of a drive to increase economic growth. But it was still uneven. Finally, in the 1990s, work teams from more central places prevented local cadre collusion with fellow villagers' wishes and even reached the more remote villages. This was implementation by coercion, compulsory abortion, compulsory sterilisation of women (men's sexual 'needs' were thought to be hampered by sterilisation), and fines for avoiding these and exceeding the number of permitted children.

Eventually, after a few more years, the policy was officially changed to allow those who first gave birth to a girl to try once more, after a period of several years, for a boy. Note the gender bias again. The planned child was the boy, the unplanned child a girl, the son lavished with attention, the daughter cherished but not as well schooled. Between them, the use of ultrasound scanners for sexual identification of foetuses and so abortions and female infanticide have skewed the balance of male to female in the population of China. But note that gender imbalance is not just a Chinese problem. It is also a problem in India for the same reasons of gender bias. In India, there was also a fierce state policy in the early 1970s of sterilisation mainly of men. Since then there has been a nominally voluntary sterilisation campaign with financial inducements aimed at women. Note too that Chinese census figures probably exaggerate gender imbalance in China because it is likely that many female children are not reported.

Harrell *et al.* (2011), comparing three rural areas, conclude that the most prosperous of the three was also the one where the incentives to have more children were absent and where fertility decline had already begun. But in the other two areas, it was under these campaigns that decline in fertility began.

Such downward coercion was deemed 'Leninist' by Greenhalgh and Winckler (2005). But since the 1990s, the Chinese government has moved from top-down planning and implementation of population fertility policy to a less direct implementation and encouragement of marketed inducements to fertility control and an emphasis on the quality, more than the quantity of children.

Greenhalgh and Winckler stress the fact that the policy was always to advance the quality (*suzhi*) of the population. In other words, fertility control goes hand in hand with the education and enhancement of the capacities of the children born — their physical and mental strengths. The balance between quantity and quality control has moved to quality because of the success of quantity control. As Hughes (2006, pp. 69–79) points out, this stress on the quality of education, including opening out to the best science and technology in the world, is in government statements couched in terms of patriotism, that it is good for the 'socialist motherland'. It is in direct line from the late Qing dynasty's self-strengthening movement of using and learning from the best foreign science and technology in order to strengthen Chinese spiritual essence — *Zhongti Xiyong*. Only now, spiritual essence is glossed as 'socialist', which means, at the least, loyalty to the leadership of a determinedly representative single Party, the CCP.

In the late 1990s, there were acknowledgements of the heavy costs of imposing the one-child family policy. This was a turn to less direct regulation. By then, Greenhalgh (2008) points out, market forces had increased the costs of having a child. Schooling even when provided 'free' to locally registered residents has an increasing number of expenses attached to it for school materials, fees for taking the increasing number of examinations, and donations or fees for improving or expanding school buildings. Health costs and the costs of supplements advertised for the care of children were also increasing. The pressures of children on their parents for money to buy advertised and trendy products further increased the costs of having children. They were often met by continuing into the post-Mao era what had become common during the Mao era, the conjugal couple both earning and leaving their children in the care of grandmothers. Women before marriage want to earn enough for a dowry in order to get married; after marriage, they want to earn enough to pay for schooling and improve the quality of their children. The importance of work for women decreases their wish to have more children. In more urban areas, gynaecological care, post-birth care for a woman to recover her body shape, parenting classes, and nursery education are available, but at a high price. And this alignment of education with wealth continues up the schooling and university ladder.

'Quality' has become a factor of income but at the same time it reinforces a meritocratic hierarchy: those who achieve high status through educational qualifications have wealth; the achievement of quality is dependent on wealth but it can also be defended as 'merit'. According to Greenhalgh, everyone has internalised the desire for better quality children, so that the ideology of quality has become a new ideology of hierarchy in which the ruder, with lower income, are lesser in the quality stakes, and accept the judgement of their inferiority. They become anxious and consumerist mothers and grandmothers.

In other words, *quality* has become a modernising version of Chinese civilisational aspiration. According to Greenhalgh and Winckler, this is China's version of what the French philosopher and social scientist of Europe, Michel Foucault called 'biopower'.

Biopower in Europe and China

In various works, Foucault took up and elaborated what others before him had established: that a new object of knowledge and of governmental concern made its appearance in eighteenth- and nineteenth-centuries Europe. Preceding theorists in the late nineteenth and early twentieth centuries had made the social (not Christendom, not the kingdom, not the Church, not the land), a distinct kind of fact for empirical knowledge and policy. The social was also the realm of new forms of literature, such as the novel and the newspaper. As a 'public' and as an 'opinion' and also as a problem, of poverty, disease and disorder, the social was and is a subject for science, for art and for policy. The very distinction between state and society that is so taken for granted in political science indicates the emergence of social sciences with 'the social' as their object of study and as something with which a government should be concerned. Foucault focused on the population as a governmental object of management in the current era, refining and modifying the previous social sciences to describe the government of life as a discursive formation he named 'biopower'.

He focused on European governmentality. But we could add that Socialism as a political doctrine and an aim derives from the emergence of the social as an object of government. It turns the object into a subject as well as an objective and makes it the force and the basis for the taking and transforming of state power, so that the state represents and serves the social. For socialists, the problems of the social are diagnosed as caused by misgovernment and by economic exploitation. The social sciences of socialism turn the state into an instrument for securing conditions of economic and political life in which the social will thrive. We can therefore see that it is possible to say that Chinese socialism is a form of biopolitics using state control.

With his concept of *governmentality*, Foucault concluded that the current mode of government in Europe has as its object not the sovereignty of the ruler, but the 'life' of the population (= biopower). It is a new kind of sovereignty. It rests in the accomplishment of what he called the 'ends', which can also be called the 'objects', of government, the main one of which is the life of the population, not just guaranteeing its bare life, as in the political philosophy of Hobbes, but life as a resource and therefore object of government, expertise and knowledge, such as medical knowledge as well as social sciences.

The point here is that population is two things. It is an object of government and at the same time it is the primary subject in the rhetoric of politics. Sovereignty is the subjectivity of the population as citizens, but even more it is the subjectivity of citizens as self-regulating individuals — whose pathologies, when they render themselves no longer self-regulating, need to be treated, medically, psychotherapeutically, and/or by incarceration in prisons and asylums. The older European sovereignty was the power to let live and to cause those who challenged the sovereign to die. This new sovereignty is, through all institutions, to make the subjects of rule live according to their own idea of freedom, which has been taught and internalised, and to exclude those who cannot be made to live as self-regulating individuals.

For Foucault, the work of *discipline* that forms such individual subjects of a population is far more extensive than the state. Discipline requires various bodies of knowledge for maintaining a social life, diffused and extended through the institutions of society including those of the state, but also those of the family, of charities, of schools, of all kinds of professional training, and more. For Foucault, the state is not separate, as it is for political scientists. It is a centralising function of disciplinary powers.

Now, let us turn to what Greenhalgh and Winckler say is biopower in China and see whether it is the same. Is Chinese 'socialism' becoming government of 'the social' in the European sense?

The government of the PRC took over the social Darwinism of late nineteenth-century social sciences, translated and influential among Chinese reformers who sought to strengthen China for what was thought to be a race war, which was a struggle in which only the fittest would survive. 'Races' were understood to be state-organised populations with their own history, biology, and civilisation. The science of population improvement in China did not include policies of exclusion or sterilisation of undesirable races as it did in Europe and the USA. But it was like European biopower in linking the family, in particular the mother, with the formation of the desired subjectivity of a resourceful population. In China, there has been far more state and Party involvement than in European biopower discipline; for instance, the correction of social problems was through ideological thought-work (*sixiang gongzuo*), but in the 2010s this was converted into psychotherapeutic counselling or social work, as in Europe. Fertility control and the promotion of quality in China focuses on the biology of sexual relations and on the responsibility of the mother for breeding. It is gender based and biased in aiming marriage policy and propagated scientific advice at women. Above all, it is encompassed and embedded in a discourse of 'quality', in which the despised stereotyped 'peasants' and half-romanticised national minorities are 'low' or 'backward'.

As a developmental state, the PRC exerts discipline including fertility control, rather than leaving the demographic transition to the processes of industrialisation and urbanisation and the dispersed disciplines that induce self-regulation. It propagates those disciplines directly by ideological promotion and campaigns, rather than indirectly through the institutions of government, such as military training and schooling, and non-governmental organisations.

Would Demographic Transition have Occurred without Fertility Control?

In 2015, the government, long aware of the burden on the single child of caring for two sets of grandparents as well as her or his parents, of the severe gender imbalance, and of the steep diminution of the working age population, implemented a two-child policy. Couples are permitted to have two children, but must still gain permission to have a third.

In fact, one advisor to the government in 1979, Liang Zhongtong, advocated a two-child policy from the start in order to maintain working age population and was allowed secretly to implement this policy in Yicheng Xian, Shanxi province. In this experiment, population in fact declined at the same rate, without the use of force (*New York Times* 31 October–1 November 2015, p. 5). In fact, official population statistics show that the rate of mortality and decline in fertility had already fallen faster since 1971 than it would after the implementation of the single-child policy (Whyte, 2015). Figure 1 relativises the impact of the one-child policy with fertility decline in general, and shows that other factors must have played important roles.

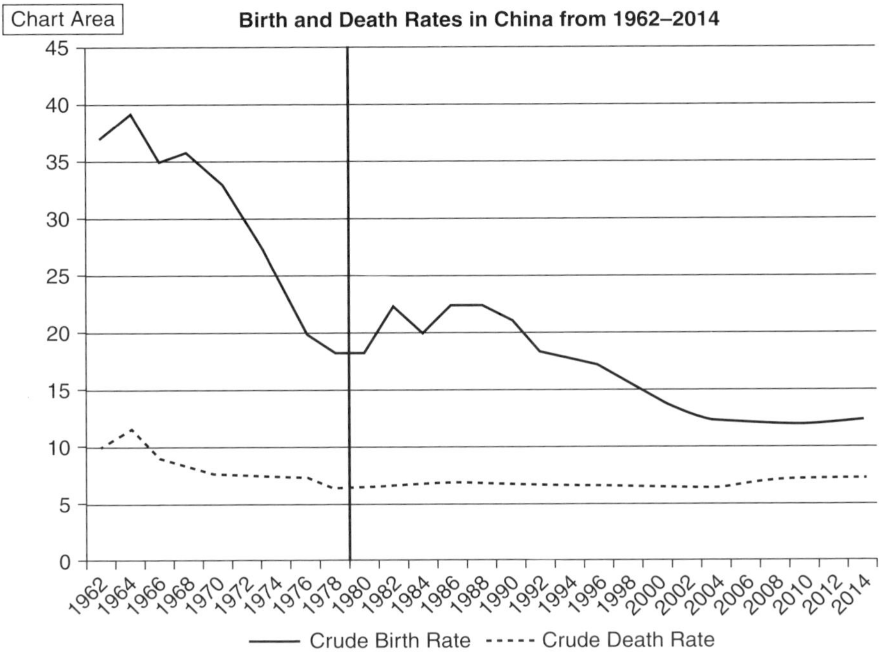

Figure 1 Chinese demographic change since 1962 per 1000 of population. (Thanks to Ben Bissell for this table, based on PRC state statistics.)

It can be argued that wherever rising incomes occurred based on work or wherever guaranteed welfare, combined with cramped living spaces, occurred, as in city work units (*danwei*), the demographic transition occurred 'naturally'. It occurred before the implementation of fertility control. But whatever other factors were involved, fertility control did reduce population growth while productivity increased, and thus enabled increases in personal income. Eventually, income and the privatisation of housing have meant increase in the living space per person and it has not been filled with more children. This has occurred not only in villages but in cities too.

It can also be argued that fertility control, since 1971, exacerbated by the one-child policy, has caused the problems of shrinkage in working age population, gender imbalance and lack of personal care for the old, which are still prevalent despite relaxation in, but no ending of, the policy of state control of fertility.

The over-arching point is that the demographic transition depended on state policies of one kind or another, from the marketisation that gave incentives to greater productivity to increased personal income to much more recent redistribution policies of state financing of rural medical cooperatives and schools in the poorest regions reducing absolute poverty.

Seminar Questions

Did industrialisation and urbanisation produce a demographic transition in China?
What were the institutional conditions for China's eventual industrialisation and its demographic transition?

Key Readings

Greenhalgh, S. 2008. *Just One Child: Science and Policy in Deng's China*. John Wiley.

Greenhalgh, S., and Winckler, E. A. 2005. *Governing China's Population: From Leninist to Neoliberal Biopolitics*. Standford, CA: Stanford University Press.

Harrell, S., Yuesheng, W., Hua, H., Santos, Go. D., and Yingying, Z. 2011. Fertility decline in rural China: A comparative analysis. *Journal of Family History*, **36**(1), pp. 15–36.

Hussain, A., Cassen, R., and Dyson, T. 2006. Demographic transition in Asia and its consequences. *IDS Bulletin*, **37**(3), pp. 79–87.

Whyte, M. K. 2015. The true history of China's disastrous one-child policy. *Foreign Affairs*, 5th November.

Yan, Y. 2003. *Private Life Under Socialism: Love, Intimacy and Family Change in a Chinese Village* 1949–1999. Stanford, CA: Stanford University Press.

Further Readings

Goode, W. J. 1963. *World Revolution and Family Patterns*. New York: The Free Press.

Hughes, C. 2006. *Chinese Nationalism in the Global Era*. London and New York: Routledge.

Hussain, A. 2002. Demographic transition in China and its implications. *World Development*, **30**(10), pp. 1823–1834.

Laslett, P. 1972. Mean household size in England since the sixteenth century. In Laslett, P. (ed.), *Household and Family in Past times.* Cambridge: Cambridge University Press.

Macfarlane, A. 1978. *The Origins of English Individualism: The Family, Property and Social Transition.* Oxford: Blackwell.

Orleans, L. 1972. *Every Fifth Child: The Population of China*. London: Eyre Methuen.

Szreter, S. R. S. 1993. The idea of demographic transition: A critical intellectual history. *Population and Development Review*, **19**(4), pp. 659–701.

Szreter, S. 2004. Industrialization and health. *British Medical Bulletin*, **69**(1), pp. 75–86.

Taeuber, I. 1970. The families of Chinese farmers [reanalysis of the Buck Land use survey 1929–1931]. In Freedman, M. (ed.), *Family and Kinship in Chinese Society*. Stanford, UP: pp. 63–85.

Tien, H. Y. (editor and translator) 1980. *Population Theory in China*. White Plains: M.E. Sharpe.

White, G. 1976. The politics of class and class origin: The case of the cultural revolution. *Contemporary China Papers 9*. Australian National University.

Chapter 5

Religion and Civilisation in China

What is 'religion'? Is there 'religion' in China, and if so what is its importance?

To answer these questions, we need to frame them with a discussion of the anthropology and sociology of religion and consider how they provide for an analysis of what is distinctive about religion in China. This will lead us automatically into a number of comparisons between religion and secularity in Europe with religion and secularity in China and indeed into a comparison between civilisations at each end of the Eurasian land mass. This will take us to the way in which the modern state in China, as well as those in Europe, use the categories of 'religion' and 'civilisation'.

A common definition of religion, first put forward during the nineteenth century in Europe, is 'belief in the supernatural'. This definition lays claims to being universal, true for all societies and cultures of human beings. But the implicit distinction between 'natural' and 'supernatural' is not made in some societies and is differently made in other societies than it was in secular Europe, where the natural sciences can establish what is 'natural'. Further, it relies on an idea of 'belief', a kind of knowledge based on propositions of truth, founded in European theological and philosophical traditions particularly in the Protestant churches, rather than on observance of ritual practices. As often seen, this common sense definition is in fact Eurocentric.

Ritual

Anthropologists have preferred to start from a distinction, made in different ways in different cultures and civilisations, between the sacred and the profane, rather than between the natural and the supernatural. It is based on the work of the French sociologist and anthropologist Durkheim (1963). The 'sacred' is distinguished from the profane by ritual. This includes prohibitions, special food, thresholds and secrecy, certain words or ways of oratorical speaking, stories (myths), prescribed actions, occasions and places, all of which are categorised as 'ritual': rituals of greeting, or of passages in the course of a life and of death — rites of passage — rituals of succession to kingship, rituals of the annual cycle, or of rain-making, or of thanksgiving. The profane, on the other hand, is everyday life, the habits and techniques of production and reproduction, including ordinary meals, of making and maintaining social life. Rituals, including those of special meals, feasting and hospitality, set practical profane life in a larger 'world', which includes a classification of all things accompanied by stories of their origin. You can treat this as a structure of knowledge, made out of myth and ritual, as did Lévi-Strauss (1978). In all such classificatory bodies of knowledge, he showed, there is an ultimate distinction of nature from culture but its content differs. Lévi-Strauss also showed that all peoples distinguish the humans, with themselves at the centre, from other beings with which they are linked in variously conceived ways. Subsequent authors and their ethnographies have shown that being of human origin involves a sense of intention. They have also found that intentionality is attributed to many other things, not just other animals, variously in different cultures and civilisations. All of these are conceptions of life, the giving and taking of life, and different conceptions of the surrounding world. All of them encompass the everyday 'profane', practical and experience-based reproduction of life, without necessarily distinguishing science from religion, or knowledge from belief, or else they make distinctions that are not the same as the ones made since the establishment of a culture of science and trust in scientific knowledge from the sixteenth century in Europe.

To perform ritual is consciously to submit to a prescribed series of actions that are ways of marking occasions and places that were established by forefathers. Even when there is improvisation and invention, adding to or subtracting from inherited rituals, their performance is an act of submission to the ways things have 'always' been done. Enhancing this sense of 'always' is the ideal world of order that rituals and their repetition enact. This too is how they encompass the profane world of chance, confusion, and immediate experience. It is an order whose roles and stories contain not just blessing but also violence as in all sacrifice. Just as important, the material objects, actions and words of ritual can be interpreted in many ways. They are full of ambivalence, but the rituals are nevertheless an ordering. As Catherine Bell has pointed out in her China-informed general treatises on ritual (Bell, 1992, 1997), this ordering is an enacted ideal and its encompassment of the world, and its ambivalence makes it an object for rival political claims to what it encompasses.

The Chinese word *li* and the ideal of rule as government through *li*, established under the first long dynasty of China as a unified empire, the Han, in the third century BC, covers not only this sense of ritual but also the rules of hospitality, diplomacy, greeting, and propriety in dress, court protocol and general manners. The order that *li* establishes is what Ames (2011), in his philosophical exposition of the Confucian classics, calls 'role ethics' — the proper conduct of relations with others in other roles, which are always pre-defined and are always asymmetrical, roles through which a person passes in the course of their life, and others that may only be reached over a number of generations of descendants. Though built on the primacy of the relations between roles, not on the primacy of self, a Chinese theory of rites (*li*) is, like all conceptions of civilisation, about constraint and the education of inner states of being, and of the proper performance of ritual as exemplary. The example of a ruler going through the rituals of mediation between Heaven and humanity is enough, according to the ideal of sage rule, to bring harmony to the universe.

Rituals that distinguish themselves from other practices can be found in every society and at all historical times, but they have a special place in the ideals of governance in China. In contradistinction to this basic focus on rituals, sociologists of religion follow the early twentieth-century sociologist Max Weber's pioneering comparison of religions, including religions in China, stressing the emergence of 'universal religions'.

Universal Religions and the Axial Age in Eurasia

Max Weber distinguished 'universal religions' from all other religious institutions. The three religions of the Book (the Bible) are among them. But so, too, are what he compared them with in his project of comparative religions. They are 'universal', he claimed, because they address a transcendental state of being, and one or more spiritual beings above and beyond the experienced world, and because they profess truths that they hold to be valid for the whole of humanity, not just for a we group. Every other kind of ritual was, for Weber, magic, including all forms of divination and what he called 'magical therapy' for healing, long life and wealth by contact with immanent spirits and demons, ancestors and what he called 'functional' gods, including patron saints, and, in China, the legendary founders of skills such as carpentry, flood control, agriculture, and smithing.

On this foundation, Karl Jaspers, a German psychiatrist, existential psychologist and philosopher of history, in the course of developing a history of thought that attempts to go beyond Western philosophy (Jaspers, 2009, original 1949) detected what he called an Axial age of transcendental thought and self-cultivation. He referred in this way to the extraordinary proliferation, independently of each other, of foundational thinkers between the years 800 and 200 BCE, followed by later founding preachers and teachers of what became state-sponsored religions (though this institutionalisation was in his view against their spirit). They include Socrates, Plato, Aristotle, and the historians and scientists of Greece, the prophets Elijah, Isaiah, and Jeremiah and we could add Jesus and Muhammed in the Middle East, Confucius and Mencius, the author or compilers of the Daoist classics (Laozi, Liezi, Zhuangzi), the egalitarian Mozi and the legalist school in China, the authors or compilers of the Upanishads, Gautama (Buddha) and the founders of Jainism in India, and Zoroaster in Persia. They founded religions or schools of thought that were widely influential and extremely different from each other, so different that the age of the mentioned thinkers in China was known as the period of 'a hundred schools of contending thought'. But for Jaspers they had one thing in common. This was their addressing universal humanity and the cultivation of an inner being to accord with an external, transcendent, absolute state of being that is a potentiality within any one who strives for human freedom (though those who do so fully and consistently are rare). For Jaspers, they constituted the birth of humanity, by which he meant a self-reflecting humanity capable in the history of thought of replacing or becoming the Being that was God. This potentiality of human being is to be cultivated by the exercise of critical reason and independent judgement, as in prophecy, as well as by humane conduct and love and respect for others. Various and quite different models of such conduct could be found in the Christian turning of God into human flesh, Daoist and Buddhist self-cultivation and perfection as harmony with the Way of the universe or a compassion for all things, and Confucian discipline through propriety and rites.

An eminent sociological follower of Weber, Eisenstadt extended Jaspers' idea of an Axial age. He argued that transcendence in the evolution of consciousness separated divinity from the everyday and practical world, as being above and beyond. The distinction hinges on the distance of moments of experience of the transcendental from everyday practicality. For Eisenstadt, rituals that had long been in existence induce such moments of apprehension of a transcendental state of being. These are the rites that mark stages in life, including birth, maturity, marriage and death, or succession to high status and entry into new roles, performed in all known human societies. The French anthropologist Arnold Van Gennep had published a hugely influential theorisation of these *Rites of Passage*, in 1909, in which he distinguished three phases that occur in all rituals: withdrawal from a current role; a central, liminal phase; and the phase of reintegration within a new role. The central phase, of being betwixt and between in both space and time, was elaborated by the British anthropologist Turner (1974, Chapters 5–7) as dwelling or travelling (on pilgrimages) in a counter-structural *communitas* — a sense of human oneness beyond the structured world. Eisenstadt locates in this experience another of Weber's ideas, of charismatic authority, where 'charisma' is grace by close relation to divinity. The transcendental is therefore universal for Eisenstadt and, as for Jaspers, it is a state of mind. It can be ritually induced. It can also be induced by disciplines of solitary self-cultivation. But in the Axial age, the experience was put into writing and the disciplines necessary for entering it were transmitted by writing as well as by preaching.

Writing is crucial for axial religions and civilisations. But the main moment of the evolution of written religious civilisations, the moment that makes some of them 'axial', is when inscribed and transmitted transcendental moments become so distant from the vernacular and practical reality that they can become sources for the criticism of practical reality. Then there is a possibility of seeing all the world of the living as *mundane*, or as another reality radically different from, though related to the transcendent. This might be related to the fact that during the axial age, large schools of literary scholars emerged. Even though not all of their followers were literate, writing and the script played an important role for the possibility of producing such a general critique of the world.

Eisenstadt distinguished among such axial civilisations different styles of bringing together the transcendental and the *mundane*, namely whether they are this-worldly or other-worldly. Confucian, Greek, and Roman civilisations are relatively this-worldly. Their followers seek perfection *in* the world. Hinduism and Buddhism (and Daoism, we could add) are relatively other-worldly, ascetic, often monastic, aspirations to a relatively impersonal state in the body and *for* the world. The monotheistic religions reconcile the City of God to the City of Man (the transcendental to the mundane) in a personal transcendence — in the persons and messages of prophets, the image of the holy city of Jerusalem, or in Sufi trance. Out of one of these, remembering Weber's Protestant Ethic, came the Great Revolutions that brought about 'modern civilisation' that, in its global (imperialist) spread, engendered many modernities through the prisms of other civilisations. Modernity, according to Eisenstadt, generalises the reflexivity of an intellectual elite and a charismatic centre, so that everywhere and everyone could, potentially, question and create new transcendental visions (2003, p. 47) and gain access to or form autonomous centres, generating a continual critical discourse, critical of current reality and of other transcendental visions (2003, p. 48).

You can see how Eisenstadt takes up and carries forward Weber's enquiry on what made the open and abstract means-end empirical rationality of modern capitalism, the Enlightenment and the social sciences possible and what still characterises them. Like Weber, but with even more widespread comparison, he is asking about something he already knows to be a global fact. There is a danger here of assuming modernity to be

European. But note that Eisenstadt also includes post-Meiji Japan as a civilisation that modernised without any axial transcendence. He is not saying that modernisation and industrialisation must everywhere stem from axial religions, let alone from Protestantism. Other scholars, such as Johann Arnason have taken up this challenge and written about 'multiple modernities' using what Arnason calls 'civilisational' analysis. For Arnason, a civilisation is a 'large-scale constellation of meaning, power and wealth' (Arnason, 2011, p. 116), for instance, referring to 'Sinic' civilisation including the Japanese, Korean, Vietnamese, as well as the Chinese states and their histories. He is critical of Eisenstadt's treatment of the axial civilisations as a type of civilisation crucially because each of the named 'axial' civilisations have had such different histories in the millennia before 'modernity'.

The axial age is, quite possibly, a fact of the evolution of civilisation and religion in Eurasia. There are many possible speculations about the reasons why this occurred in such different parts of the Eurasian continent at around the same time.

A recent and plausible one is put forward by Morris (2010). It is part of his much longer history of the emergence, expansion and shifting of core regions of social development in the history of the human species. These core regions are all in temperate zones of the Eurasian continent that have the environmental advantage over all others in the number and variety of domesticable plants and animals. Out of these zones, he notes, Axial thinkers accompany what he calls the emergence of 'high-end sovereign states'. 'High-end' means having a bureaucracy and a standing army and relying on a tax-generating and collecting system rather than just on alliances with lesser kingdoms and vassalage (feudal) ties to noble families that raise their own armies. Sovereigns of these high-end states rely on a mediating relation to divinity rather than claiming themselves to be exceptional shamans to establish superiority to their peers. The bureaucracies of these mediating and highly armed sovereigns included advisers and ministers who came from minor lineages, were not nobles or royal, but were highly accomplished in the arts of literacy. In sum, 'universal religions' and schools of thought were the product of scholars, separate from the sovereigns of states but needed by them, for instance, in guiding them in the arts of achieving long life, good rule or just effective rule, or (in China) immortality as a sage. But also and at the same time their advice was available to anyone who could read or who could hear the preaching and other ways by which their thought and methods for self-cultivation were transmitted. So now we have to ask what if anything was peculiar to religions in China.

Religion in and of China

The Chinese word *zongjiao*, which translates as 'religion', is an even more recently coined term in Japanese and Chinese (late nineteenth century) than the current usage of 'religion' in European languages (since the sixteenth century).

One anthropologist who conducted a critique of the accepted English use of the word religion in social studies was Freedman (1974). He was one of the most innovative explorers of Chinese religion. Because he focused on rites of passage, on the honouring of ancestors, and on the family and relations of kinship and marriage, he has been understood to have neglected class and state hierarchies. This is wrong. In fact, he took into full consideration the complexity of relations between high textual and judicial authority and common rites of passage (he paid far less attention to temples, festivals and gods).

Freedman tried to link all he knew, from historical sources and his own and other anthropologists' observations, into the premise of a single Chinese religion. According to his conception, rituals are heightened expressions of often conflicting principles by which Chinese social relations are organised — principles that he called 'jural', like but not reducible to actual laws. He sought to discover within rituals observed in China a Chinese model of how society works according to its often conflicting rules; the varieties of this modelling are so great that each is conceivable as a fraction or a variant of a greater model that only social science can put together. He was empirical enough to demand of himself proof in China (not in general theory) that there *actually is* a single underlying model. He took as strong hints that there *is* such an underlying model of models by such general cosmological principles as *Yin* and *Yang*. In sum, he sought in China a definition of 'religion' suitable to China based on observed rites of passage and local organisation of families and ancestral lines.

But his search for a 'Chinese' model of models of how society works was driven by a basic premise that there is a single Chinese ethnicity (here, he equated 'Han' with 'China') and therefore there had to be a single Chinese religion, if only we could find it empirically. He did not consider other than Han ethnic nationality and he did not think that the so-called 'Han' nationality varies and crosses the border regions of China into surrounding areas. Neither did he consider the tumultuous history of what counts as 'Chinese', that it could be the result of imperial expansion and partial assimilation of external religions and civilisation into the one or many civilisations that can be found in the now tightly bounded territory of China. Indeed, his was an ahistorical conception of Chineseness.

In a partial, but historical defence of Freedman, it is important to note that unlike Europe, from the twelfth century onwards, whether under conquering or indigenous dynasties, a single Chinese empire has been unified and is now an empire-nation. From the end of the twelfth century, the imperial capital, wherever it was built, was not just a centre of rule of a single empire, it was also the centre of mediation between earth, humanity and heaven — a cosmological centre and its capital city.

The relationship between religion and politics could not be clearer. A telling comparison can be made with another relationship between religion and politics at the other Western end of the Eurasian continent, starting from the Roman adoption of Christianity as a state religion and then the breaking up of the Roman empire and of Christendom into Eastern (Orthodox) and Western (Catholic and then Protestant). What was played out in every European, Western and Eastern, Christian empire and nation were variations on the fraught relations between religious and sovereign law, between the powers of the Church and the powers of the Prince, between what is of God and what is of Caesar.

Despite this contrast, each was at the centre of a world-defining civilisation, in Europe it was Christendom, in China it was *Tianxia* — 'All Under Heaven', with the emperor as chief mediator between heaven and earth, as elaborated in Chapter 2. Neither conception was based on the idea of a people or of an ethnic identity. One key point that can be seen in Freedman's anthropology of Chinese religion is the strong tendency in modern social sciences and also in governmental policy to ethnicise religion, to treat what claims to be universal as a claim coming from a nationality, ethnically defined — be it the self-asserted Christianity of US manifest destiny, be it the eastern Christianity of Russians as its chosen people, be it the Church of England, or the policy toward minority nationalities by means of an other-ascribed identification with 'their' religion (such as 'Muslim' minorities in Europe or in China). But this is an effect of the emergence of modern, nationalist states.

Religion as Policy and the Privileging of Confucianism

The history of the term *zongjiao* and the way it is used today in China is closely bound up with state policy and also with Confucianism. It was Jesuits who first brought the European, sixteenth-century conception of 'religion' as an almost secular category, to China and brought back to Europe a high esteem for Confucius. As Jensen (1997) points out, Jesuit Christians accommodated themselves to Chinese life under the last Ming emperors by becoming Chinese *literati* (their term for the Chinese *shenshi* or *junzi*). They became as learned in the classics associated with Confucius as the Chinese who passed the imperial service examinations. When these Jesuit literati translated into Latin what they had learned, they referred to the teaching of Confucius and what preceded it as *religio sinensium* (Chinese religion) (Jensen, 1995, p. 123). According to their own construction of Confucius' prehistory, the most important element was a universal characteristic that they found in China as everywhere else, namely an intimation of monotheism. In China, they found it in Shangdi (supreme deity) and then the Tian (heaven) whose principles Confucius expounded, after which they gave as the Chinese name for the Christian God Tianzhu (the Master of Heaven).

The Jesuits had at first assumed the ascetic life and clothing of Buddhist monks (*heshang*). But in assuming the new status of literati, they held as far superior what they now described as the order (Italian *legge*) of the master, to whose name they added the honorific *fu* to make Kongfuzi, coining a brand new term both in Chinese and, as Confucius, in Latin and then in the languages of Europe. They depicted the gods of Buddhism and Daoism as inferior, along with the Egyptian and Roman gods. Confucius thus joined the classical philosopher heroes, Socrates, Plato, and Aristotle. Eventually, in the Europe of the eighteenth century, Confucius became a philosopher who shed the universal light of reason. He joined the European emergence of secularity from post-Reformation Christianity. You can see how this eventuated in Weber's conception of universal religions and Jaspers' philosophical humanism.

The Jesuits thus did many things. They brought with them a new category, 'religione', that could include any institutions of worship and belief, and applied it to the teachings of Confucius. In doing so, they turned the teachings that in China were simply called *rujiao* (a great variety of teachings and these as just one set among others, such as *fojiao* and *daojiao*) into an 'ism'. And they conveyed this 'ism' back to Europe as an enlightened secular system of thought, even though it was also a 'religion'.

In their assumption of Confucianism as the highest reach of pre-Christian Chinese civilisation, the Jesuits picked up something that was already happening in China, namely the reforming and anti-Buddhist studies and propagations of the Donglin Academy of *rujiao* (Jensen, 1997, pp. 51–52). The Donglin academicians continued their Ming dynasty mission with great success through the Qing dynasty. Donglin scholars' influence in the Qing court increased the stress on the *ru* classics, accompanied by the development of an apparatus of careful textual scholarship to authenticate what was and was not written by the claimed master. In this way, the preservation of the authentically ancient came into tension with the observations of anomalies and irregularities not only in texts but also in customs and in the skies, from the observation of which the imperial state drew up a calendar for the whole empire. Great sophistication was required to justify ancient texts to the present of current change and deterioration. Scholars drew a parallel between the inevitability of corruption compared to the ideal past depicted in the classical texts, leading to the necessity for reform of the human heart–mind (*xin*), including rectification of social custom, and observations of anomalies in the skies leading to the necessity for a rectification of cosmology, using astronomical instruments introduced from Europe by the Jesuits. Along with this textual sophistication was a renewed emphasis at court on ritual.

This was a ritual of spirituality to govern the popular personifications of moral and cosmological principles.

There is also a link between the Jesuit's unifying image of Confucianism as a natural or universal human civilisation heralding Christianity and the revolutionary intellectuals of twentieth-century China. Revolutionary intellectuals could either condemn something brought together by the Jesuits or turn it on the contrary to a Chinese humanist and moral civilisation (Jensen, 1997, pp. 268–269). The late Qing reformers, led by Kang Youwei, sought a spiritual and unifying renewal in their own readings of the classics associated with the figure of the sage. They conceived of them as distillations of an essence of the country (*guocui*). When the dowager empress Ci Xi was finally convinced of the necessity for reform in 1905, she abolished the imperial examinations and in 1907 introduced a 'state religion' (*guojiao*) based on the symbolic figure of Confucius as the prophet of Chinese modernisation (Jensen, 1997, pp. 158 and 175–177).

The favouring of Confucius was combined with a modern curriculum and the confiscation of popular temples to turn them into schools. But the combination of prophetic and singular Confucianism with modern science favoured by Kang Youwei did not prevail. The sharp distinction of science from religion imported from Europe began to exclude Confucianism from science. Confucianism continued to be considered a moral philosophy, an encapsulation of moral practices at the heart of China, as China's most famous twentieth-century anthropologist Fei Xiaotong argued in *From the Soil* (see Chapter 1). But more radical reformers, in favour of social Darwinism and European enlightenment, considered Confucius to be a burden to be rejected in favour of a new morality in the new modernising temporality of a break with the past. The temporalities of death rituals and divination, of ancestor worship and festivals of local protector gods and their temples, which are variously the temporality of familial reproduction (ancestral time), the temporality of cults of heroes of justice and responsiveness (heroic time), and the temporality of constant movement from and return to sage rule, which could be a millenarian project led by sectarian prophets — all these were sidelined by the new temporality of progress and modernisation and turned into 'superstition'.

The end result has been a social scientific and policy-making distinction between science and religion, in which the anthropology of ritual is marginalised, and the distinction between religion and superstition is used to deal with these rituals.

The Current Situation

'Religion' and 'superstition' are used by the People's Republic of China (PRC) government in ways that are quite similar to their use in every other modern state, despite great differences in ritual practices and religions. 'Superstition' is a supplementary and negative category of 'religion' established in Europe before it was translated into China as *mixin* — 'errant, or confused, beliefs'. It connotes an extra religiosity, less moralising, more rule-bound. In the new temporality of progressive realisation of a promising future, called modernisation, 'superstition' is cast further back than religion in schemes of development produced by the human sciences and applied in the art of government. In human sciences of the nineteenth and early twentieth centuries, superstition is a remnant of the ethos or the rationality of (now outdated) knowledge that preceded the emergence of what Weberians call 'universal religions'. Superstition corresponds to what Weber called 'magic'. It is a remnant of what is supposed to have passed away. It is false knowledge or, in the language of criminality used in policing, it is chicanery and fraud.

'Religion' in this evolutionist sense is by contrast an instrument of good government. In China, it is part of the disciplining of intention among the population to be governed, whereas 'superstition' is backward and subject to ideological and educational reform as well as to more violent acts of policing. Where superstition is backward, religion is a useful discipline for achieving the goal of modern civilisation — *wenming*. Respect for the elderly and therefore of ancestors is a necessary element of social welfare. But in addition, the goal of *wenming* requires advances in knowledge and production, in all senses of the word, not just economic production but also production of public opinion, action and responsibility. For such advances, 'religion' can be useful but 'superstition' is a hindrance.

In the hierarchy of *wenming* and the improvement of the quality (*suzhi*) of the population through the hierarchy of schooling and higher education, modern civilisation in China looks down on the ritual practices officially defined as 'superstition'. But despite this there has been an extraordinary resurgence of these practices in the last 30 years. It is a basis for contestation over civilisation within Chinese villages. Ritual life asserts its own morality and civilisation. It can be a source of judgement of the low morality or for the legitimation of political leaders, as anthropologists of temples and their festivals have pointed out (Steinmüller, 2010; Chau, 2006; Feuchtwang, 2001, Chapter 8).

Seminar Questions

What is the historical relation between the category of religion and the 'invention' of Confucianism?
Does a Chinese religion exist?

Key Readings

Eisenstadt, S. 2003. *Comparative Civilizations & Multiple Modernities*. Leiden: Brill.

Freedman, M. 1974. On the sociological study of Chinese religion. In *Religion and Ritual in Chinese Society*, A. P. Wolf (ed.). Stanford, CA: Stanford University Press.

Jensen, L. 1997. *Manufacturing Confucianism: Chinese Traditions and Universal Civilization*. Durham: Duke University Press, pp. 31–76.

Further Reading

Ames, R. 2011. *Confucian Role Ethics: A vocabulary*. Hong Kong: Chinese University Press.

Arnason, J. P. 2011. Response to comments and criticisms in the special issue devoted to his work *European Journal of Social Theory*, **14**(1), pp. 107–118.

Bell, C. 1997. *Ritual: Perspectives and Dimensions*. Oxford: Oxford University Press.

Bell, C. 1992. *Ritual Theory, Ritual Practice*. Oxford: Oxford University Press.

Chau, A.Y. 2006. *Miraculous Response: Doing Popular Religion in Contemporary China*. Stanford: Stanford University Press.

Durkheim, E. 1965 [1912]. *The Elementary Forms of Religious Life*. New York: Free Press.

Eisenstadt, S. (ed.) 1986. *The Origins and Diversity of Axial Age Civilizations*. New York: SUNY Press.

Feuchtwang, S. 2015. Chinese religions. In *Religions in the Modern World* (3rd edn), L. Woodhead, H. Kawanami, and C. Partridge (eds.). London and New York: Routledge.

Feuchtwang, S. 2001. *Popular Religion in China: The Imperial Metaphor*. London: Curzon.

Goossaert, V. and Palmer, D. A. 2011. *The Religious Question in Modern China*. Chicago: University of Chicago Press.

Jaspers, K. 2009 [1949]. *The Origin and Goal of History*. London: Routledge.

Lagerwey, J. 2010. *China: A Religious State*. Hong Kong: Hong Kong University Press.

Lévi-Strauss, C. 1978. Comparative religions of non-literate peoples. *Structural Anthropology 2*. Harmondsworth: Penguin (Chapter 5).

Morris, I. 2010. *Why the West Rules — for now: The Patterns of History and What They Reveal about the Future*. London: Profile Books.

Shahar, M. and Weller, R. P. 1996. *Unruly Gods: Divinity and Society in China*. Honolulu: University of Hawai'i Press.

Steinmüller, H. 2010. How popular confucianism became embarrassing: On the spatial and moral centre of the house in rural China. *Focaal: Journal of Global and Historical Anthropology*, **58**, pp. 81–96.

Turner, V. 1974. *Dramas, Fields, and Metaphors: Symbolic Action in Human Society*. Ithaca, NY: Cornell University Press.

Wolf, A. P. (ed.) 1974. *Religion and Ritual in Chinese Society*. Stanford, CA: Stanford University Press.

Yang, C. K. 1961. *Religion in Chinese Society: A Study of Contemporary Social Functions of Religion and Some of their Historical Factors*. Berkeley: University of California Press.

Yang, Mayfair Mei-hui (ed.) 2008. *Chinese Religiosities: Disjunctures of Modernity and Nation-state Formation*, Berkeley: University of California Press.

Chapter 6

Statehood and National Independence

What kind of nationalism was created in China and what kind of modern state was created in the course of the republican movement? To answer these questions, we should start from the last dynastic state of China. This will bring into question a comparison with European nationalism, as part of European imperialism. From there, we can fruitfully consider a comparison between Indian and Chinese republican states in modernity.

A Land Empire

In Chapter 2, we have looked at the workings of the imperial bureaucracy. Imperial, dynastic China, was a unification of states and an expanding continental, land empire, within which the absorbed states were ruled through appointed headmen, called *tusi*, or as a princedom of the dynastic family. The last dynasty of China, the Qing, achieved the greatest expansion of the empire in its history. Peter Perdue's history of this expansion (2005) focuses on the northern frontier regions in which four empires interacted, the Tsarist Russian empire, the Mongol, the Manchu and the Chinese. From the frontier, the main issue, according to Perdue, is what he calls the *political ecology* of conquest, military organisation and technology, means of transport as well as weapons, plus bureaucratic administration, particularly the logistics of support of the military at the frontier. And what it shows is a movement in the seventeenth–eighteenth centuries toward many of the characteristics of modern statehood: a firming up of borders, an efficient bureaucracy, and well-organised military force based on conscription. The main concern of each imperial regime was with food provision and therefore with the regime of taxation and storage of grain and the maintenance of grain farming in the regions at the frontier where the troops were billeted in long-term military colonies.

This political ecology involved a symbiosis between three kinds of economy defined as types of economic appropriation: the pastoral, the mercantile and the agrarian. Pastoralists are herders, though most herders also raise grains. Their mobility and expansive terrains are their main characteristics, based on fast transport — horses, camels, reindeer, etc. Their tribal heads muster armies and form allegiances to the most powerful such army of riders and they become controllers of trade routes, becoming mercantile empires, which can conquer agrarian empires. The greatest of these was the Mongol empire. The history of China's vast northern (and western) border regions is the history of trade, tribute, diplomacy and intermarriage and of military technologies and forces borrowed from pastoral alliances and mercantile empires.

The Manchu empire, after its conquest and absorption by and of the Chinese empire, showed its superiority by eventually defeating the Mongol successors to the huge Mongol empire of the thirteenth and fourteenth centuries. It was superiority based on an innovative system of taxation and an improved empire-wide granary system not only for famine relief but also for the stabilising of grain prices, such that the new settlers in the new frontier regions of the empire in northwest China could be relied on, despite their relatively low yields compared to the main grain regions of China, to supply the military colonies in Gansu and further west. It was also based on diplomacy; strategic treaties with the Russian empire allowing the Qing/Manchus to focus on the Zunghar Mongols after having suffered an epic defeat at their hands in 1731. Apart from the grain taxation and storage system, another innovation of the Qing was the sharpening of frontiers into borders, not only in the northwest but also in the southwest of the Chinese landmass. In other words, the Qing became a more centrally efficient bureaucracy, a greater military power, and a more firmly bounded and far larger territory than any previous Chinese empire, much like the chronologically contemporary absolute monarchies in Europe. But the European monarchies were at war with each other over religious confession and for maritime empires. The comparison between the two was discussed in Chapter 2.

Perdue issues two challenges. He questions the distinction between empire and nation-state. And he challenges the idea that nation-states spread from Europe, since the Qing had already some of the features of a modern state (p. 527). In other words, China under the Qing was already becoming an empire-nation, while European absolute monarchies were becoming maritime empires.

Goldstone (2002) adds to this the fact that the princedoms and other kinds of state, including absolute monarchies of Europe in the same period included only one that approached what we might now understand as a nation, namely Portugal.

But the formation of modern so-called 'nation-states' was still to come and in China the empire-nation was to become a republican state through a movement of nationalism.

A racialised rivalry for empire drove the overseas imperialism of European monarchies and their civilising missions in their colonies, while the Qing empire was still a Heavenly mandate of central rule of the world through tributary, trade, and marriage arrangements with 'barbarians'.

The Chinese sovereign (the emperor) had been responsible to Heaven (*Tian*) and to his subjects according to tenets of good rule, such as the classical precept of *cang fu yu min* 'storing wealth among the people', as mentioned by Perdue (2005, p. 530). The Chinese monarch was not a divinity (like Roman emperors), but had a mandate, as 'Son of Heaven', to mediate between Heaven and Earth. The empire was treated as *Tianxia* — 'All Under Heaven' — in which Heaven was a set of eternal principles that act much like 'natural law' did for Christian Europe but Heaven was within the universe and was not predicated on an external creator deity (Zarrow, 2005, p. 23).

The Qing empire in its last one and a half centuries, from the eighteenth century onwards, was weakened from within by the turning of its military organisation of Manchu banners into sinecures. In the nineteenth century, it was further weakened by European gunboat diplomacy and by huge internal rebellions. It was eventually overthrown by a nationalistic republican revolution. Despite the fact that the Qing was as Chinese as other dynasties, the republicans treated the Qing as a foreign dynasty that had weakened a Chinese people that needed to be strengthened nationally, which also meant ethnically and racially, to overcome humiliation by imperial powers. The first republican government established a secular and a nationalist state. It was secular in that it replaced heavenly mandate with the history of a people among other peoples, struggling for sovereignty and strength, conceived as a Darwinian struggle for survival and the survival of the fittest races. To see whether and how this fits, comparatively with the formation of other modern states, we should consider first some general theories of nationalism and of secularism.

Three Theories of Nationalism

Among theorists of nationalism a bone of contention is precisely whether nationalism and its formation of a state marks a sharp departure from the past, or has a long history of emergence. Two theorists, Ernest Gellner and Benedict Anderson, emphasise what is new in the nation-state, while Anthony Smith emphasises the strong precedents without denying that something new was forged in the making of modern states and their nationalism, which preceded and followed their establishment.

Gellner (1983) argued that large-scale industry and the rise of a literate middle class were the conditions for nationalist movements of *emancipation* from feudal and religious bonds. The key event was an intellectual revolution, the Enlightenment, and the romantic reaction to it, so on the one hand the universal humanity of the reasoning individual and then the reaction, which was to search for a blood and soil local nature. The intelligentsia — well-educated public intellectuals and educators — among the middle class conducted research on local cultures in music, myth, language dialects and the figurative arts and created art-songs and other compositions in music, published poetry and fiction and produced fine arts using the results of this research, forging new forms to appeal to the growing middle class. They built a folk or popular base for their more distinguished fine art and the civilisation of what they could call a 'people'. 'Culture' was the new designation of this self-consciousness and differentiation of peoples. Histories were selectively rewritten. These histories and their geographic territories as well as their cultural inheritance were, once an emancipatory state was formed, to be taught in new kinds of school and through the extension of literacy. This basic task of the nationalist state was driven by two needs according to Gellner. One was the need for a new kind of social cohesion. The second was that the industry required a mass, literate work force. Gellner's theories apply as much to 'developing', colonial and ex-colonial, as to European metropolitan states.

Anderson (1991) argued that nationalism and nation-states emerged out of settler states' declaring independence in Latin America against their imperial monarchies, Portugal and Spain. Such nationalism was virulently racist in relation to the peoples with whom the settlers had married and whose land they had colonised. And you could further add that the individualist modern subject was born not in Europe but among slaves in the slave plantations of the Caribbean, who were uprooted and forced to work out how to survive as slave workers in the first large-scale industries of the world, without the need for or provision of literacy (Mintz, 1996).

Anderson's general theory of the emergence of the nation as an imagined community is that its preconditions are what he calls 'print capitalism' and the break into a new kind of narrative time from the recyclical time of cosmological liturgies. Print capitalism was a combination of the translation of ritual liturgies from sacred languages, such as Latin and Hebrew, into the languages of common speech and the industrialisation of writing by printing and the manufacture of paper and book binding. The new narrative time was what he called 'homogeneous empty time' in which every reader could presume themselves to be co-present with the other readers of the same language, a national language, and its temporality from past to future, picked out in events of emergence, current promise but deficiency in the light of that promise, and work for future generations to realise that promise.

Smith (2003) showed how an existing ethnicity is powered by the idea of a chosen people in nationalist movements and their states, giving a sense of sacred destiny to a secular narrative. The USA is a good example, with its myths of manifest destiny and the city on the hill. These stories invoke an historical destiny, not one of divine judgement and salvation or damnation, but of the judgement of history, its territory as homeland and landscape, and its people. For Smith, many of the ingredients of traditional ritual are preserved but now myths of origin are of a people among other peoples, whose symbols regarded as sacred include the raising of the flag and the erection and days of memorials to the dead geniuses and heroes of the formation and future of the people, their election and their land, their mission as a destiny for and in the world but of 'us' as distinctive, as what makes us different from others.

Modern states, the world over, are either secular or a mix of secular government with religious authority and tradition. So, to put the Chinese republic into comparative perspective, we now consider what kind of authority the modern state claims for its justification and legitimacy in general terms.

The Secular State and its 'People'

Asad (1999) provides a suitable framework for comparison and contrast. He confines himself to secularism as it emerged from monotheism, arguing that secularism is itself indebted to the European and southern Mediterranean contexts of Reformation and Redemption in Christianity, and that its main contemporary problem is with one of the other two monotheisms, Islam. By contrast, China's ritual practices and doctrines and its clerical religions of Daoism and Buddhism are polytheistic. They do not enter Asad's history, but Asad does set a standard for comparison, which can be adapted to or contrasted with China's polytheism and secular substitution for Heavenly legitimation of rule.

Two of the most important public tests of a state's legitimacy in European countries are derived from Christianity, according to Asad. One is the notion of a sovereign body of law to which all are equally subject, except that the source is now said to be human (the will of the people, the choice of the people). The other is the narration of a story, one that is shared by learning, principally in schools, about a past of suffering and emancipation by miraculous events, except that again the source is now heroic human action (in uprising, civil war, war against another nation or empire or against an enemy within). These stories are constantly re-told or re-invented in political rhetoric and in demonstrations of protest. Even though it is now without the mythic truth of God and His Messiah, Redeemer or Prophet, the secular myth is still a project of redemption — of the realisation of human progress against evil in humanity (Asad, 2003, pp. 60–61).

European secularism starts from the pairing of state and the society of its citizens. What distinguishes the modern state from previous states is the mutuality of recognition between state and society in which one depends on the other. Asad observes that every (civil) society recognised by a state must be exclusive, not just inclusive. Inclusivity is anyway graded. The authority of having the right to speech and of being heard in public is confined to those deemed capable of and competent to make decisions. So the history of (civil) society-state relations is one of fights for inclusion, for citizenship and suffrage, against restrictions by property, gender and educational qualifications, a history of battles over rules of competence and qualification to make decisions about government. Another issue of inclusion may be added: control of the borders of immigration, and the granting of citizenship and of belonging to minorities within the borders of territorial sovereignty.

A government of a modern state calls upon a citizenry as a 'public', a general public of several subsidiary publics. It brings public opinion into being by constantly appealing to it in political rhetoric. The public and its opinion, quantified in opinion polls, are called upon to legitimate the existence of a government or a party aiming to govern a state and of rule through that state. But this call upon 'the public' or 'the people' leads to a permanent quandary. Does the popular sovereignty that a state is supposed to represent pre-exist the state? Or is popular sovereignty (the public) called into existence by nationalism, such as movements for independence which fight for the right to form a state and when that is won nurtures this 'people' through the state? Is the public and (civil) society of a state a necessary fiction, summoned variously and with unintended consequences by those who rule or have access to ruling through that state? All these questions can be answered in the affirmative, and none of the answers is the only true one. The 'people' has a past, but is also a creation by a modern state. The issue cannot be resolved. It is a political as well as an academic issue, whether an identity, supposedly shared with other citizens, is 'ethnic' (pre-existing the nation, or several nations sharing a territory that makes up the public or the people) or just a question of citizenship by birth and residence in the state's territory.

Legitimacy rests on a state's relations with the public in whose name it rules. Tests of legitimacy are not necessarily conducted and performed through the usual mechanisms of democracy, principally the vote. They also work through a populist appeal, which can take the form of treating leadership as inner, charismatic, arising from the natural qualities of a people as nation or as race, or as civilisation, including religious civilisation.

Bhabha (1990) identifies another prevalent tension in the story a people-state constantly retells. It has a pedagogic project, in which the state and its political classes, the elite, guide the nation or public into its future. So that which might be 'the people' is always in a state of not-yet existing, or of having existed but also having to be recreated in an ambivalent present. The present is one of multiplicity. The state's hegemonic ideology appeals to a reality that is always a reality yet to be realised, despite the powers of the state and its school system. Ideally, civil society is the formation of public opinion by listening and by persuasion; citizens persuade and listen to each other; politicians listen to and are accountable to citizens. But in the everyday and the occasional performance of civil society, such as elections or demonstrations, all current traditions and organisations take part, including, despite the secularity of the state, religious organisations. They create some of the most prevalent spaces in which public opinion is formed, repeating or reminding themselves of past demonstrations or riots or timeless senses of the world that they say they have inherited even as they re-invent them. In sum, there is a permanent tension between the pedagogic and the performative creation of the people of a state.

What makes the state secular is not the absence of religious doctrine or authority so much as the category 'religion', which, just like the category 'culture', has the effect of multiplying members of a people into 'communities' of its religions and cultures, and therefore many relative centricities of claims to truth — many truths — under a state's jurisdiction. Secular in reality means just that all states are governments of pluralities of culture and of religious observation, sectarian or doctrinal belief.

Dynastic states in China had also governed over a plurality of religious teaching, but the masters of these teachings were either disputants over truths about the universe and how to live, or keepers of methods to prolong life. They were not cast into a relativity of beliefs and practices, each for their collective selves (communities). But the secular state makes religion a matter of each citizen's conduct, opinion or claim to ultimate truth, turning the adherent citizens into 'communities' of belonging.

Our truth, what we know is best for us, is our version of the human world, according to our story of emancipation or redemption. It is a localised version of religion allowing others to have their versions, or claiming superiority over them. But at the same time it contains a notion of shared principles and values, indeed a way of life, that 'we' not only prefer but advocate to the rest of the world, such as the American way of life. Of course, no one can entirely agree what it is. Nor can we say what that was generations ago, whether it was anything like the same as what its proponents say it is now. Nevertheless, we can share a sense of belonging through the symbols, buildings, landscapes and focal points we say we share. A combination of several of these makes up a necessarily plural 'nation'. And the world system of nation-states and multi-nation-states is also a system of rival claims to human truth and decency, ideologically justifying the powers of each state or of its peoples' struggles against the overweening and immoral powers of their own or other states.

Promotion of the ideals of *civil* society is secular in another sense. To be civil is to be prepared to listen and to be persuaded and to insist on others listening and being prepared to be persuaded. That is not only a claim to persuade the world, it is also different in kind from a religion of an already known truth, goodness, and beauty. To be civil is at odds with any dogma of universal truth, be it couched as religion or not. But religious doctrine can, unless it is tightened into a sectarian dogma, also recognise other forms of conscience and activity in civic duty and society, and its followers can be prepared to hear the same sense of duty and authority of conscience in others.

Having thus established the interplay between civic and other, particularly religious, publics authorising rule in a modern state, we can now turn to a comparison of this interplay in the two largest states in the international system.

Religion and Democratic Nations: UK and India

Van der Veer (1999, pp. 15–43) draws attention to the religious movements in both Britain and India that formed the public that made up the forces that still support the states of UK and independent India.

In Victorian Britain, Christian movements brought into existence a public opinion that included both Evangelicals, such as Methodists, and new kinds of adherence to and propagation of Roman Catholicism, including Anglican Catholicism. These Christian and other completely secular movements formed the nationalities that make up the British Isles and the nations that formed the UK: Scotland (whose emblem is Saint Andrew), Wales (St. David), England (St. George) and Ireland (St. Patrick). The same mix of movements was also active in India, cumulatively in the formation under British imperial rule of the Indian Civil Service and the promotion in India of the English language and of the Christian and Enlightenment traditions.

The Indian elite's response to them and to the British promotion of Christian civilisation was to found equivalent Hindu movements of the book, the Upanishads with or without their commentaries, as a return to a pure Hinduism shorn of the 'barbaric' practices condemned by the English, such as a widow casting herself upon the bonfire of her husband's corpse (*sati*). Such purifying fundamentalism turned the privileged castes and the priestly elite into scientific elites of spiritual superiority to the crass materialism of the colonisers. Hindu civilisation had been intimately linked to European civilisation in the linguistic grouping of Indo-European languages including the ancient languages of Sanskrit, Greek and Latin, a combination racialised as the Aryan race. But in their grouping, European writers condemned Hindu civilisation as a static and backward remnant of a common past surpassed long since by the dynamic Europeans. Now the Hindu Aryanists claimed older, purer *and dynamic* precedence over their European younger brothers.

Van der Veer has extended this into a comparison of secularism in India and China, (2014, Chapter 6 in particular) focusing on state formation and intervention in the management of religious differences and reduction of what are deemed to be the false or backward practices of magic and superstition. Both secularisms are emancipatory and violent in the sense that they seek to make and enforce change, in creating a nation rid of imperialist rule and rid also of traditional forces holding back progress. Indian state neutrality, rather than atheism, is inherited from British colonial rule and the turning of its caste and religious traditions into religious communities tempered by a spiritual non-violent anti-communalism forged by Gandhi. On the other hand, Chinese Communist state atheism continues the dynastic state suspicion of popular religion and deepens it into an anti-imperialist pro-science self-strengthening attack on popular temples and for certain periods on all religions in what was itself a form of millenarian movement under Mao. But beyond and after Mao, the Communist state has had to accommodate a huge revival and revitalisation of popular religions and the spread of Christianity by a mixture of heavy policing and cultural policy that includes the promotion of Confucianism as a national spiritual heritage (see the preceding chapter on religion).

Going over the same material but with his own emphases, Duara (2015, Chapter 6) shows that redemption from the humiliation of colonisation or military defeat has non-Christian equivalents in India, China and the religious societies of the Sinic region (Japan, Korea, Vietnam, and Indonesian and other overseas Chinese associations). They include the spiritual tradition espoused and enhanced by Gandhi and Buddhism espoused by Ambedkar in India, the Confucian syncretism with Buddhism and Daoism in China and with Christianity in Korea, and the moral politics of mobilisation through the figure of Mao in China. For Duara, it is of prime importance that these spiritual movements also transcend national boundaries. He is writing about secularism and its spiritualities, but against national exclusiveness, even while recognising that transcendental inclusiveness can always be closed down.

Chinese Nationalism

In the story told by Chinese republicans and nationalists, the father of the nation is Sun Yat-sen, founder of the party that organised the alliance of forces that overthrew the dynasty. Sun Yat-sen's major slogan was: *Tianxia wei gong*. 'All Under Heaven', (the cosmological conception of the empire of the heavenly mandate) is public, or is the public, or is a public good.

Gong is the character used in the Chinese translation of 'republic': *gonghe guo*, and 'republic' is itself a transformation of the Roman Latin of *res publica*, the things of the public realm. Sun's slogan is a Chinese secularisation.

In China, a nationalist, anti-Manchu movement overthrew the imperial state and set up a republic. Rival republican movements eventually polarised into civil war between the Nationalist and the Communist Parties and their respective allies. Both were secular, both laid different claims to Chinese history and its nations and religions. The Communist Party was and is deliberately atheist, but its position toward the Confucian tradition is ambiguous: condemnation in the tradition of May Fourth 'Mr. Science and Mr. Democracy' and subsequent Mao-period Anti-Confucian campaigns contrast with adaptation of Confucian values in Premier Liu Shaoqi's 1939 booklet *How to be a Good Communist* and since the 1990s in the promotion of filial duty. The Nationalist Party (Guomindang) was and is (in Taiwan) a secular and multi-religious Party, but it too promoted a Confucianism that had been modernised for a state that ruled in the name of a people and its civilisation. It was Confucianism that promoted Confucius as a prophet for a new age and as a cult of morality for that new age, first by the Qing reformer Kang Youwei, then by Jiang Jieshi (Chiang Kaishek) through the school system in what he called the New Life Movement. Kang Youwei's promotion of Confucius as a prophet and for a state religion was in direct response to the Anglican Church as a state religion of Britain's constitutional monarchy, and to the new kinds of school created in China by Christian missions (Zarrow, 2005, pp. 27–29). Now the Chinese Communist Party (CCP) is also claiming its 'Chinese' credentials as rulers of a people through the promotion of a modernised Confucian tradition and its ceremonies (Billioud and Thoreval, 2015).

Another important response to Christian missions in China was a new kind of Buddhism, a worldly Buddhism — formed on the Mainland in the 1920s, now flourishing in Taiwan and spreading back into the PRC. Daoism, Christianities, and Islam have also spread and at the same time they have been regulated by the state both in the People's Republic and in Taiwan. There were religious movements — indeed they were the primary movements — against the imperial dynasty in the eighteenth and nineteenth centuries: the Muslim rebellions in the northwest against Han colonisation of the new territory of the Qing empire; the syncretic Christian Chinese Taiping rebellion that established for a few years its imperial capital in Nanjing until the Qing state defeated it with the aid of British and German military advisers; the anti-Christian and secretly imperial-supported Boxer rebellion in north China based on syncretic sectarian organisations combining Buddhism, Daoism and the efficacy of local temple gods. But none formed 'communities' to be governed as part of the Chinese people. So how may we, as it were from the academic outside, characterise Chinese nationalism?

Chinese State Patriotism

There was something like an ethnic nationalism in late Qing dynasty China and the beginnings of a movement against the Manchu rulers. As Harrison (2001) puts it, there was a sometimes deeply motivating, sometimes a more rhetorically manipulative opposition to the Qing as a foreign dynasty. Opposition could range between reform of the imperial state and replacement of the dynasty with a native emperor, or something more radical, a Chinese republic. At this time, a *relativising of Chinese civilisation* in the world grew, purified and strengthened by means of scientific learning, the incorporation of the latest military and industrial technology, and the defeat of foreign dominion in China. This meant a reform of education, learned from various European, North American or Japanese models. It meant the promotion of vernacular speech and writing based on it, of mass literacy, of physical exercise, of standing straight, and of creating a school system, including uniforms that were military. As in every nation-state, the school system became the principle means for conveying a unifying ideology and sense of sharing a common history and destiny.

Anti-imperialism took the form of the party itself that could lead China's emancipation from imperial domination. This was as true of the Guomindang (the Nationalist Party) as it was of the CCP. The party was identified with both people and state, creating a constitution and a body of law.

In China, patriotic anti-imperialism was politically imposed and to a large extent supported through a single party, be it the Nationalist Party (until democratisation of Taiwan in 1987) or the Communist Party. It is a strong appeal to loyalty to the political centre that holds China together and claims to unify it. So Harrison at one point calls it '*state patriotism*', though this should be *party-state patriotism*.

But we must also enquire what was the 'public' or the 'people' mobilised into either these or other patriotisms in China, what stories they told or learned of their history as a possible nation.

Nation as History

Duara (1995) compared Chinese with Indian nationalism, but did so in order to question the conventions that bind modern historiography to the space and time of the nation-state. Duara concedes to the historians and theorists of the modern state and of nationalism that late imperial and republican state building in China strengthened and hardened boundaries defining a sovereign territory. But which boundaries were hardened while others were softened within them depended on different currents of nationalist movement and reform. There were different regional centres of Chinese nationalism, different centres of a claim to act for and be at the core of a Chinese civilisation, and different movements stemming from such claims. In the history of China's civil wars and uprisings in the twentieth century, there are many counter-histories to the current history of the Chinese state written by historians at various times of various ideological supremacies. At the very least, each can be considered a variation or alternative to the history promulgated through the school system of the Chinese or the Indian state at any one time.

Duara also takes up the commonly observed characteristic of nationalisms everywhere, namely, that they claim at once to be primordial (that the people has always existed) and yet also claim to break from the past. Theorists like Gellner (1983) had argued that the break from the past is like a qualitative supercession into modernity; indeed, the prime characteristic of modernity is to establish itself as a newly self-conscious development, of progress into a future, including the creation of a modern state and a modern economy of a people. For Duara, claims of a break with the past are suppressions of possible alternative claims to a past. What modernisers repress as backward is in fact another claim to the present of the same population of subjects and citizens. Similarly, Anderson (1991) had stated that a new kind of writing of history and sense of shared time was inaugurated by print capitalism in seventeenth-century Europe and its mercantile colonies, particularly in Latin America. The writing was of course in the language of the vernacular, not a sacred language such as Latin, or ancient Hebrew, or ancient Arabic, or classical Chinese. Against this, Duara (1995) points out that in India and in China, a sense of imagined community and history, a similar sense of shared history and of being simultaneous in a common present, had been true already for the Brahmanic caste in India and for the Confucian literati in China long before European print capitalism and its historiography entered India and China (China of course had print far earlier anyway). But in both civilisations, when turning to oppose domination by foreigners, there was a movement to extend literacy and schooling from its formerly exclusive privileged status. Duara argues that the resulting sense of history retained quite a lot of its much older claim to universality and was foreshadowed by the challenges to that universality faced by dynastic writers when invaded by bearers of other civilisations. He argues, somewhat contentiously, that these challenges produced an identical sense of ethnicity to that produced in the modern narratives of China. He also argues, against Gellner, that self-consciousness is peculiarly modern, claiming that it is a particular tenet of the Englightenment individualism and in particular its Hegelian dialectic of history. Readers must judge for themselves whether the newly coined 'culture' and consciousness of its being 'our' heritage as distinct from those of distinct others comes with this rationalist self-consciousness or on the contrary derives from the romantic European counter-movement. In any case, Duara makes two strong points. One is that in every case, ancient and modern, a local sense of community is felt and experienced in relation to a larger more inclusive community and that the latter is therefore claimed in different ways that are not always consistent with each other and that therefore there are claims and counter claims to a civilisation as there are to a history and its narration. The other is that modern historical narratives are not simply local but contain assertions and aspirations to transcendent and universal humanity, among which the Enlightenment universality is just one.

In fact, something similar could be said of all claims to a human way of life, that through the idea of humanity, the culture or civilisation or way of life promoted in China, or India, or the USA or the countries of Europe, in each case claims to be a truth and a moral universe for all other humans, as well as coming from one particular section of humanity. Secular universality uses a reinforced notion of humanity into which cosmological ideas such as the idea of Nature as well as History are fed just as God, Prophecy and Redemption were fed into European secularity.

The Chinese Race-Nation

Most interesting for comparative study, Duara (1995, 2009) contrasts the religiosity of Hinduism with the stress on what he calls *discent* in China (1995, pp. 75–78). Dissent to dynastic and to imperialist rule was based on an idea of the Chinese people, a newly racial idea using the suffix for line of descent (*zu*) for the new translation of 'people' (*minzu*) referring to the ethnic Han and the multi-national nation of which they are the great majority. The doctrine of social Darwinism in the system of peoples in the world as a struggle for the fittest to survive was adopted by both Indian and Chinese intellectuals. In China, national essence was conceived in a new notion of descent, racial descent as the generalisation of lineal descent, to include all those who had a line of descent from a primordial ancestor, Peking Man or the Yellow Emperor and his people (Mair, 2005). The movement of self-strengthening that started in the last decades of the Qing and continued through to the present day seeks through schooling, mass exercises, and military organisation to strengthen a national essence (*guocui*).

Of course, Hinduism is not just spiritual, it is also racial, and there is no absence of religion in China. As Duara himself points out, Chinese popular religion and popular religious sects have been revived in claims to regional and moral superiority and condemnation of a current regime and its suppressions. Nevertheless in China, no claim to a single 'Chinese' religion has been made as it has by Hinduists in India. Confucianism is claimed by some members of the political elite and parents who send their children to private schools to define Chinese civilisation and its state, just as the political elite of the literati did in late Qing dynastic China. But there are other claims to be made to Chinese civilisation. Can we say that Chinese nationalism is instead driven by the idea of a Chinese race?

The resolution of two currents in China — unification of a multiplicity and evolutionary or developmental ambition and sense of superiority — conceives of China as multi-national-racial-ethnic, like the UK except that the Chinese flag used stripes and stars, not the signs of patron saints, to form the combined patriotism of the nation (see the illustration in Harrison, 2001, pp. 107, 145 and 153), including the nations that had conquered China, the Manchus and the Mongols. But there was in addition another way of conceiving the Chinese people to be led by a Party. As Smith (2008) pointed out, among workers in Shanghai, a much more class-based, and place-of-origin-based anti-imperialist nationalism prevailed, which became the basis of Communist Party nationalism, which puts the hammer and cycle among the stars in the flag.

Nationalism of any sort, once it has achieved state power immediately becomes involved in inter-state relations, in particular in regional alliances and rivalries (Duara, 2009). Chinese nationalism cannot be understood without this regional context. Now, Chinese industrialisation is both regional and international, part of a set of alliances with states and economies of the East Asian region that had once been the Co-Prosperity Sphere unified by Japanese military empire and its anti-Western puppet regimes in East and Southeast Asia.

All nations define themselves against others, and most vividly against neighbouring rivals within a region. So, for Chinese nationalism, both popular and state-didactic, the principal other is Japan, the more distant other is the USA. And it is in the projection of naval force in the South China Sea that these rivalries are most dangerously explosive.

Seminar Questions

Was the Chinese nationalism formed during the first half of the twentieth century similar to the nationalism of other multi-national modern states such as Britain's and India's?

Is Chinese secularism and nationalism a transformation or a continuation of Chinese civilisation?

Key Readings

Anderson, B. 1991. *Imagined Communities: Reflections on the Origin and Spread of Nationalism*, Revised. London: Verso.

Asad, T. 1999. The moral state: Religion, nation-state, secularism. In *Nation and Religion: Perspectives on Europe and Asia*, P. van der Veer and H. Lehmann (eds.). Princeton: Princeton University Press, pp. 178–196.

Bhabha, H. 1990. DissemiNation. In *Nation and Narration*, H. Bhabha (ed.). Routledge. (Chapter 16).

Duara, P. 1995. *Rescuing History from the Nation: Questioning Narratives of Modern China*, Chicago: University of Chicago Press, Chapter 7 'Critics of Modernity in India and China', pp. 205–228 [see, a slightly revised version here http://ignca.nic.in/ks_41015.htm].

Duara, P. 2009. *The Global and the Regional in China's Nation-formation*. London: Routledge (Chapter 9 'Visions of history, trajectories of power: China and India since decolonization', pp. 186–199).

Duara, P. 2015. *The Crisis of Global Modernity: Asian Traditions and a Sustainable Future*. Cambridge: Cambridge University Press (Chapter 6).

Gellner, E. 1983. *Nations and Nationalism*. Ithaca, NY: Cornell University Press.

Harrison, H. 2001. *China (Inventing the Nation)*. London: Arnold (Introduction and Chapter 4), pp. 1–6, 88–131.

Perdue, P. C. 2005. *China Marches West: The Qing Conquest of Central Eurasia*. Cambridge, MA: Harvard University Press.

van der Veer, P. 1999. The moral state: Religion, nation and empire in Victorian Britain and British India. In *Nation and Religion: Perspectives on Europe and Asia*, P. van der Veer and H. Lehmann (eds.). Princeton: Princeton University Press, pp. 15–43.

van der Veer, P. 2014. *The Modern Spirit of Asia: The Spiritual and the Secular in China and India*. Princeton and Oxford: Princeton University Press (Chapter 6).

Further Reading

Asad, T. 2003. *Formations of the Secular: Christianity, Islam, Modernity*. Standford, CA: Stanford University Press.

Billioud, S., and Thoreval, J. 2015. *The Sage and the People: The Confucian Revival in China*. Oxford: Oxford University Press.

Callahan, W. A. 2004. *Contingent States: Greater China and Transnational Relations*. Minneapolis: University of Minnesota Press.

Duara, P. 2009. *The Global and the Regional in China's Nation-formation*. London: Routledge (Chapter 1, The global and regional constitution of nations: The view from East Asia, pp. 21–39).

Goldstone, J. A., 2002. Efflorescences and economic growth in world history: Rethinking the "rise of the West" and the Industrial Revolution. *Journal of World History*, **13**(2), pp. 323–389.

Karl, R. E. 2002. *Staging the World: Chinese Nationalism at the Turn of the Twentieth Century*. Durham, NC: Duke University Press.

Kuhn, P. A. 2003. *Origins of the Modern Chinese State*. Stanford, CA: Stanford University Press.

Levenson, J. R. 1965. *Confucian China and Its Modern Fate: A Trilogy*. Berkeley: University of California Press.

Mair, V. H. 2005. The North(west)ern peoples and the recurrent origins of the 'Chinese' state. In *The Teleology of the Modern Nation-state: Japan and China*. J. A. Fogel (ed.). Philadelphia: University of Pennsylvania Press.

Mintz, S. 1996. Enduring substances, trying theories: The Caribbean region as Oekumen. *Journal of the Royal Anthropological Institute*, **2**(2), pp. 289–311.

Scott, J., Tehranian, J., and Mathias, J. 2002. The production of legal identities proper to states: The case of the permanent family surname. *Comparative Studies in Society and History*, **44**(1), pp. 4–44.

Smith, A. D. 2003. *Chosen Peoples: Sacred Sources of National Identity*. Oxford: Oxford University Press.

Smith, S. 2008. *Revolution and the People in Russia and China*. Cambridge: Cambridge University Press.

Zarrow, P. 2005. *China in War and Revolution* 1895–1949. London: Routledge.

Chapter 7

Revolution and Maoism

Aside from the end of the last dynasty in 1911, the Communist revolution is perhaps the most significant event in the twentieth century in China. This chapter will deal first with revolutions in world history, discussing broader frameworks of comparison. The second part deals with the various interpretations and explanations of the Chinese Communist revolution. The third part then deals with specific features of the Communist revolution, namely the personality cult of Mao Zedong and the particularities of guerrilla warfare. Both aspects are set within broader interpretive frameworks dealing with revolutionary struggle in the twentieth century.

Revolutions in World History

Major popular revolutions, such as the French revolution, the Russian revolution and the Chinese revolution, all tried to overthrow the ancient regime, the old political order of the same countries. The explanation of the origins of revolution is a major topic in the historiography of France, Russia, and China. Different explanatory frames emphasise origins in elite politics, popular nationalism and class relations, for instance. Revolutions are often seen as central for modern national identity — for instance, the importance of the French revolution for modern French identity (Schurmann, 1968, prologue). Their consequences might be judged according to the kind of political integration they produced, the social revolutions they entailed, and/or the economic development that followed.

Barrington Moore, in his magnum opus on *The Social Origins of Dictatorship and Democracy* (1966), provides a comparative framework for the reasons and consequences of modern revolutions. His main argument is that social conditions, and, in particular agrarian class relations, determine the chances for the development of democracy, fascism and communism. Democracy, he argues, needs a 'bourgeois revolution' (1966, p. 430) — in other words, 'no bourgeoisie, no democracy' (p. 418). He identifies the emergence of a relatively independent bourgeoisie replacing a landed aristocracy as a necessary condition for the development of democratic participation. This further implies that commercial agriculture replaces former 'feudal' relations in the countryside, weakening the landed aristocracy. In the process, moreover, a coalition between the aristocracy and the bourgeoisie has to be prevented through a revolutionary break with the past. Using this basic framework, Barrington Moore goes on to compare a number of countries: In England, the landed aristocracy first started commercial farming; the enclosure movements destroyed the peasantry, but the old aristocracy allowed for a 'bourgeois impulse' and a moderate development of a new bourgeoisie. The kind of political system that emerged from this situation was a moderate democracy that retained a strong aristocratic influence. In France, the revolution put the new bourgeoisie in opposition to the aristocracy, but the peasantry remained a relatively strong social class and hence a limiting factor in democratic development — determining just how far the revolution could go. In the United States, the victory of the industrial North over the Southern plantation owners opened the possibility of liberal democracy. In Japan, transition towards industrial modernity did not happen via a 'bourgeois impulse', but rather through labour repressive agriculture, a reactionary alliance of powerful landowners and a weak new bourgeois squeezed the peasantry. Similar to Germany, this revolution from above led to fascism. China, finally, was characterised by relatively weak landed elites and emerging bourgeoisies against a very numerous and strong peasantry. The peasantry led a revolution from below that would ultimately result in communism.

In Barrington Moore's framework, only a strong bourgeoisie can create democracy. Societies, which for some reason failed to develop a strong bourgeoisie, either ended up with fascism (Japan) or communism (China).

In the first case, the (emergent and weak) bourgeoisie connects with the elite, in the second, the bourgeoisie connects with the peasants. It should be emphasised that in this outline, democracy requires not only the emergence of the bourgeoisie as a new social class but also as a violent revolution.

In sociological history, there are various schools that focus on the different pathways of European governments, trying to explain the differences between constitutionalism (Great Britain and France) and absolutism (Prussia, Austria-Hungary and Russia). One can separate here a school that focuses on classes, of which Moore is one representative, (others include, Anderson, 1979; Brenner, 1987), and another school that focuses on the contingencies of political development and, in particular the different forms of militarisms in the development of states (including Skocpol, 1976, 1979; Mann, 1986).

Interpretations of the Chinese Revolution

The different factors that played a role in the Chinese revolution have been subject to much debate (Esherick, 1995). There is, however, broad agreement on the fact that most peasant rebellions in China before the Communist revolution were largely defensive in nature, very often based on the discontent of local populations at high taxation. These factors probably also played an important role in the 1920s and 1930s, in particular in the regions governed by the Nationalist Party (the Guomindang). But the Communist revolution also represented a historical novelty led by urban intellectuals, rather than peasants (Bianco, 2001; Perry, 1980).

The central question then is — what explains the success of the Communist army and party that led to their victory over the Nationalist Party and ultimately the establishment of the People's Republic of China?

Chen Yungfa (1986) provides a useful summary of previous debates about this question. The main factor that distinguished the Communists from the Nationalist Army was that the Communists were much more successful in mobilising China's peasants. From the end of the Long March in 1935, through the Japanese War and the Civil War to the establishment of the People's Republic in 1949, the Communist Party easily mobilised much larger numbers of ordinary people. What then was this support based on?

One main argument emphasises the role that mass nationalism, especially in the resistance against Japan played here (an example is Johnson, 1962). Yet, in this explanation, socio-economic factors are neglected. Other explanations would emphasise precisely those socio-economic factors, in particular the appeal of land reform for poor farmers (Selden, 1971 is an example). Yet, these explanations, in turn, ignore the contradictions in the stated goals of the Communist Party: in fact, during the war the Party generally retreated from the goal of land reform. What is more, the Communist Party frequently made strategic concessions to 'peasant capitalism', to smallholder marketing and local strongmen. Perhaps most importantly, this line of thought does not take into account the organisational and bureaucratic challenges the Communist Party faced — basically 'how' it organised the peasants. Perhaps, the most important innovation of the Communist Party lay in its organisational strategies, which emphasised continuous, spontaneous mobilisation of local peasants and their obedience to imposed authority, together with military struggle against the enemies of the party (Tetsuya Kataoka, 1974). The organisational development of the Communist Party included a whole series of new institutions: mass associations, rural administration, village militia, and Party branches. In all these institutions the party practiced techniques of 'controlled polarisation' that aimed at the creation of a new rural order. The central polarised opposition was between the 'basic masses' (*jiben qunchong*) and the 'feudal forces' (*fengjian shili*). This opposition was constantly rehearsed in 'struggle meetings', and enforced by the presence of party cadres in villages. Party officials were supposed to rectify emerging contradictions within the new mass associations, the militias, party organisations, and government administration. But party officials also often cooperated with the old elite, when strategically necessary.

For the same reason, Chen speaks of 'parochial mobilisation', implying that mobilisation was in the first place not for abstract and general aims, but often motivated by personal and particularistic links. At the same time, the new mobilisation of the Communist Party aimed at the ultimate destruction of traditional personal and particularistic bonds and their replacement with the new general (and personal) links of comradeship. In this way, the party used and harnessed personal networks and localism for their larger cause.

As far as it goes, Chen's explanation focuses on revolutionary cadres and emphasises their success in the process of the revolution, but it does not take into account the origin of the revolution — what actually did motivate people to think of revolution? Nor does it deal with the situation of the rural (and urban) economy before the civil war.

There is a whole different set of factors that also played an important role in the historical build-up of the revolution, which have more to do with workers than with peasants, more with the coastal city than the rural hinterland, more with Shanghai than Yan'an. These (urban) factors have more to do with the social and cultural background against which new revolutionary ideas first emerged, rather than the political and military success of the revolution at later stages.

In his book on *Revolution and the People in Russia and China* (Steve Smith, 2008), Steve Smith provides such an analysis that privileges the framework of 'modernity' instead of, 'capitalism' (and in that sense also represents a general trend in historiography). Smith suggests a comparison of St. Petersburg from the 1880s to 1917, and Shanghai between 1900s and 1940s. During these periods, both cities experienced rapid urbanisation, driven by significant inflows of rural labour migrants. Earlier studies focused on proletarianisation and wage labour. But industrial capitalism did not only mean changes in the sphere of production. People living in those cities experienced broad changes in their worldviews and identities. Smith's focus is more on the subjective experience and critical reflection on modernity, rather than on the 'objective' processes of political economy. Altogether, this explanation of the roots of the revolution focuses less on capitalist exploitation than on a crisis of the entire social order, epitomised in the new experience of urban life, consumer culture, anonymity and the spread of the nuclear family and literacy. He compares the 'identity crises' people experienced in St. Petersburg and Shanghai in the following fields: native-place identity, individuality, gender identity, and nation-state identity in turn.

In these different arenas, the populations of St. Petersburg and Shanghai experienced a breakdown of the old order and the formation of a new commercialised mass culture. In both places, these experiences were also fundamentally related to the impact of transnational and global influences — modernity in Russia and China included a re-positioning towards a Eurocentric world. It was in the confrontation with westernisation and cosmopolitanism that new senses of nationalism and political identity developed in both places.

Yet, even though all these experiences were to some extent similar in both St. Petersburg and Shanghai, there were also differences given that there was more local industrial development in St. Petersburg, when compared with the presence of foreign investment in Shanghai. Smith emphasises that for the same reasons the focus of the Russian revolution was more on class identity, whereas in China it was a class-inflected national identity.

Smith's work deals much more directly with cultural difference and the localised experience of modernity, when compared with the outlines of Chen or Moore. Whereas the latter had focused on large-scale social comparisons, Smith emphasises the experience of modernity.

Aside from the large-scale interpretations of the reasons, process, and results of revolution, social scientists have also analysed specific features of modern revolutions; in the following, we briefly discuss two outstanding characteristics of the Maoist revolution in China.

Personality Cult and Partisan Warfare

The German sociologist Max Weber famously distinguished three types of authority: traditional, charismatic and rational-legal. He defined charismatic authority as 'resting on devotion to the exceptional sanctity, heroism or exemplary character of an individual person, and of the normative patterns or order revealed or ordained by him' (Weber, 1947, pp. 370–390). That is different from traditional authority, which is a repetition of previous generations, and from rational-legal authority, which is based on formal rationality, separate from substantive purposes. Because of its reliance on one person, charismatic authority can either disappear with the person, or become routinised by successors into traditional or rational-legal authority. Populist politics always rests to some degree on charismatic authority; and radicalism possibly corresponds to personal identification with leaders and their charismatic authority. As with Stalin and Kim Il Song, the charismatic authority of Mao as a leader was rehashed in symbolic exchanges between the people and the leader (Brooks, 2000; Ssorin-Chaikov, 2006; Kwon and Chung, 2012).

The personality cult around Mao became a central problem in Chinese communist politics. While the cult was often employed as a means of mobilisation, it was also a central problem in the interactions between elite level leadership, bureaucracy, and grassroots implementation. Inside party and government, a constant debate was taking place on the benefits and drawbacks: on the one hand, the personality cult was useful to mobilise ordinary people, yet at the same time, it was dangerous because overemphasising the person of the leader opposed socialist ideals (Leese, 2011). But aside from the charismatic authority of Mao Zedong himself, there were other features of Maoism that clearly distinguished it as a political movement: its radicality as a left-wing political movement, requiring complete identification with the cause of the movement.

This is well-captured in Carl Schmitt's *Theory of the Partisan* (1962). This series of lectures (delivered to an audience of academics in Franco-era Spain), deals with the history of partisan warfare, as a crucial form of modern war and politics. Schmitt defines the 'partisan' by the following four features. All of these features distinguish the partisan from the soldier in a standing army. First, irregularity: membership and social organisation are not fixed according to unequivocal institutional rules. Second, increased mobility: partisans are always on the move, and they change positions frequently and relatively independently. Third, intensity of political engagement: partisans' engagement with their cause is substantial and deep (this compensates for the irregularity of their organisation). And fourth, the telluric character of the partisan. From the Latin word for earth (*tellus*), this refers to the ties to the soil of autochthonous populations; populations that are defined by their geographical particularity. Partisans are very often peasant populations whose motivation to fight includes the wish to defend their land and people against oppressors and intruders.

Schmitt describes the development of the 'theory of the partisan' starting with the Spanish, Tyrolean, and Russian guerillas resisting the Napoleonic armies. The citizen-army that Napoleon led across Europe was itself based on a fundamental identification with the national cause and the person of the leader. This corresponded to a new and more intense participation of ordinary citizens in the resistance, and led the Prussian General Clausewitz to his famous formulation of 'war as a continuation of politics'. Later, Lenin would recognise the fundamental importance of partisan war for the cause of socialism. Here, the identification with the cause turned to new extremes; enmity had become absolute and no more 'bracketing' of war was possible. Maoism, finally, meant that partisan warfare became a normality through which civil wars and wars of resistance were fought in the twentieth century.[1]

The distinctiveness of partisan warfare shows in various aspects. Spatially, it ties down warfare to the particularities of the landscape — often being a local, the partisan is intimately familiar with geographical conditions, often in rough terrain, and for these reasons guerilla groups could resist large regular armies (e.g., in Algeria, in Vietnam). In terms of technology, partisans try to keep up with the technological advancement and armaments of regular armies, but generally have difficulties doing so because of their peripheral condition. Partisan warfare also implies an inter-locking of local and global political contexts; partisan struggle relates to wider geo-political interests and takes place within this broader landscape. In their radicalisation of struggle, the final objective is the complete annihilation of former social structures — the 'old order' — and its replacement with a new society. If previously war often proceeded like a chivalrous contest, the partisan knows the enemy (in the abstract) and aims to destroy him completely. In this sense, partisan warfare implies a continuation of Schmitt's classic conceptualisation of 'the political'.

In his 1927 volume *The Concept of the Political*, Carl Schmitt had defined politics in a radical way: 'The specific political distinction … is that between friend and enemy.' It is remarkable how similar this definition is to the following sentence by Mao Zedong: 'Who are our enemies? Who are our friends? This is a question of the first importance for the revolution' — which is from the 1926 essay 'An Analysis of the Classes

[1]The last step in the development of partisan warfare in Schmitt's (1962) lectures are the French generals under the leadership of Raoul Salan, who resisted the negotiations the French government had started with Algerian independence fighters, and then started the paramilitary *Organisation de l'armée secrete*. One might see the new wars of the twenty first century and contemporary terrorism as further developments of the genealogy that Schmitt describes.

in Chinese Society' and became the first sentence of the Little Red Book (*The Collected Sayings of Chairman Mao*). Noting this parallel, Dutton (2005, 2008) suggests an analysis of Maoist politics in terms of Carl Schmitt. Dutton offers radical insights both into the history of 'the political' in modern China, and the particular mechanisms of what he terms 'commitment politics' under Maoism. The radical nature of political commitment under Maoism — constantly being involved in a war between friends and foes — 'produced a life both extremely dangerous but also utterly life-affirming. It gave purpose to one's existence and offered a sense of belonging that would fill one's soul' (Dutton, 2005, p. 313). But the friend–foe opposition also became a core mechanism of the mass campaigns and the state-building efforts of the party. In constant rectification campaigns, the core problem became how to distinguish between friends and enemies. This was not only obvious in the constant re-appearance of 'traitors' and 'class enemies', but also in the inner process that Communist Party members had to undergo through self-observation and self-criticism.

Seminar Question

Compare different explanations for the reasons of the success of the Chinese Communist revolution in establishing the People's Republic in 1949.

Key Readings

Chen, Yung-fa. 1986. *Making Revolution: The Communist Movement in Eastern and Central China 1937–1945*. Berkeley: University of California Press, introduction, pp. 1–9.

Harrison, H. 2001. *China (Inventing the Nation)*. London: Arnold, Chapters 7 and 9, pp. 169–189, 207–225.

Moore, B. J. 1967. *Social Origins of Dictatorship and Democracy: Lord and Peasant in the Making of the Modern World.* London: Allen Lane, Chapter 9, pp. 453–483 (also read the preface, pp. xi–xix).

Smith, S. 2008. *Revolution and the People in Russia and China*. Cambridge: Cambridge University Press (Introduction).

Further Readings

Anderson, P. 2010. Two revolutions. rough notes. *New Left Review*, **61**, pp. 59–96.

Andrew, A. M., and Rapp, J. A. 2000. *Autocracy and China's Rebel Founding Emperors. Comparing Chairman Mao and Ming Taizu*, Rowman and Littlefield.

Bianco, L. 2001. *Peasants Without the Party: Grass-roots Movements in Twentieth-Century, China*. Armonk: M. E. Sharpe (Chapter 7).

Brenner, R. 1987. The Agrarian Roots of European Capitalism. In *The Brenner Debate*, Aston, T. and Philpin, C. (eds.), Cambridge: Cambridge Univeristy Press.

Brooks, J. 2000. *Thank you, Comrade Stalin!: Soviet Public Culture from Revolution to Cold War*. Princeton: Princeton University Press (Chapter 4: 'The Economy of the Gift').

Dutton, M. 2005. *Policing Chinese Politics: A History*. Durham, NC: Duke University Press.

Dutton, M. 2008. Passionately governmental: Maoism and the structured intensities of revolutionary governmentality. *Postcolonial Studies*, **11**(1), pp. 99–112.

Esherick, J. W. 1995. Ten Theses on the Chinese Revolution. *Modern China*, **21**(1), pp. 45–76.

Johnson, C. A. 1962. *Peasant Nationalism and Communist Power: The Emergence of Revolutionary China, 1937–1945*. Stanford, CA: Stanford University Press.

Kataoka, Tetsuya 1974. *Resistance and Revolution in China: The Communists and the Second United Front*. Berkeley, CA: University of California Press.

Kwon, H. and Chung, B-H. 2012. *North Korea: Beyond Charismatic Politics*. Lanham, MA: Rowman and Littlefield.

Leese, D. 2011. *Mao Cult: Rhetoric and Ritual in China's Cultural Revolution*. Cambridge: Cambridge University Press.

Mann, M. 1986. *The Sources of Social Power*, Vol. i: *A History of Power from the Beginning to 1760 AD*. Cambridge: Cambridge University Press.

Schmitt, C. 2007. *Theory of the Partisan: Intermediate Commentary on the Concept of the Political*. New York: Telos Press Publishers.

Schurmann, F. 1968. *Ideology and Organisation in Communist China*. Berkeley: California University Press.

Selden, M. 1971. *The Yenan Way in Revolutionary China*. Boston, MA: Harvard University Press.

Skocpol, T. 1976. France, Russia, China: A structural analysis of social revolutions. *Comparative Studies in Society and History*, **18**(2), pp. 175–210.

Skocpol, T. 1979. *States and Social Revolutions: A Comparative Analysis of France, Russia, and China*. Cambridge: Cambridge University Press.

Ssorin-Chaikov, N. 2006. On Heterochrony: Birthday gifts to Stalin, 1949. *Journal of the Royal Anthropological Institute*, **12**, pp. 355–375.

Tilly, C. 1990. *Coercion, Capital and European States, AD 990–1990*. Oxford: Blackwell.

Weber, M. 1947. *The Theory of Social and Economic Organization* (transl. Talcott Parsons). Glencoe, IL: Free Press (pp. 370–390 on Charisma).

Chapter 8

Socialism

This chapter introduces debates in the sociology and political science of socialism, including topics such as the transformations of local society, the relative reach of the central state, and the distinction between 'reds' and 'experts'. These questions are discussed for the case of Maoist China and compared mainly with Stalinism in the Soviet Union.

Overview of Sino-Soviet Relationships

Because the Soviet Union will be the main comparator in this chapter, it will be helpful to start here with a brief overview of the relationship between the People's Republic of China (PRC) and the Soviet Union between 1949 and 1976. After the establishment of the PRC, the relationship was initially very close. The policies drafted in the 1950s often followed Soviet outlines, in particular in their emphasis on heavy industry, and in those years the Soviet Union sent a number of advisors to China. Aside from heavy industry, the main objective was to build bureaucratic structures; the main ideological targets were also similar, and included the mobilisation of labour, gender equality, and atheism.

But slowly political differences also developed. These became apparent after Khrushchev denounced Stalin in a famous speech 'On the Personality Cult and its Consequences' in 1956. Khruschev then ushered in a 'thaw' politics, distancing himself from Stalin, and aiming at 'peaceful co-existence' in the international arena. These changes were seen with suspicion in China. In particular, the international outlook was quite different, with Mao still favouring a more confrontational position towards the USA.

The Soviet Union, in turn, did not support China's internal policies, in particular the 'Great Leap Forward', in which Mao's Party rejected the Soviet ministerial vertical command of industry establishing a parallel and lateral Party committee control of ministerial firms. These differences culminated in 1960 in a split between the two countries. In order to pay for the industrial plants that the Soviet Union had loaned to China, grain revenue was commandeered from Chinese farmers by Party-led collectivisation and mobilisation that became a kind of terror that led to useless rural iron and steel production, harvest failure and a mass famine in 1959. The Sino-Soviet split was formalised in 1960 in the midst of the famine. The split lasted after reversal of the Great Leap rural policies and prepared the ground for China's rapprochement with the United States. This culminated in US President Nixon's visit to China in 1972, and ensuing 'ping-pong diplomacy'.

During the Cold War, the main powers fought proxy wars, supporting different smaller local powers, mainly in the Third World, including, for instance, the Korean War of 1950–1953 and the second Vietnam War in 1979. The crucial importance of the third world arena for the cold war has only been recently recognised by international historians (Westad, 2006).

One very important distinction between the Soviet Union and Maoist China had to do with the different forms of organisation that are epitomised in the definition of the new bureaucrats: cadres or 'political commissars'.

Reds and Experts

The new bureaucracies of the Soviet Union and the People's Republic were staffed by a new kind of bureaucrat. These officials had to combine 'ability and virtue', they had to be both capable to take over formal positions in the bureaucracy and be leaders in political combat. Similarly, it is normal for elected representatives in legislative assemblies and the ministers promoted from their ranks to combine ability, leadership and virtue without already being experts. But their administrative bureaucracies serve them as experts, whereas in the Soviet Union and the People's Republic, Party cadres led state officials at all levels of administration and were to be exemplars of all these qualities. In this particular new combination, they were different both from 'traditional' and 'modern' bureaucrats in the classical definitions of sociologist Max Weber.

Traditional bureaucrats worked through extended networks of mutual involvement and personal relationships; their bureaucracy was guided by a shared sense of values and a certain ethos. Modern bureaucracy, according to Weber, means the spread of formal rationality; behaviour had to be adjusted to rational norms and rules. Both are schemes of organisation geared towards routinisation. Managers and cadres are opposite to bureaucrats in the sense in which their action is primarily not geared towards routinisation, but instead to constant change. And whereas managers try to adapt to constant change using administrative techniques and rational organisation, cadres reverted to human solidarity. Here the shared values are not an 'ethos' of the organisation, but rather a political ideology. And cadres had to use this ideology to manipulate the thoughts and sentiments of followers. So, the solidarity of the cadre was in some way similar to traditional bureaucrats — who were also guided by a set of shared values — yet, different to a traditional bureaucrat, a cadre had to constantly adapt to new situations and partake in political combat. While the new cadre bureaucracies also established further division of labour according to technical expertise, the organisational coherence of many units was based on personal relations (Schurmann, 1968, pp. 162–172).

The development of organisational and managerial structures within the Chinese Communist Party (CCP) has often been interpreted as an oscillation between 'reds' and 'experts' — the two sides of the institution of the cadre (who had to be both 'red' in terms of political ideology, and an 'expert' possessing technical knowledge). These opposite sides are embodied in the leadership of Mao Zedong ('red') versus Liu Shaoqi, and later Deng Xiaoping ('expert'). The main objective of either side was mass mobilisation versus bureaucracy-building; some writers have described this as 'institution' versus 'organisation' (Selznick cited in Schurmann, 1968), or even mechanic solidarity versus organic solidarity (Kipnis, 2008, pp. 179–183).

On a broader comparative level, there are similar differences between Maoism and Stalinism: whereas, Maoism tended to emphasise political mobilisation, Stalinism put higher value on the construction of an effective bureaucracy. The differences here are partly due to the different social bases of Maoism and Stalinism in China and Russia: while, Maoism was largely peasant-based, Stalinism put more emphasis on the urban working classes (yet, both were led by educated elites).

The differences between Maoism and Stalinism must be seen on the background of very contingent local histories that cannot be subordinated to a simple distinction between 'red' and 'expert'. Soviet Russia had gone through its most intense periods of mobilisation from the 1920s to the 1940s, already before the establishment of the PRC. The Soviet Union encompassed a much larger diversity of ethnic groups; and even though the classification and political representation of China's non-Han 'minority peoples' (*shaoshu minzu*) was originally modelled on Stalinist theory, the PRC would not contemplate a federation of republics such as that of the Soviet Union. If ideologically both countries were internationalist, the undercurrents of Chinese (Han) nationalism became different from the Cold War opposition of Russia/the Soviet Union to the capitalist West, mainly because of the different geopolitical positioning of both countries. By the 1970s, the Soviet Union had been relatively successful in terms of establishing a socialist 'welfare system' of education and health. The turmoil of the Cultural Revolution (1966–1976) contrasted much with the years of stagnation under Brezhnev (Rozman, 2010, 521ff).

Socialism also simply lasted longer in the Soviet Union, and by the 1980s, the Soviet Union, in its major cities of Moscow and Leningrad had a larger urban class that was in many ways dependent on the system. At the same time, China was still predominantly rural and therefore a lesser percentage of the population had relatively stably benefited from socialism. The bureaucratic nature of the Soviet Union, on the whole, remained less compatible with the Chinese society. For similar reasons, reforms turned out to be more difficult in the 'mature' Socialist society of the Soviet Union. Ultimately, the focus of the Bolshevik party was more on urban elites and bureaucratic construction when compared with Maoist mobilisation.

So far, we have taken a macro-perspective on Chinese society. In the following we will discuss several approaches that put the social development of rural China at centre stage.

Local Governance: Cellularisation and Involution

Chinese Maoism has been described as a form of totalitarianism; Cold War polemics aside, the central question remains how to understand the extraordinary social transformations that took place under Maoism. Early analyses in terms of totalitarianism emphasise the radical ideological transformations and the 'penetration' of local societies by an extended bureaucracy (Schapiro and Lewis, 1969).

Against such arguments that compare the Maoist state in China to totalitarianism, Shue (1988) argues that the reach of the socialist state in China was limited. Contrary to its proclaimed aims, it entrenched peasant localism and the 'cellularity' of China's rural society.

Shue proposes a centre-periphery approach that focuses (a) on the extent of social integration; (b) on the patterns of social and structural division and (c) on the relations of the developing state apparatus to both social integration and socio-structural division. The aims of the centre had been assumed to be ever greater integration and penetration of the periphery. Befu, for instance, had suggested a typology of states in which 'the modern state of Communist China … controls practically every sphere of peasant life' (quoted in Shue, 1988, p. 44). The core problem of such an approach is that it is empirically wrong as Shue points out. Conceptually, power is imagined as a zero-sum game in such an approach: what the central government gains in power, the village loses. But power does not have to exist in fixed amounts and it is conceivable that both central government and village-level government gain power at the same time. And finally such an approach does not focus on the particular social struggles, units and groups at the periphery of state power.

This is particularly significant for the conditions under which the Chinese revolution took place: a large percentage of the population was still illiterate; large parts of the countryside were relatively underdeveloped (in particular, in terms of mass communication and technology) and local bureaucracies remained relatively inefficient. For all these reasons, it was simply not possible to quickly build a surveillance state of the proportions of Eastern European states at the same time. Hence, it is useful to take the gap between the countryside and the city into account, and focus on the particular conditions of rural society and the peasantry as a social group. The Maoist revolution, in fact, made residential and occupational mobility impossible, and welfare was closely tied to villages and rural communes. To understand what happened to rural communities, Shue refers to William Skinner's model of standard marketing areas. Skinner (1964) had argued that the standard marking areas had been the fundamental social units of traditional China. These were defined by the periodical peasant markets that still exist in many parts of China and which are generally held on every second, third, or fifth day of the Chinese lunar month. Every family goes regularly to one market, and if households are distributed equally on a plane, the standard marketing areas form hexagons. Aside from its economic importance, Skinner had also argued that the standard marketing areas are fundamental social units — basically the units of the face-to-face society in which most families were known and in which the same dialect was spoken. In later publications, Skinner also dealt with the changes that Maoism had brought to the periodical peasant markets. He described how policies toward rural marketing could be taken as an example of the cycles of policy changes under Maoism. Policies oscillated between mass mobilisation, based on "normative power (persuasion, exhortation, manipulation of symbolic rewards)" and economic recovery, based on "remunerative power (material rewards, appeals to self-interest)". According to Skinner, the national policy cycle went at least 11 times back and forth (Skinner, 1985, 395ff).

What is important to note is that the standard marketing areas in most parts of China roughly corresponded to the new administrative units of the people's communes (*renmin gongshe*). Shue points out that, just like the earlier marketing areas, the people's communes and other rural units drew clear boundaries between insiders and outsiders. They were also largely self-sufficient in economic and social terms. In the normative cycles, they were units of collective mobilisation. In the remunerative cycles, they were units of marketing of products including the produce of households' private plots. Yet, different to the 'half-society' of the peasant — the small society of the little tradition that could not be understood in isolation from the 'great tradition' (Redfield) — Maoism pushed local society further towards a relatively small 'complete society'. She describes this process as an 'encapsulation' or a 'cellularisation' of local societies that become more and more 'vertically segmented'. Her central argument is that the Maoist state, against its own intentions, effectively strengthened the solidarity of peasant communities against outside ('statist') domination.

Political integration was partly ideological and partly organisational, to use Schurmann's terms. Once the turmoil of the Great Leap Forward was settled and its hugely over-sized and unmanageable Communes were broken up, the organisation of rural production was through 'teams' (*xiaodui*), which were neighbourhoods or hamlets, the basic unit of cooperation and joint work and budgeting. A number of teams made up a 'brigade' (*dadui*), often a large village, the basic unit of rural industry and of grain storage and distribution. 'People's communes' (*renmin gongshe*) sometimes coinciding with the area of what had been administrative townships or with the area of a standard marketing centre contained several brigades and organised more specialised industry and services.

The same structure of organisation existed throughout the People's Republic, but income was distributed (according to a tally of workpoints for each household) at team or brigade level, overseen by the commune. Income and all rural welfare such as payment of income to the aged without family support varied according to local production levels. The ideal was that a commune should be self-reliant. So this was organisational but not economic integration, whereas in the Soviet Union standardisation of incomes had been achieved even in the equivalent to brigades, collective farms and rose to be equivalent to the wage grades on state farms. Soviet farmers were close to having been proletarianised and fully integrated into a central planning system, though that was still one that depended on fixers and corrupt practices to show that targets had been met.

Ideological integration in the People's Republic was through the top-down organisation of the Party, whose lowest cells were at the level of the brigade. But its members were not integrated into a firm structure of planning. Formal plans were in fact the result of bargaining between provinces and regions determining how much revenue from production and its sales through agreed prices should go to the centre and how much at the regional or provincial or lower levels.

Local officials had to combine administrative activism and local political and economic entrepreneurship. Team and brigade leaders and brigade Party cadres were local farmers, subject to the peer-pressure of fellow collective farmers as well as to their superiors and their ambitions to rise by performance according to 'red' virtue standards and the current political line, to be studied in the latest editions of the Party newspaper, The People's Daily (*Renmin Ribao*). Farmers worked collectively, but their teams were the same as what had been local descent groups, sharing the same ancestors. They lived in family households that shared the work-points of their members and the debts to the team if they needed welfare payments to raise them to the minimum needed for survival. The house built on collective land was owned by the family household and the household land included a plot on which the family could raise poultry, pigs, and vegetables both for their own consumption and for sale in local markets.

The main consequences of all this were that the vertical segmentation and localisation of peasant society were strengthened; and the penetration of the village periphery by the central state was seldom direct and never complete. Maoism in the countryside in fact entrenched peasant localism and cadre departmentalism.

An ethnographic example from rural Guangdong province seems to confirm Shue's argument: before the 1950s, local society was characterised by a plethora of local organisations, temple associations, powerholders, and gentry. The Maoist revolution in fact replaced this diversity of local powerholders with a relatively monolithic government apparatus. But teams of young, sometimes urban, cadres who were sent down to the countryside, had to work together with members of local society.

Campaigns had to be adapted to local conditions and bureaucratic efficiency remained fairly low. Such a situation, in which the local state and local society became deeply intermingled with local society, Helen Siu describes as 'state involution' (1989). Siu's notion of 'state involution' broadly supports Shue's arguments about cellularisation; but different to Shue, Siu also emphasises the changes in ideological discourse that took place. This is also the main criticism that other scholars have brought forward against Shue's arguments. On the basis of his long-term research in rural China, Jonathan Unger, for instance, points out that Shue plays down the changes in ideological discourse (Unger, 1989). Even though there might have been a lot of eclecticism in the ways in which the messages of the centre were taken up in local society, surely something fundamental about the general discourse changed during the Maoist era.

Yet, some observers have used Shue's focus on the relative 'subsidiarity' of local political units in China, to describe their adaptation to changing environments in the reform era that began in the 1980s. Shirk (1993), for instance, argues that it was precisely because of the spontaneous organisation that local units had mastered during the Maoist era that allowed them to adapt to a new, volatile, environment in the 1980s — and that, this institutional adaptability ultimately was a main factor that explains their economic success since then.

Urban and industrial organisations were far more unified. All urban residents were organised into either work units (*danwei*) that were also units of residence, recreation and welfare under the authority of various ministries of industrial production or of education or civil and military centralised organisation. Or they were organised into neighbourhood units, decreasing in number and importance, within which mainly women and the infirm were also organised into neighbourhood factories. The work unit was also a unit of ideological formation, the creation of a socialist person, as well as the lowest level of Party organisation (Bray, 2005).

Narrative Approaches to Socialism

The radical re-organisation of society that was implied in the socialist revolutions of the twentieth century also meant a radical re-description of the world. Hence, language and narrative can also provide interesting perspectives on comparative socialism.

In fact, language, discourse, and narrative were in many ways crucial for the success of socialism and for its working in general. The Russian cultural critic Boris Groys makes the point that language was in fact the 'universal currency' of communism. Whereas in capitalism, capital was the universal currency, ultimately determining thought through processes of commodification, in communism, language fulfilled a similar function: the correct analysis and the right narrative ultimately determined the right measurement of and approach towards the world. For the same reason,

Groys describes communism as a 'kingdom of philosophy' (Groys, 2009). The definitions he uses of capitalism and socialism are perhaps too monolithic; but it is undeniable that the speeches of Communist leaders such as Khrushchev, Castro, and Mao often were particularly long — perhaps more so than the speeches of leaders of liberal democracies — and they had to be studied at all levels of Party organisation.

Various scholars have described the uses of narratives that the Communist regime made in China (Apter, 1993; Apter and Saich, 1994; Liu, 2009, Chapter 6). Revolutionary discourses created new realities in various ways. In perhaps the most obvious way, the Maoist revolution introduced a whole new set of names — the names of institutions and places, for instance. But beyond that, it also introduced new narratives, story-lines according to which life histories and local memory could be transmitted.

For instance, land reform in the first years of the People's Republic created new identities that were the bases of the main rural mass organisation, peasant associations. These identities, which marked every resident's file and identity card until some years into the post-Mao reforms, were the class identities that made them friends or enemies of the revolution: landless labourers, poor peasants (tenants with no land of their own), lower-middle peasants (who owned some land but not enough to live on), middle peasants (who owned sufficient land to live on), rich peasants (with more than enough to live on, some of it rented out) and landlords (who rented out their land, though this included not just town-based absentee landlords but also poor widows who depended on rent for a poor living). The latter two categories were 'enemies' even if they belonged to the same descent group as their neighbours. The first four categories were organised into peasant associations, later excluding 'middle peasants' from 'poor and lower-middle-level peasant associations' mobilised for class struggle and the furtherance of socialism. These class labels were reinforced by the personal narratives of class struggle performed in meetings to attack landlords and oppressors in sessions for 'speaking bitterness' (*suku*) or 'remembering bitterness and appreciating sweetness' (*yiku sitian*). Poor and landless peasants recalled bitter experiences of hardship at the hands of landlords. Present sweetness was having land or later collective income and the promise of a glorious future of socialism. It was a shock when some urban youth volunteering to live in the countryside in the years of cultural revolution realised that the bitterness some villagers spoke of was the famine of 1959–1961. Narratives that similarly contrast the bitter past with the glorious present and future are presented today in films and TV serials that recall the humiliations China suffered at the hands of the imperial powers and from which it has now recovered to become a global power. Farquhar and Berry (2004) show its prevalence over the whole Chinese-speaking world. Indeed, it is a trope common to most nationalist movements, with which patriots of all kinds can identify. What might be peculiar to the People's Republic was that it was personalised and institutionalised at the village level.

Seminar Question

What are the main differences between Maoism and Stalinism?

Key Readings

Bernstein, T. 2010. Introduction: The complexities of learning from the Soviet Union. In *China Learns from the Soviet Union, 1949–Present*, T. P. Bernstein and Hua-Yu Li (eds.). Lanham, MD: Lexington Books, pp. 1–26.

Bray, D. 2005. *Social Space and Governance in Urban China: The Danwei System from Origins to Reform*. Stanford, CA: Stanford University Press.

Rozman, G. 2010. Concluding assessment: The Soviet impact on Chinese society. In *China Learns from the Soviet Union, 1949–Present*, T. P. Bernstein and Hua-Yu Li (eds.). Lanham, MD: Lexington Books, pp. 517–526.

Schurmann, F. 1968. *Ideology and Organization in Communist China*. Berkeley: University of California Press, pp. 162–172 on the cadre and pp. 220–238 on Bureaucracy and management.

Shue, V. 1988. Introduction. In *The Reach of the State: Sketches of the Chinese Body Politic*. Stanford, CA: Stanford University Press, pp. 1–8.

Further Readings

Apter, D., and Saich, T. 1994. *Revolutionary Discourse in Mao's Republic*. Boston: Harvard University Press.

Apter, D. E. 1993. Yan'an and the narrative reconstruction of reality. *Daedalus*, **122**(2), pp. 207–232.

Bernstein, T. P. 1967. Leadership and mass mobilisation in the Soviet and Chinese collectivisation campaigns of 1929/1930 and 1955/1956. A comparison. *The China Quarterly*, **31**, pp. 1–47.

Farquhar, M., and Berry, C. 2004. Speaking bitterness: history, media and nation in twentieth century China. *Historiography East and West*, **2**(1), pp. 116–143.

Groys, B. 2009. *The Communist Postscript*. London: Verso.

Kipnis, A. 2008. *China and Postsocialist Anthropology*. Norwalk, Conn.: EastBridge.

Liu Xin. 2009. *The Mirage of China: Anti-humanism, Narcissism, and Corporeality of the Contemporary World*. New York: Berghahn Books, Chapter 6, pp. 133–171.

Westad, A. 2006. *The Global Cold War: Third World Interventions and the Making of Our Times*. Cambridge: Cambridge University Press (esp. pp. 160–170 and 396–407).

Siu, H. F. 1989. *Agents and Victims in South China: Accomplices in Rural Revolution*. London: Yale University Press.

Schapiro, L., and Lewis, J. W. 1969. The Roles of the monolithic party under the totalitarian leader. *The China Quarterly*, **40**, pp. 39–64.

Shirk, S. L. 1993. *The Political Logic of Economic Reform in China*. Berkeley: University of California Press.

Shue, V. 1988. *The Reach of the State: Sketches of the Chinese Body Politic*. Stanford, CA: Stanford University Press.

Skinner, G. W. 1964. Marketing and social structure in rural China: Part I. *The Journal of Asian Studies*, **24**(1), pp. 3–43.

Skinner, G. W. 1985. Rural marketing in China: Repression and revival. *The China Quarterly*, **103**, pp. 393–413.

Unger, J. 1989. State and peasant in post-revolution China. *The Journal of Peasant Studies*, **17**(1), pp. 114–136.

Chapter 9

Post-Socialism

This chapter discusses the changes Chinese economy and politics underwent in the 1980s and 1990s. The main debates about the transition from socialism deal with China's relative economic success and the changes in the political regime, including the questions of social pluralism and managed authoritarianism. The main comparator is Russia, but other post-socialist countries are also drawn upon.

The Maoist political and ideological project of the Chinese Communist Party (CCP) only lasted for two generations. Older loyalties and ideologies, including those of kinship and local religion re-emerged in 1961 during the first decollectivisation, and they have been re-emerging since the second decollectivisation in 1980.

The ending of the Cultural Revolution decade after the death of Mao in 1976 was the victory of the Party-institution tendency and for repeating the same reforms that had been used for the recovery from the Great Leap famine, as Yang Dali (1996) has argued. Those reforms became what Maoists had predicted they would become: a restoration of capitalist economics. The reforms, beginning with gradual decollectivisation of agriculture, went on to dismantle the whole ministerial administration of the economy. The result has been an extraordinary growth of all kinds and sizes of manufacturing industry, light, service, and heavy, of household savings and purchasing power, and the production for export or re-export and the importing of consumer goods to meet and stimulate market demand.

The shortness of the period of what we can call a Maoist state and its politics of mass mobilisation should not make us think that the Maoist state and emphasis on political will are entirely gone. Many of its features still exist, in particular the CCP and its monopoly of authority and control of state power, though now at an indirect remove from economic and social organisation. The use of work teams and police to conduct campaigns persists. On a more popular plane, collective will and ideals of social justice are recalled. They are mixed with the new, reforming state and its institutions on the one hand, and the revival of older, including pre-Republican, loyalties on the other.

In the post-Mao era, members of transformed local elites and transformed poor peasants became leaders of revived institutions of kinship and popular temples and festivals, or became supporters of Confucian virtues as well as the more recent ideals of service to the people and collective responsibility cultivated during the revolutionary decades.

What is Post-Socialism?

Post-socialism, in the outline of various observers, refers to the shared practices, institutions and ideologies in formerly 'socialist' countries. Even though the People's Republic of China (PRC) is still 'socialist' according to its self-description, it shares many of the features of the post-socialist countries of Eastern Europe and the Former Soviet Union (SU).

In their introduction to the edited volume, *Post-socialism: Ideals, Ideologies and Practices in Eurasia* (Hann, *et al.*, 2002), Chris Hann, Caroline Humphrey and Katherine Verdery discuss the usefulness and application of the concept. Chris Hann points to the similarities in the social transformations that formerly socialist countries underwent. The transition 'away from socialism' generally implied a renewed focus on markets. With this a number of crucial questions arose: what are the pathways of privatisation? How did the transition towards a market economy change the balances between agriculture and industry? In which ways were new consumerist lifestyles established in different countries? How did new movements of ethnicity and nationalism compensate for the demise of the socialist order?

Caroline Humphrey emphasises three points that point to the value of the label of 'post-socialism': First, it can help us to think about the heritage of actually existing socialism. Second, the label opens up a good field for comparison. And finally, the label should emphasise that the changes of post-socialism have not been unidirectional — there has been a resurgence of communist parties in a number of countries; and historically various twists and reversals followed the end of socialism. Fundamental generational changes are taking place in many post-socialist countries — and that is also true for a new generation of observers who focus on different issues than the first generation of students of 'post-socialism'. There are regional re-orientations taking place, with much of the former Eastern Bloc now looking towards the EU and NATO, whereas the nations of East Asia have to deal with the rise of China. New authoritarianisms and nationalisms have also emerged in the 'post-socialist' world (which will be discussed further below).

Katherine Verdery points out that post-socialism might also be usefully compared with post-colonialism. Both intellectual fields mark a temporal transition, as well as a conceptual field. In fact, the expansion and influence of the SU in particular might also be said to have been 'colonial' in some way. Similar to colonialism, various forms of socialism operated as 'civilising missions' of a centre towards its peripheries. The centre exercised its dominance not only in terms of administration, but also in politics of knowledge and representation.

Yet, while there might be similarities to imperialism and colonialism, the expansion and influence of the SU and of China was also in some ways fundamentally different when compared with the colonial policies of Great Britain and France, for instance. Surely, global capitalist competition played a very different role in both processes; while it was an integral part of modern imperialism, capitalism was the foil against which socialist societies operated during the Cold War. Accordingly, some have argued that the label "Post Cold War Studies" would be more appropriate than "post-socialism" (Kwon, 2011).

The Transition

The recent histories of the 'transition' in China and the SU show striking contrasts. In China, the cultural revolution came to an end in 1976, the same year in which Mao Zedong and Zhou Enlai died. In the next two years, Deng Xiaoping emerged as the new paramount leader (even though he would never hold the offices of chairman or prime minister). Under Deng's leadership, large changes took place. One of the most significant policy changes would be the return of farmland from rural collectives to individual households, in the so-called "household responsibility system", which was introduced in the early 1980s. The same decade would see the promotion of small industries, the "Township and Village Enterprises" (TVEs), and the opening of Special Economic Zones in China's coastal areas. The era of "Reform and Opening" that was declared was interrupted by the student uprising of 1989 that was brutally repressed by the central leadership. The Southern Tour of Deng Xiaoping in 1992 marked the beginning of further opening of the Chinese economy, progressive privatisation of state companies and the encouragement of foreign investment. On this Southern Tour, Deng Xiaoping famously announced that development as measured in Gross Domestic Product (GDP) growth is the "absolute principle" (*ying daoli*) for China. Even though the following decade saw a further re-invigoration of economic privatisation, pillar industries still remained government owned, according to the principle of "grasping the large and releasing the small" (*zhuada fangxiao*).

Throughout this transition, the Communist Party of China remained in power. On the whole, the gradualism of the transition from collective ownership to private entrepreneurship led to huge economic growth, an increase in household savings and in finance and the banking sector.

The gradualism of the transition in China is often compared with the suddenness of reform in the SU. Previous to the transition, the SU had experienced almost two decades of relative stability and stagnation during the Brezhnev era (1964–1982). In the 1980s, the new president Gorbachev slowly began policies of *glasnost* ("transparency") and *perestroika* ("restructuring"). But these policies eventually led in 1991 to the collapse of the SU and the Communist Party. The former SU broke up into a large number of member states out of which the Russian Federation under Yeltsin was the biggest and most important one. Following the recommendation of International Monetary Fund (IMF) and World Bank economists, the Russian Federation then implemented economic policies that have been often described as 'shock therapy'. They included rapid privatisation that led to a decrease in welfare, a fast increase in the number of the unemployed, and a sharp drop in household savings and finance in the banking sector. On the whole, the results of the transition in Russia were a shrinking economy, impoverishment and insecurity.

Comparisons and the Role of Markets

It is a core assumption of neo-classical economics that market economies are more efficient in the allocation of resources than planned economies. But the results and pathways of such transitions have been very different, and so important insights about the functioning of markets might be drawn from different post-socialist transitions.

Before the transition, both the Union of Soviet Socialist Republics (USSR) and the PRC shared an emphasis on heavy industry, guaranteed schooling, medical care, and security of low income. Within limits, both countries managed to raise life expectancy and literacy. As emphasised in the previous chapter, the USSR had become more industrialised and state-organised when compared with China, which remained more rural and agrarian. Per capita income in China was much lower when compared with the SU.

Transition increased relative inequality in both countries, but in China, absolute income levels increased, whereas in USSR they decreased for the majority of the population.

The comparison between the 'shock therapy' in Russia and the gradual changes in the Chinese political economy is very common, and it might sometimes blind us to the fact that the Chinese economy was in several ways fundamentally different when compared to Russia. Vietnam is to some extent a more appropriate comparator for China, in particular because both countries were predominantly rural and started their transitions towards more diversified industrial economies during socialism. In both countries, the planned agricultural economy returned to household farming, emphasising a fair distribution of land for the purpose of income security. In both countries, one major economic challenge had to do with the further development of industry outside the agricultural sector. The reduction of employment in the official sector and in State-Owned Enterprises (SOEs) together with the reduction of agricultural land due to expansion of industry and urbanisation led to high unemployment and 'surplus labour' both in China and Vietnam. The further growth of the economy was then mainly dependent on an increase of economic activity and new entrepreneurship. Governments aimed to foster diversification and economic liberalisation, in particular through large-scale investments in infrastructure. Even though there were some new institutions of welfare and social insurance, the main source of social insurance remained family savings (which was very different from Russia, where the state welfare sector was much bigger).

The so-called "Washington Consensus" of the IMF and other economic advisers heeded by Yeltsin in Russia was that macroeconomic stability could be achieved by a strict monetary policy and balanced government budgets by the liberalisation of prices and the privatisation of SOEs. But as we have seen, following these guidelines led to a massive fall of GDP. Price liberalisation that was supposed to lead to more efficient allocation was implemented too suddenly with seriously disruptive impacts on supply networks and uncertainty. The lesson was that price controls on staple products could be justified. Indeed, rationing, fixed purchasing prices, and price controls were maintained in China for more than a decade. A dual price system (part controlled, part fluctuating) for staple food and crucial means and materials of production was maintained. It did guarantee standards of living and production in key economic sectors, while at the same time it was an engine for corruption, in which 'two-way merchants' (*erdao fanzi*) with access to fixed-price resources could sell them at fluctuating but higher market prices. Consumer prices in China remained relatively stable, whereas in Russia price controls were removed immediately with disastrous consequences.

Reasons for the Chinese Economic Miracle

The gradualism of the policy of 'reform and opening' is one reason for the Chinese economic miracle of sustained GDP growth. Among other reasons that should be brought to attention are high rates of state investment at provincial and lower levels, more than at central budgeting levels, to finance infrastructure projects, such as roads and high-speed rail links, or special economic zones and industrial parks, and for maintaining the remaining, large SOEs. A further reason is the large-scale migration of surplus labour to industrial production in all sectors, competing for jobs and keeping the costs of employment low: in short, cheap labour. Another important reason is foreign direct investment which is one of the things attracted by cheap but literate labour, especially for manufacturing export (70% of China's exports are value-added exports). Since 2008, China has become the world's number one exporter of manufactured goods. As a result, China has the world's largest dollar reserves creating a symbiosis between the economies of the PRC and the USA. US debt and the value of the US dollar is supported by the PRC's import of parts from and export of finished products to the USA — supporting, rather than taking jobs out of the US labour market.

But the rate of growth in export earnings has slowed, leading to a crucial question that Chinese policy-makers have faced for two decades: how can the Chinese economy continue creating jobs for the laid-off workers from SOEs and the surplus labour from the countryside without relying so heavily on export industries? The answer is greater self-sustained growth, increased domestic markets and domestic consumption. For this reason, government campaigns have urged people to save less and spend more, but this is only feasible if basic income, housing and welfare are secured by other means.

Standard explanations for Chinese economic growth point to local institutional innovations, such as the TVEs that were partly or mainly owned by local government units, decentralisation of government and selective financial control. Yet, all these explanations contradict standard explanations of economic growth, which would include the following factors that were arguably not present in China: private ownership, security of property rights, financial liberalisation, and political reform.

Huang (2008) points out that in China, especially in the 1980s, seemingly inefficient policies (such as public ownership and financial control) performed underlying efficient functions. Against much accepted knowledge, Huang describes an environment that effectively favoured private entrepreneurship. On the basis of a large amount of empirical data he points out that TVEs were effectively not publicly-owned. In fact, Huang argues it was thriving private entrepreneurship in the countryside in the 1980s, which created the new Chinese capitalism. He sees this entrepreneurship as based on financial reforms in the countryside. Furthermore, he maintains that the security of proprietors increased substantially, and all this took place in an environment in which policies became more credible and predictable, and the political system was as a whole 'directionally liberal'.

He contrasted this development model with the urban focused development epitomised by Shanghai since the late 1990s. According to Huang, the latter is mainly led by SOEs, whereas indigenous private-sector business remained stifled by extreme regulations and restrictions. Accordingly, the share of labour income to GDP remained low, while GDP increased, household incomes did not. Wages for employees in government and SOEs were high, but asset income was amongst the lowest in the PRC. All this led to the income of the poorest segments of the population decreasing since 2000. This kind of development model, Huang argues, is also linked to low rates of innovation: the number of annual patent grants decreased substantially when compared with Zhejiang and Guangzhou that were much more heavily invested in private industry. And ultimately, according to Huang, this development model systematically favoured corruption because of the tight links it promotes between government and business.

Hence, for Huang, there are two Chinas: an entrepreneurial, market-driven rural China, and a state-led urban China. In the 1980s, rural China was leading in economic development, and a form of capitalism was promoted that was entrepreneurial, politically independent, vibrantly competitive in its conduct and virtuous in its effect. But since the 1990s, urban China has gained the upper hand, and since then Chinese capitalism tends toward political dependency on the state and corruption.

It should be noted that Huang and others describe the years between 1989 and 1992 as a watershed. Marked by the Tiananmen riots and Deng Xiaoping's 1992 Southern Tour, this watershed marks the establishment of a new form of authoritarian capitalism that has since been consolidated.

Politics and International Relations

The Chinese economic reforms from 1978 ended hostility to both the USSR and the USA. Then the successors to Brezhnev in the USSR began their own reforms, principally those of Gorbachev opening to the world economy and making structural changes in the system of planning and rule in 1985. The unforeseen outcome of these reforms was the secession from the Soviet bloc of the east European states (Latvia, Lithuania, Estonia) and of Byelorussia, Ukraine, and Georgia in the west of what had been the USSR and in the far east, on the borders with China, independent states in Kazakhstan, Uzbekistan, Kyrgyzstan, Turkmenistan, Tajikistan and Mongolia. A more profound outcome was that the Russian Federation, the remainder of the USSR after its dismemberment into independent states, from Yeltsin onwards sought financial aid and with it the neo-liberal economic and political model of the USA, the sudden simultaneously political and economic reform starting in 1991. By that time, the more piecemeal but escalating economic reforms and even slower political reforms in China, led by the same one Party and in the same one territory of the PRC, were showing very successful economic growth.

It was the end of the bipolar system of treaties backed by the deterrent of mutually assured destruction between the SU and the USA and their respective alliances. At first, it seemed like unification of the globe into the world capitalist system with one supreme power, the USA. But US military supremacy has won it no wars, in Vietnam or in Iraq, and its increasing indebtedness — including debt to China's foreign exchange reserves and purchases of US bonds — indicates something else. The world system is not uni-polar but multi-polar, as the November 2008 meeting of 20 powerful economies to deal with the world financial crisis indicates.

The transition has also led to new kinds of politics, which have been identified by various writers as new kinds of authoritarianism. In a pair of articles, Ferdinand (2007) traces the initially quite different trajectories of the two countries, Russia and China, and their later convergence and growing partnership.

The first article describes the results of their domestic policies of reform: two huge economic crises in Russia resulted. The first in 1992 came from the sudden shock of privatisation and democratisation leading to enormous inflation and devastation of incomes, and a fall in GDP much worse than the US Depression after 1929. The second was a further financial crisis in 1998. It was followed by recovery under the rule of Putin. This is in contrast to China's well-known story of high growth rates despite inflation (less severe) in the 1980s. Ferdinand notes that in Russia's case, the first and most dramatic economic reform was in industry, leaving agricultural organisation — state farms and collectives — intact for longer and slower reform — the opposite of China's reforms starting in agricultural organisation with growth in private markets in which the main players were town and village small-scale enterprises. Another contrast: Russia invited foreign investment with no geographic restrictions from the start while China started very cautiously with a few Special Economic Zones. He also notes that despite the dramatic falls in income in Russia, the average income per person in Russia is still higher than that in China. Note also a curious reversal: whereas Russian economic strength had been in manufacturing industry for export to the Soviet bloc countries, its main exports are now primary products, oil and gas principal among them; whereas China has become the factory of the world and its trade politics are principally concerned with bartering infrastructural and industrial projects for the raw materials its economy needs. Both countries need to move into high-tech value-added manufacturing.

Ferdinand concludes that both states are best characterised as capitalist 'developmental states', models of which were the Japanese and South Korean with their close relationship between huge business conglomerates and government. More importantly, he concludes further that both states are sufficiently strong economically and politically confident and assertive of their own sovereignty to insist on their own models of democratic development.

The second article ('Sunset, sunrise: China and Russia construct a new relationship', *International Affairs*, **83**(5), pp. 841–867) describes the resulting international partnership between the two countries.

It is now a partnership of convenience, not dependency, between two emerging major economies among others. There have been major fluctuations of mistrust and trust between the two — principally over oil supply deals from Russia and scaremongering about a yellow peril of illegal Chinese immigration in the far eastern parts of Russia. Nevertheless, the border disputes that had raised hostilities to such a high level have been completely settled. China's initiative in forming an international meeting called the Shanghai Cooperation Organisation (SCO) has been successful on its own terms, not that of an alliance but of mutual agreements on security and other matters with the new countries of the far eastern ex-USSR and with Russia. Other countries are keen to establish more than observer status with the SCO. Russia and China have, in addition, entered on what Ferdinand describes as a programme of constructing popular support and understanding of each other in each other's countries, going beyond the realist, interest-based relations of earlier post-reform years.

He detects two countervailing tensions. The SCO is based on the same principles established in 1955 at Bandung Indonesia among the Non-aligned nations, the developing countries distinguishing themselves from Europe, USSR, and USA, led by the PRC and India. On the other hand, China is much more dependent on exports to the developed countries than is Russia. Nevertheless, there is convergence and mutual construction of partnership.

Beyond what Ferdinand writes, there remains the question of the remnants in both countries of a history of socialist revolution and of economies that were built by state and collective organisation, the Russian much more advanced economically, the Chinese much more based on Mao Thought. Both have been disaggregated and turned into forms of capitalist economy. But the same Party leads in China, and a very controlled two-party arrangement has been constructed under Putin in Russia, including the remains of the Russian Communist Party.

Balzer's 'Managed Pluralism'

Since the end of 'real existing socialism', many observers have discussed the notion of 'civil society' in post-socialist countries. We will deal with this notion in more detail in Chapter 15. In relationship to the comparison of the transition in China with the SU Russia, here, we will briefly review the alternative concept of 'managed pluralism' suggested by Balzer (2004). While 'civil society' often implies an opposition between state and society, Balzer suggests 'civic society' instead, implying that the objective here is a 'partnership with the state', or at least an interrelationship, rather than opposition. 'Civic society', including professional groups, trade unions, and social organisations is dependent on the state to some extent. Additionally, Balzer points out, there is the 'private sphere' of economic organisations that interact in markets, and are also dependent on the state. Both spheres continuously interact with state institutions, sometimes in politics of contestation.

After the demise of communist ideology and charismatic authority in China and Russia, a new pluralism of social groups and organisations has emerged. Yet, this pluralism remains 'managed', argues Balzer: only players acceptable to the regime can participate and only certain issues are allowed to be openly debated and contested. In terms of religious groups, media organisations, and trade unions, the regimes at the same time encourage and limit diversity.

Contestation might take place in a number of ways, including strikes and rural protests (both of which are arguably more numerous in China). It might also take the form of lawsuits and judicial process, cultural contestation, or ultimately political contestations and elections, direct elections at the local level only in China whereas in Russia, highly controlled multi-Party direct elections for central government occur.

This situation could, Balzer writes, move in either of two directions. They could become the basis for what he calls 'democracy', as distinct from authoritarian or charismatic leadership. He thinks that in both countries there could be a movement from authoritarian to democratic interdependencies. Economic growth has created an alternative source of power, the power of wealth and over economic resources, as distinct from power over state political, coercive and ideological resources. Economic activity has become a realm of relative freedom of action. It has also led to a rise in the number of managers and, in China, of new rich village entrepreneurs, and of private patrons of cultural, historical and heritage projects, and non-governmental organisations. Finally, it has led to increased prospects of social mobility and new kinds of prestige.

Much depends on the relative growth of new middle classes in both countries. We will take up the question of democracy in China in Chapter 17.

Balzer suggests that there are three crucial conditions:

1. Middle class support for political opening occurs only when convinced that extending the franchise does not empower the disadvantaged population to demand significant income redistribution.

2. Middle classes become active agents only when their size achieves 'critical mass' and they judge that their economic interests are threatened by the cronyism of the authoritarian regime.
3. Professionals experiencing downward social mobility are not likely to provide leadership for a liberalisation movement.

As of now, the other tendency prevails: both Russia and China are state-dominated. Both states, Russian and Chinese, are authoritarian regimes setting strict limits on what is legitimate organisation; for instance, what are the limits of religious toleration — the key case in point is the exclusion and suppression of Falungong. Here, Balzer notes the exclusion in Germany of the claim of Scientology to be a 'religion' as if this were a parallel, but could add the contrast that the sect is treated as a counter-revolutionary (i.e., anti-Party) organisation in China, whereas Scientology is seen in Germany simply as a socially harmful sect.

Under Putin, the organisation of opposition parties, as well as media of opposition to the ruling party and to government policy, has been so severely curtailed that his regime approaches the continuing monopoly of legitimate power held by the CCP in China. The Party in China opened itself to those who could through local elections show themselves to be more popular and responsive to villagers and town-dwellers than the incumbent Party Secretary, and to those who had, alternatively, shown themselves to be successful entrepreneurs and successful scientists.

Authorising this is the Party doctrine of the so-called Three Represents, whose author is officially Jiang Zemin. They are the core of Jiang Zemin Thought, studied by anyone who is recruited into the Party. The three things the Party represents are very similar to what modernisation is as a project for the Chinese people: the Party represents the most advanced forces of production (i.e., technical and scientific advances for new industries, including agro-industry), the most advanced culture (i.e., the best educated and having the best quality of civilisation), and the broadest interests of the majority of the Chinese population. The Party, in short, stands for the optimistic prospect of making China an advanced economy and culture and the Party insists on being the channel for the advancement of political representation. People do in fact further their careers by joining the Party.

Alongside this is the dark side of political power, the use of force and its legitimation for private gain, not public good. Balzer rightly holds out the possibility of increasingly close links between state security services, private security firms and criminal gangs in a vicious circle of increasing personal and property protection and the escalating need for protection. Against this linkage, there has been an increasing number of protests to insist on local power holders obeying the law and making sure that economic corporations' breaches of the law are punished. These protests appealed through journalists, through offices of letters and petitions, and through the procedures of the legal system as well as to senior state officials and Party authorities to rectify abuses of the law and of personal power.

In sum, Balzer points to prospects of a convergence of Russian and PRC politics: in both, managed pluralism and uses of sub-contracted force link state and corporations. Under changed conditions, greater political freedoms could flourish as economic freedoms increase.

Narratives of the Heroic and the Quotidian

We concluded the last chapter with a review of the new narratives of the Maoist era. Post-socialism similarly can be seen as a new master narrative. The literary scholar Tang Xiaobing (2000), for instance, argues that the post-Mao era is an era where the 'quotidian', everyday life, is given priority over the 'heroic' moments of Maoism. In the Maoist Era, every detail of everyday life had to be subordinated to the singularity of the 'hero' (e.g., Mao, or the model worker Lei Feng), and ultimately to the homogeneity of life under socialism. This homogeneity found its realisation in realist art and the representations of Maoist mass culture, which effectively denied or subordinated individual production and consumption (expression) in favour of joint production of a new self, working toward a collective abundance.

Since the end of Maoism, however, the homogeneity of workers' socialism has been replaced with the heterogeneity of everyday life. Individual production, consumption, and sentiment are the 'new normal' (Tang, 2000, pp. 273–294), and when compared with the heterogeneity of everyday life, Maoist heroism and its drive towards homogeneity are denied or relativised and remembered nostalgically. The ‘anti-utopia’ of consumerism has replaced socialist utopianism.

As a literary critic, Tang Xiaobing describes this transition mainly in literature, comparing socialist realism and the literature that has emerged in China since the 1980s. But beyond the field of literature, it might be argued that this time (a time with no real heroes) is a time of cynicism and insiders’ irony (cf., Yurchak, 1997, 2003; Steinmüller, 2011). In general assessments of the era, both insiders and outside observers decry the decline of public morality in a society that some observers have called a ‘post-belief’ society. In the era of Reform and Opening, there has been without doubt also a relaxation of political control, and a new pluralism of social organisations, consumer choices and lifestyles. But it remains questionable whether an entire society or era can be usefully described as ‘ironic’ or ‘cynical’. Such a description always relies on the opposite foil of a ‘golden age’ of ‘great unity’. In any case, looking at ironic and cynical gestures and positions can provide insights into central political, social, and moral dilemmas in contemporary Chinese society (see, contributions to Steinmüller and Brandtstädter, 2016).

Seminar Question

Compare the transition away from socialism in China and Russia.

Required Readings

Ferdinand, P. 2007. Russia and China: Converging responses to globalization. *International Affairs*, **83**(4), pp. 665–680 and Sunset, Sunrise: China and Russia construct a new relationship. *International Affairs* **83**(5), pp. 841–867.

Hann, C., Humphrey, C., and Verdery, K. 2002. Introduction: Postsocialism as a topic for anthropological investigation. In *Postsocialism: Ideals, Ideologies and Practices in Eurasia*, C. Hann (ed.). London; Routledge, pp. 1–28.

Balzer, H. 2004. State and society in transitions from communism: China in comparative perspective. In *State and Society in 21st-century China: Crisis, Contention, and Legitimation*, P. H. Gries and S. Rosen (eds.). London: Routledge/Curzon, pp. 234–256.

Further Readings

Bramall, C. 2004. Chinese land reform in long-run perspective and in the Wider East Asian context. *Journal of Agrarian Change*, **4**(1), pp. 107–141.

Bramall, C. 2007. *The Industrialization of Rural China*. Oxford: Oxford University Press.

Chan, A., Kerkvliet, B. J., and Unger, J. (eds.) 1999. *Transforming Asian Socialism: China and Vietnam Compared*. Lanham, MD: Rowman & Littlefield.

Duara, P. 2010. Chinese reforms in historical and comparative perspective. In *Reform and Development in China: What Can China Offer the Developing World*, Yao, Y., and Wu, H.-M. (eds.). London; Routledge, pp. 71–81.

Goody, J. 2004. *Capitalism and Modernity*. Cambridge: Polity (Introduction).

Huang, Y. 2008. *Capitalism with Chinese Characteristics: Entrepreneurship and the State*. Cambridge: Cambridge University Press.

Kennedy, S. 2011. *Beyond the Middle Kingdom: Comparative Perspectives on China's Capitalist Transformation*. Stanford, CA: Stanford University Press.

Kwon, H. 2011. *The Other Cold War*. New York: Columbia University Press.

Naughton, B. 2006. *The Chinese Economy: Transitions and Growth*. Boston: MIT Press.

Liu, X. 2009. *The Mirage of China: Anti-humanism, Narcissism, and Corporeality of the Contemporary World*. New York: Berghahn Books, Chapter 7, pp. 172–198.

Nolan, P. 1995. *China's Rise, Russia's Fall: Politics, Economics and Planning in the Transition from Stalinism*. New York: St. Martin's Press.

Pei, M. 1994. *From Reform to Revolution: The Demise of Communism in China and the Soviet Union*. Cambridge MA: Harvard University Press.

Shirk, S. L. 1993. *The Political Logic of Economic Reform in China*. Berkeley: University of California Press.

Steinmüller, H. 2011. The state of irony in rural china. *Critique of Anthropology*, **31**(1), pp. 21–42.

Steinmüller, H., and Brandtstädter, S. (eds.) 2016. *Irony, Cynicism and the Chinese State*. London: Routledge.

Tang, X. 2000. *Chinese Modern: The Heroic and the Quotidian*. Durham, NC: Duke University Press.

Wang, H. 2003. In *China's New Order: Society, Politics, and Economy in Transition*, Huters, T. (ed.). Boston, MA: Harvard University Press.

Wang, H. 2009. *The End of the Revolution: China and the Limits of Modernity*. London: Verso.

Yang, D. 1996. *Calamity and Reform in China: Rural Society and Institutional Change Since the Great Leap Famine*. Stanford, CA: Stanford University Press.

Yang D. 2004. *Remaking the Chinese Leviathan: Market Transition and the Politics of Governance in China*. Stanford, CA: Stanford University Press.

Yurchak, A. 1997. The cynical reason of late socialism: Power, pretense, and the Anekdot. *Public Culture*, **9**(2), pp. 161–188.

Yurchak, A. 2003. Soviet hegemony of form: Everything was forever, until it was no more. *Comparative Studies in Society and History*, **45**(03), pp. 480–510.

Zhang, L., and Ong, A. (eds.) 2008. Introduction: Privatizing China. In *Privatizing China: Socialism from Afar*, (2nd edn.). Ithaca: Cornell University Press, pp. 1–20.

Chapter 10

Property Relations and China's Contemporary Economy

One of the conventions of neo-classical economics is that the nearer an economy is to a perfect market system, the better it is for growth and efficiency. At the same time, they recognise that there are what they call 'externalities' to markets and admit that there is a possibility of market failure. These include inability to cope with ecological damage. Or dealing with the poverty that comes from being laid off without being able to find another job despite willingness to find work, or supplementing pay that is so low it is below the poverty line. Further, the capitalist imperative to form monopolies in order to seek profits through prices above what would be market rates in 'free' competition always creates 'imperfections'. Innovation can create a temporary monopoly; indeed, the advantage of being able to set a price for a new product or fashion or the raised productivity an innovation allows is part of capitalist competition. Market ideology assumes that competitors would soon reduce that advantage. But monopoly advantages are created without the virtues of innovation, for instance by cartels or for another instance by the privatisation of state monopolies, creating longer term imperfections. Such imperfections are a necessary part of the functioning of a capitalist market economy, the seeking of advantage and profit, even though market perfection is part of the science and the ideology of capitalist economics. So, since the onset of political economy in the work of Adam Smith, economists have acknowledged that the state has vital functions in establishing and maintaining a market economy, whether in liberal or more social democratic economic theories.

Despite these qualifications, the efficiency of an economy is still often measured against the ideal of a market economy that assumes perfect information about costs, supply, demand, and competition. Thus, in the Cold War, state socialism and its planned and administered economies were, according to this ideal, bound to fail. That they did not and instead industrialised and grew, while their states became militarily powerful and threatening, was a cause for a war of economies, aided by governments, including that of the prime mover, the USA, to prove that market economists are right. And so, the wasteful deficiencies of planning in increasingly complex economies were exacerbated by the strains of military expenditure in the escalation of investments in Mutually Assured Destruction. There were, in addition, the hot proxy wars of Africa, Indochina, Afghanistan, and Latin America in the so-called Cold War, not forgetting the Sino-Soviet rift in the late 1950s and the huge forces lining the border with China. All this told on the Union of Soviet Socialist Republics (USSR's) economy and when it also induced economic reforms in the People's Republic of China (PRC), the eventual victory of the governmental promoters of free markets was a cause for celebration. The sense of triumph was justified because the reforms in the ex-USSR and in the PRC were aimed at joining the world economic system of capitalism. So we now live in a global economy of different kinds of capitalism, two of which are what has emerged in Russia and the PRC.

We must ask 'what is the PRC's kind of capitalism?' This is not only a question about the current state of the Chinese economy, it is about what kind of an economy it has become in the decades since the dismantling of the command economy of Mao's time. A starting point to answer this question is property rights.

Property rights are, according to free market economists, the basic facilitator and indicator of competition-driven efficiency. At their foundation is private ownership by a legal person who is seldom an individual. Even the mass of consumers who are private property owners in the sense that they possess wealth for spending, are often to some extent jointly managed household budgets. As for the main economic actors of intermediate demand and of supply, the legal person must be subdivided into different kinds of person from the shareholder, through managing director, to the employee. Even so, an economic unit that owns means of production, distribution or exchange, including finance, is nominally and ideally a legal person that can be bought, sold, and dissolved or stripped through the sale of shares (in a market of shares).

Ownership of a legal person should ideally be entirely alienable with no residual rights. The income from its activities should be entirely made from receipts greater than expenses — namely, profits — according to prices that are not distorted by anything other than other such economic units' (including households') supplies and demands, and the stock (or capital) in hand, including households' savings. In short, market reform on this model is privatisation, selling all state assets to units of absolute ownership that thrive or fail in ideally undistorted market conditions.

Some Useful Distinctions among Property Rights

Even absolute private property is never simple. It is always a 'bundle of rights'. For instance, lawyers and economists distinguish *use rights* from *ownership rights*. Thus, leaseholds are use rights, usually in land or a building. Theorists of firms distinguish between *executive powers* and *ownership rights*. And within firms, there are also the *rights of the workforce* even though according to neo-classical economics they are treated as one category of the factors of production. So, the assets and factors of a private firm are in fact a number of distinguishable rights or legitimate powers: ownership rights, use rights, executive powers, and workforce rights. Finally, there are the rights of the government to revenue in tax from the benefits of ownership rights (dividend payments) and the sale of assets (capital gains), from income, from sales, and from profits. All these rights are written into law, such as the law of leasing as distinct from the law of ownership, and the laws on workers' councils or on health and safety and child protection authenticated by the International Labour Organization (ILO) of the United Nations. Executive powers are upheld in contracts with the appointed managing director and in the constitutions of firms. Taxes are always also defined in law or by government directives and statements, such as plans and budgets. Finally, there is the right of the consumer, be it an intermediate, which is a firm, or a final consumer, such as a household. These take the form of actual, written, or implicit contracts.

Each of these rights and responsibilities expresses *a relationship* between government, owner, leaseholder, manager, worker, and consumer. In short, property rights are also relationships through the material activities and physical assets of that property which is a firm or enterprise or piece of land, or the capacity to work (the physical strength and skill employed), and the wants and needs of final consumers.

In the light of property rights, then, the question about the nature of the Chinese economy becomes a question about the relations and the balance of powers among these categories: government, owner, leaseholder, manager, worker, and consumer. With any right in law the question is whether and how it is sanctioned and implemented, with what powers of enforcement. The same question turned inside out is whether a law or policy directive disguises what actually goes on. The question therefore is not so much about law, but *what are the relationships of power and control over property*. Did the dismantling of the command economy in the PRC lead to a full-scale privatisation of economic units of production and consumption, commerce and service, and to a rule of law? What relationships of power and control are emerging?

Here, a comparison of the PRC's marketisation reforms with Russia's is instructive.

Marketisation in Russia and China

The Russian government under Boris Yeltsin, elected to the Russian Soviet in 1991 and then retaining power in 1993 by a military-backed *coup d'etat*, chose to heed free-market economists and to reform by privatisation. Sale of public assets to private ownership — initially workers' shares in the enterprises in which they were employed — created huge windfall profits for those with the connections to arrange with banks the means to buy shares from the workers and then profit greatly from their operation as private monopolies. The sudden impoverishment of most of the population was collateral damage of these market reforms. Between 1990 and 1994, the male mortality rate in Russia soared by 32%, life expectancy went down below 58 years, lower than Pakistan, and population decline increased. Healthcare spending by the state fell to less than 5% of its budget, half that of Lebanon. Female survival rates became so much greater than male that there were 15% more women than men in Russia (Anderson, 2007, pp. 11–12).

Under the elected government of Putin from 2000, some of the sold state assets, principally oil and gas, were brought back into government control, and some of the owners of these assets became ministers (Anderson, 2007, p. 6). Government control, accompanied by all kinds of coercion, of strategic private or part-private corporations, succeeded in reversing the indications of demographic and economic decline. But now, instead of manufacturing being prominent, Russia depends on the production and export of primary products, whereas China has become the manufacturer to the world.

Chinese economic reforms had nothing of the suddenness of what Yeltsin brought about in Russia. They were piecemeal. Reforms were introduced in small increments, after their unpredicted outcomes were noted and then recognised in further policy and finally in law. Law was not the precondition of reform but the consolidation and generalisation of each reform experiment. Some reforms were not even initiated by the central state, but by lower levels of the state hierarchy and then recognised by the centre.

We can begin to describe the economic reforms as *incremental decentralisations of agency from government to managerial control, without relinquishing residual state rights of ownership*. It is important to note that the Chinese system, as distinct from the Soviet system, was already decentralised. Control of production had already been partially relinquished by central and provincial governments. But now it was relinquished further to managers. In the countryside, it was already in the hands of the heads of the 'collective' units of account: teams, brigades, and in rare instances, communes. In the course of the reforms, this was further decentralised to households, the targets of which were set by their 'collective' units.

Property in Land and the Agrarian Reforms in China

There are two kinds of ownership of land in the PRC: collective and state-owned land. Nominally, as very many other states, the PRC has a reserve power to requisition land. Local governmental authorities in built-up municipalities own the urban estate as state land. The other state land is that on which state farms operate. But the far larger proportion of rural land is collectively owned: administrative villages (*xingzheng cun*), which have replaced brigades (*dadui*), are the title holders of the arable land and the land upon which village industries operate, while the land on which village houses stand is separately managed as an indefinite leasehold to the villager until the whole family has moved elsewhere, when this land returns to the village for redistribution to current villagers.

The first set of economic reforms was in the countryside. They started in about 1980 with a contract between the village administration and households to produce planned quotas of crops. At first, these were experimental initiatives by lower levels of government in the provinces of Anhui and Sichuan. This eventually became the outright leasing of agrarian land to households. Households' leases were eventually extended to 30 years under the 1998 Land Administration Act so long as the households remained on the land. The 2003 Rural Land Contracting Act sanctioned sub-contracting so that leaseholders sold sub-leases of their land-use on what is *a market of land-use rights*. This occurred most in the richest and least in the poorest regions (Naughton, 2007, pp. 247–248).

The first decade of reforms constituted a golden age for farmers: prices for agricultural products were deliberately raised as an incentive to production, while the prices for farm inputs (tools, fertiliser, and pesticide) were held down, and production of food and industrial raw materials did, as intended, increase rapidly. But then, with the privatisation of State-Owned Enterprises (SOEs) (to which we shall come later in this chapter), and the deregulation of prices, the costs of farm inputs increased faster than the prices paid for farm outputs and the gaps between agricultural and industrial producers grew.

There are economists, Chinese economists among them, who say that the Chinese economic development, including both agricultural productivity and the solution to problems of environmental degradation, depends on there being a market in land, as on exclusive and total rights of ownership. Other economists, such as Joseph Stiglitz, say other issues are more important, and privatisation of property rights is not a priority and may not be necessary (Sanders, 2005, p. 131). Sanders' article contains a very useful overall description of the different kinds of property right in rural land.

First, all land in China is at the final disposal of the state: *a state property regime*. Most states in the world retain a legally well-constrained right to dispose of land by compulsion. But in China that right is extensively used and only gradually have laws been introduced to restrain state requisitioning of land and to regulate compensation to the dislocated.

The small fraction of the total run as state farms, often experimental, Sanders calls a *state ownership regime* combining ownership and use rights. We will take up this and his other categories and bring them up to date.

But by far the largest fraction of farmland use rights was distributed to farmers in two ways. Most land was distributed in the early 1980s to households as 'responsibility land' (*zerentian*), on which farmers had to grow what they were contracted by the village administration to sell to the state at a fixed price, but over and above that and on any land left farmers could grow what they liked and sell it at market prices. After a time, all prices were determined by the market, including what farmers were contracted to sell. Then, the village administration ceased to assign quotas of what to grow and sell. Instead, government extension and work teams began forcibly to encourage farmers to adopt certain crops or animals to raise for sale. There has been a government-led transformation of subsistence to cash cropping and thereafter the formation of agro-industrial enterprises.

Small plots of land distributed to households as 'rationed land' (*kouliangtian*) and as 'private plots' (*ziliu di* — as during most of the years of collectivisation), were for farmers to grow whatever crops and raise whatever animals they wanted. But eventually, the distinction between responsibility land and private plots vanished. This mix of basic ownership and of user rights, Sanders classifies as a *partially-privatised common property regime*.

Not all land was distributed in this way. Some village administrations, with the support of the farmers, elected to remain collective, the land remaining a jointly managed agricultural enterprise. Further, during the 1990s, other villages pooled their responsibility land to form large specialised farms in which each had a share, the form of which varied. Sanders classifies these as a *common property regime*. In the second decade of the new millennium, this regime was promoted as a key part of a policy of village 'urbanisation', since nearly all villages were under the administration of the nearest city.

Lastly, some upland land remained open to use by anyone for hunting, grazing or gathering. This is *open access*, although formally it is state-owned land.

So out of the user rights of Chinese farm and forestry land, the Chinese government has created four regimes: *state ownership*, *partially privatised*, *common*, and *open access*. To these, we must now add *agro-industrial consolidated leaseholds*. Cash-cropping is increasingly being turned into agro-industrial rural enterprises. But there were also many other rural industrial enterprises when the reforms began, and they grew extremely fast in number and variety after they were auctioned to bidders who could offer the highest fees to the collective which is now an administrative village. In the next section, we will turn to the fate of these rural enterprises.

Purchase or requisition of rural land is to convert collectively owned land into state-owned land, leased by urban governments to property developers whose purchase of the leasehold is at a price far higher than the compensation paid to villages and villagers for the same land. The difference provides the urban government with revenue for the construction of infrastructure, the implementation of central policies, that in the main are not centrally funded, but also sometimes to the personal benefit of officials involved with the development companies and always to the chagrin of villagers. This is how the rapid urbanisation of China has occurred.

For land under cultivation, the village administration has the power to dispose of it at a price paid by the urban authority, distributing the proceeds to the farmers registered as resident in the village. For land under their residence, each household disposes and negotiates its price or compensation with either the Land Exchange or Requisitioning Office or directly with a sub-contractor appointed through the urban authority. The decision to turn village land of either kind into urban estate is a policy decision implemented by the urban authority, not the choice of the village or the household.

Since 2004, all urban leasehold sales for purely private development are made through public auctions, with details of all transactions posted to the public on the internet, including state-owned urban land sales, organised by urban land bureaux. But the public auctions are themselves open to corruption, which is to say private gain at the expense of urban government revenue.

Township and Village Enterprises (TVEs)

Industrial enterprises in villages and townships had been encouraged under collectivisation, at the level of brigades and communes. They included food-processing, the processing of other products, such as silk fibre, or tea or tobacco leaves, production of building materials, such as cement, bricks and tiles, and many others.

Oi and Walder (1999, 'Introduction') detect three quite different paths of industrialisation in rural China in the process of de-collectivisation. One path of disposing of these assets was through auction to those who had accumulated personal savings and remittances from migrant and overseas relatives. Over time, these assets were replaced by others, to produce other products or for more efficient production. All assets except for the land on which they stood have come into the ownership of joint shareholding or partnerships.

Another path was through the village or township retaining not only ownership but also managerial control of enterprises and using the profits to finance local infrastructural projects, rather than reaping revenue through fees from enterprises. Most of these also became shareholding companies, in many of which the local state retained some or the majority of shares.

In between were enterprises that went by auction to, or were expanded enterprisingly by a local Party secretary or official, one way or the other exercising managerial control in the purchasing and expansion of assets. They had the personal connections and privileged access to bank loans to bid for the collective assets or to start new enterprises. But these too became shareholding enterprises over time.

Oi and Walder note how reforms presented cadres and officials with material incentives to use their connections for entrepreneurial activities rather than bureaucratic control. The reforms turned cadres or officials into state entrepreneurs, lining their own pockets but also using their profits for further investment in what were deliberately local job-creation and infrastructural schemes.

Gregory Ruf (in Oi and Walder) tells the story of how the biggest of the main lineages of a village in Sichuan from before Liberation (1949) had remained dominant despite the removal of its collective land and despite removal of its traditional leaders. It remained dominant through the new peasant leaders that were recruited into the militia in the first years of the PRC, and continued so in the post-reform administrative village. The Party Secretary, a member of this dominant lineage, during the reform period used his good connections to expand rather than to auction off the village industries. He turned the village into a corporation of several enterprises, including two brick kilns and a distillery, an orchard and a transport team, by selling shares in the corporation to all the families in the village. Those who could not afford the price of a share got a share anyway and paid its price in instalments from the proceeds of the grain they sold to the government procurement station as part of their contracts with the village administration.

Ruf describes the village corporation as a large family. The village enterprises were staffed by close lineage kin and affinal relatives (related through marriage and through daughters and sisters). They were supported by the rest of the village because they provided jobs for the whole village, as it moved from work on the land to work in industry.

In a few years, the kilns and the distillery came into increasing competition with newly started and better quality kilns and distilleries in other villages. The Party Secretary then began to recruit shareholders from the local town and expertise from the city of Chengdu to diversify into zinc refinery (the initial contact was a scholar accompanying the anthropologist Ruf — Fn. 46). Over the 1990s, this trend of extending ownership of the enterprises through shareholding beyond (but still including) the villagers continued. Then some were leased to managers who controlled the decisions on production and output.

What did not change is that the land on which they are built remained the freehold of the village, which charged the enterprises a fee. Meanwhile, some families saved and made contacts through which they could raise funds to start their own private enterprises.

Even in this example of one village, what emerged is a variety of forms of ownership and control. In the country as a whole, there is far more variation, including variation in the nature of collective (or village) wealth, on the basis of its leased industries, and what it has done with that wealth. For instance, in a very wealthy village in coastal southern Fujian, more than half of whose registered households were in fact residing and doing business in Hong Kong, enterprises in the village were all private. Village infrastructure of school building and road paving was in the hands of the village leadership but that leadership had become the leadership of the single village lineage and its segments (Tang Dong, studied by Wang Mingming and Stephan Feuchtwang until 1991).

In another very wealthy village, in the north near Tianjin city, studied by Nan Lin and Chih-jou Jau Chen (chapter in Oi and Walder), the Party Secretary was extremely enterprising and controlling, as in the Sichuan village of Gregory Ruf, but not on the basis of any larger kin organisation, just his personal and kinship network. Even though he overstepped the boundaries of what was tolerable at the time and was imprisoned for being involved in beating to death an accountant accused of mislaying just under 30,000 Rmb, the four groups of village enterprises that he had established continued after his removal. They had made the village a highly publicised model of getting rich quickly. But at the end of the 1990s, like many other collective enterprises, the four groups were on the verge of being sold to their managers.

As they grew, the increasing ranges of activity of Township and Village Enterprises such as these met with increasing competition with enterprises expanding from elsewhere including cities. The result for many was financial failure. Others diversified into industries that served as suppliers to larger city enterprises, spreading into a number of markets, producing, transporting, cash cropping, forming groups of enterprises, always providing jobs for villagers, but over the years leasing ownership of assets, though not ownership of land, to managers and shareholders — including overseas investors.

Residual rights of land ownership and the exacting of local taxes, often called fees, are still in the hands of the village or township. But whatever paths they followed, rural industries that survived became joint shareholding firms whose managers were often ex-cadres and their links with local government turned officials into fellow entrepreneurs. Some of these became township or urban enterprises as townships came under city administrations, the rest failed in competition with urban enterprises. The abolition of agricultural tax by the central government was the last incentive to households to increase agrarian productivity and it was offset by the increasing costs of industrially produced inputs, such as pesticides, fertilisers, vehicles and tools. Since 2014, the policy experiment, centrally approved and then generalised, has been to induce villagers to lease their land to agro-industrial enterprises, whose consolidation of farmland reaps the advantages of scale in production and marketing.

Household Property, Kinship and Territory as Moral Community

The most numerous property right units are families in rural households and long-leaseholding residents in cities. The case study in this section, focuses on rural households and how they use their income and property to form larger moral communities. In the following section, we will see how urban businesses also form trust through inter-personal relationships, though they are not institutionalised as they have been in some villages.

Brandtstädter (2003)'s study of what families do with their property rights and income is based on three villages in southern Fujian. Southern Fujian is one of the areas that quickly benefited from overseas connections and rural–urban migration and wage earning to turn from being a marginal area of the Chinese collective economy to being one of the most productive and rich in China.

She makes a point made by others in their studies of both rural and urban enterprises that interpersonal ethics are used to create predictability in a market that is highly unpredictable on its own. It is probably true to say as she does that in all capitalist economies, enclaves of greater predictability are created as moral communities.

She adds further examples to those given by Ruf and others, when she points out that the administrative villages, despite elections of their heads, are not trusted as institutions of a moral community. Trust is created and reinforced by non-official standards and means of forming relationships.

Official leaders are either suspected of graft or else they are respected *personally* as managers, not as officials *per se*. This has changed in some villages where elections are conducted according to law and not manipulated, so that the elected leader is genuinely a popular choice. Village representative committee leaders and small group (village section) leaders are not paid officials anyway.

Families prefer to establish business partnerships with families linked to them through marriage. This is a reinforcing of links already made through gift exchange and the rituals of marriage. Note how this is entirely compatible with the trend, noted by Yan Yunxiang in northeastern China (Yan, 2003), toward smaller domestic units of couples with their children and possibly one or other of their parents and away from patriarchal hierarchy. The emphasis is on friendship within kinship or the forming of trust in relationships that can weather the storms of price fluctuation, business failure and restarting business.

The formation of a moral economic community goes beyond interpersonal networks in these villages. Neighbourhood beyond the family and beyond immediate neighbours has been recreated, becoming a political-economic community based in either lineage or local temples and their festivals. As in Tang Dong, mentioned above, remittances from migrants created large corporate funds and properties, ancestral halls, schools, old people's recreation centres, temples, roads, bridges, market buildings leased to businesses, on land leased in effective perpetuity to the lineages or the temple, turning the locality into a shareholding corporation of all resident households. The lineage or temple corporation is a political unit, replacing the producers' collectives of the Mao era, run by its most capable managerial members, often endorsed by election to the formal position of village head.

A great deal of income is spent on weddings: the displays of gifts, house building and furnishings for which the couples themselves negotiate and have themselves contributed. In addition, households contribute monetary donations to the building and refurbishing of ancestral halls and temples, churches and mosques, whose grandeur is the pride of the locality. Is this a separate gift economy, as Mayfair Yang (2000) has argued? Brandstädter argues that it is separate from the rest of the economy, but not as an alternative economy, rather as the construction of moral enclaves within it.

Small and Medium-Sized City Enterprises

In the cities, a similar pattern is evident from David Wank's study (in Oi and Walder) of non-state enterprises in the special economic zone of Xiamen city in Fujian province.

He measures the efficiency of personal networking against the *nirvana* model of market efficiency (Demsetz, 1969), so called because it is a never reached ideal, and finds that, through their network improvisations, entrepreneurs create property rights in the enterprises they form and maintain a high level of efficiency despite there being at the time no clear law of private ownership. They create enterprises and through them seal relationships with government officials, banks, and other entrepreneurs. He shows that what he calls 'the cultural model', which is the set of moral standards of reciprocity, honour and trust transmitted and continually renewed in changing circumstances, secures what elsewhere laws and legal sanctions secure. Entrepreneurs of domestic private or joint foreign-domestic enterprises secure a relationship with an official high enough to be able to make firm (*ying*) decisions because they, the officials, have good connectivity (*lianlao*) with other government departments, can grant the necessary licenses, and introduce the entrepreneur to bank personnel. The officials benefit from gifts. But in addition, through their links to entrepreneurs they conduct their own partly official, partly sub-official entrepreneurial activities. These networking private and state entrepreneurs never resort to litigation in cases of breaches of agreement. To do so would be a failure to act like a capable person (*zuoren*). Instead, they continue to resort to whatever sanctions they can exert through interpersonal relationships.

In other words, capable entrepreneurs can get things done without any clarity in law. Instead, the law catches up with what they have already done. They are, indeed, constantly taking the risk of going beyond the law, finding loopholes, because that is where most profit can be made. But they do make use of membership of state-sanctioned non-government organisations, such as chambers of commerce or associations of young entrepreneurs, to make representations about other people not having acted honourably.

Government officials and state enterprises used the same means to set up companies that used state-owned assets, leasing them to managers or to joint stock shareholding cooperatives. They then went further to transfer all the profitable activities to private managers, meanwhile bankrupting the remaining state enterprise holdings. These privately managed former state enterprises grew by forming groups of several relatively small enterprises linked by overlapping directorships and personal networks, shifting assets from one to the other, just as the village enterprise groups did, using one to finance the losses or expansion of the other.

A law was eventually passed to deal with these facts on the ground. The 1994 Companies Act turned all state enterprises into legal persons (*faren*). It also made the transfer of their assets to private legal persons punishable. But with a sufficiently high government official condoning it, the risk could still be taken. Instead, the state's residual rights came in the form of an interest, which could be a share in the private firm, based on powers of licensing and opening the way to privileged access to loans, to information on the market, and to new development policies. As Wank writes (p. 260) 'Rather than heralding a further step toward greater clarification of legal rights to property, it seems, corporatisation (turning state enterprises into legal persons) has stimulated the spread of network strategies to higher levels of the state structure.'

He concludes that networking arrangements 'stimulate commercial activity that would otherwise not occur' (p. 261); they are an alternative means to doing the things that law as a framework for market activity provides. They are used to gain privileged access to information, which is always sought for rent seeking (extra profits) and tax-avoidance.

Semi-legal activities, gifts verging on bribes, and the occasional use of force to get things done sounds like the *nomenklatura-mafia* about which Russians speak and write. But Wank points out that the Russian protection rackets and their government sponsors are just plunderers, whereas corrupt Chinese government officials are shareholding entrepreneurs, interested in the banquets and karaoke girls with which they are entertained, but also on the look-out for opportunities for profit-making activities from which they and their boss (*laoban*) friends can together make more money.

To repeat Oi and Walder's conclusion (p. 21), these piecemeal reforms have turned bureaucrats, by ever-changing incentives, into entrepreneurs in great numbers rather than, as in Russia, a few plundering monopolists in hierarchies of threat over local, small enterprises. Nevertheless, in China, large enterprises have often replaced small by their economies of scale and by deliberate government policy.

Large Enterprises and Financial Regulation

The ownership and control of SOEs has gone through several phases since they were both owned and controlled by the state and its territorial-administrative divisions jointly with industrial ministries in the command economy years.

The first phase was to cede control to enterprise managers and to allow enterprises to retain profits instead of remitting all profits to their controlling ministries. From 1993, smaller SOEs were leased and then turned into shareholding enterprises, as described above. As pointed out by Guo Sujian (2003, pp. 565–566), this policy of 'letting go the small' (*fangxiao*) was to relieve the state from responsibility for losses, and at the same time try to invigorate enterprises with investments from outside state funds, including workers' wages since workers of these enterprises were induced, under duress, to buy shares, while other shares could be bought by outsiders.

Under the supplementary policy of 'seizing the big and letting go the small' (*zhuoda fangxiao*), the largest were kept in state ownership, with managerial control, but the industrial ministries were abolished. The resulting large state enterprises were regulated. The regulator was modelled on the Japanese Ministry of International Trade and Industry (MITI). In 2003, a new Commission was formed, charged with turning the state enterprises into something like the great multi-functional corporations in South Korea, *chaebol*, or again like Mitsubishi and the other *zaibatsu* in Japan. This new commission is the State Asset Supervision and Administrative Commission (SASAC), which had by 2005 turned the 196 large state enterprises under its regulative administration by mergers into 169. There are other large state enterprises in regulatory administration of a similar kind at the level of province and municipality.

None of these large SOEs is subject to bankruptcy, as are all other enterprises. They also have privileged access, without networking, to bank loans and to stock markets. They are quoted on foreign stock markets, but foreign shareholders are held down to a minority holding. They tend to be concentrated in the parts of the economy that are protected from takeover by private enterprise: banking, natural resources such as oil and forests, railways and airlines.

Furthermore, 60–70% of shares quoted in China's two stock exchanges, Shanghai and Shenzhen are not tradable and are held by state institutions. Transfer of shares to foreigners has to be approved by the State Economic and Trade Commission and Ministry of Finance. The stock exchanges are closely regulated: for instance, short selling is not allowed; the size and the frequency of new issues are set by the government. There was a limit of 10% on share price movement (Guo, 2003, p. 13).

From the beginning of 2007, in conformity with entry to the World Trade Organization, foreign banks can operate in China with greater freedom. They can buy into the state banks. But they can only be minority shareholders. The banks have their own state regulator, which is no longer the central bank — the People's Bank of China — but another Commission, the Banking Regulatory Commission.

Urban as well as rural households, driven by uncertain welfare and social security, have long-standing habits of saving. This gives the banking sector a lot of financial strength, alongside insurance companies, even while they incur bad debts in loans directed by the Party for infrastructure projects by central, municipal and other local governments.

The regulatory administration has the responsibility of making sure that the huge state-owned industrial enterprises are profitable and that banks reduce the proportion of their assets made up by non-performing loans, which in a more law-regulated and free-market economy would have bankrupted them. There are constant government attempts to cut down on 'zombie industries' and 'bad loans' held by SOEs.

The point to draw from all this is that the Chinese state has kept under its control the transfer of assets of the largest enterprises in key areas of the economy, even while sharing their ownership with private and particularly foreign shareholders. They provide at national, provincial and municipal levels a portion of their profits as revenue for state projects.

Government has an incentive to make sure they make profits in order to generate revenue that it can spend on infrastructure and welfare.

Chinese economic growth has been heavily dependent upon export. Further, the huge extent of foreign direct investment in Chinese industry makes it vulnerable to the repatriation of profits rather than their reinvestment in China. So, since the early 2000s, it has been the policy to stimulate the domestic market by urging savers to spend and by urbanising the population and turning agriculture into a consolidated agro-industry.

The whole process of the privatisation of the Chinese economy and the issue of how this has been at the expense of public good and public goods is detailed empirically and argued at a theoretical level by Lin Chun (2008, 2009) in two articles. Chinese privatisation shows that both privatisation and the creation and maintenance of public goods are political matters, meeting the need to find and promote political measures to ensure just rewards for enterprise and for the creation and maintenance of public good, anywhere in the world.

Conclusion

To put all this extraordinary variety of property rights together, here are six points.

1. Through ultimate ownership of land, all levels of state have the power to compel a change of use on present leaseholders of their user rights, with liability only to legally determined compensation payments.
2. Through standing commissions for the regulation of the commanding heights of the economy, the state retains some planning powers as well as through shareholding in banks and SOEs at the national, municipal and provincial centres.
3. Retention of a single Party as the only policy-making channel means that policies are made and disseminated through the Party hierarchy, which includes branches not just at all levels of the state and in all state agencies, but also in villages, urban communities and the larger economic corporations, including foreign-owned enterprises — with powers to appoint or to dismiss holders of executive positions (such as a Party Secretary or a manager in a large corporation).

4. Through taxation, through its budgets, through the revenues from its SOEs and through large and small infrastructural projects and the powers to commission firms to execute these projects, state agencies at all levels make crucial economic decisions.
5. Through permits to operate and through personal links to entrepreneurs, by which the operation of laws can be mitigated or evaded, state agents also participate in making economic decisions.
6. Through providing access to banks and loans, state officials are entrepreneurs.

Bearing these six conditions in mind, we should also distinguish two kinds of state power. The first is to direct the economy (of a village, or of any larger scalc locality, up to the nation). The second is that of state agents who simply engage for their own and for local benefit in entrepreneurial activities. Much (though not all) of the use of powers to permit (for instance the purchase of land-use-rights) in law and to evade law is both for personal benefit and for preference of family and friends. But even then, some of the actions of the Party Secretary as entrepreneur in the village studies cited also benefited the rest of the village and promoted the economic development of the village as a whole.

Seminar Questions

Weigh up the importance of the law and the market on the one hand and interpersonal relationships, including kinship and friendship on the other in economic management in China.

Does the state in China retain extraordinary powers to direct its economy, compared to other states, including those described as 'developmental' or 'post-socialist' states?

Key Readings

Anderson, P. 2007. Russia's managed democracy. *London Review of Books*, 25th January.

Brandtstädter, S. 2003. The moral economy of kinship and property in southern China. In *The Postsocialist Agrarian Question*, C. Hann (ed.). Münster: Lit Verlag, pp. 419–440.

Guo S. 2003. The ownership reform in China: What direction and how far? *Journal of Contemporary China*, **12**(36), pp. 553–573.

Lin, C. 2008 and 2009. Against privatization in China: A historical and empirical argument. and Challenging privatization: A conceptual and theoretical argument. *Journal of Chinese Political Science*, **13**(1), pp. 1–27, **14**(1), pp. 21–48.

Naughton, B. 2006. *The Chinese Economy: Transitions and Growth*. Boston: MIT Press, pp. 299–304.

Oi, J. and Walder, A. (eds.) 1999. *Property Rights and Economic Reform in China*. Stanford, CA: Stanford University Press (Introduction and chapters by Ruf, by Chen and Lin, and by Wank).

Sanders, R. 2005. Organic agriculture in China: Do property rights matter? *Journal of Contemporary China*, **15**(46), pp. 113–132.

Further Readings

Cai, H. 2009. China's Land Market Auctions: Evidence of Corruption?. http://www.grammatikhilfe.eu/geographyAndEnvironment/whosWho/profiles/henderson/ChinaLandMarketAuctions.pdf [accessed 17 February 2014].

Chang, H. 1999. The Economic theory of the developmental state. In *The Developmental State*, M. Woo-Cumings (ed.). Ithaca and London: Cornell University Press.

Demsetz, H. 1969. Information and efficiency: Another viewpoint. *Journal of Law and Economics*, **12**(1), pp. 1–22.

Nonini, D. 2008. Is China becoming neo-liberal?. *Critique of Anthropology*, **28**(2), pp. 145–176.

Shigehise K. 2013. *The Asian Developmental State and the Flying Geese Paradigm*. United Nations: UNCTAD Discussion Papers No 213 (Accessible free on the internet).

Yan, Y. 2003. *Private Life under Socialism: Love, Intimacy and Family Change in a Chinese Village 1949–1999*. Stanford, CA: Stanford University Press.

Yang, M. 2000. Putting global capitalism in its place: Economic hybridity, Bataille, and ritual expenditure. *Current Anthropology*, **41**(4), pp. 477–495.

Chapter 11

The Countryside and Migration

China like so many European states on the eve of the industrial revolution was an agrarian empire. But unlike the remaining serfs of Europe in the seventeenth century, and in some places such as Russia even later, Chinese farmers were not tied to their land (the 'manor' in England) in the sense that transfers of land were also transfers of those that cultivated it. Land had been a commodity, bought and sold, in China since at least the Tang dynasty, eighth–ninth centuries. Its cultivators had been owners or tenants of owners of land. In a closely linked contrast, the cultivation of land defined the second highest status according to the Confucian ideology, on a par with the freeholding 'yeomen' of Britain, whereas the serfs of Britain were the lowest class of commoner. Then in the nineteenth and twentieth centuries, the emergent social sciences of rural sociology, anthropology and folklore in Europe, China, India, and Latin America, following movements of nationalism and the formation of modern states, the cultivators of the land were called 'peasants'. In China, this had a striking effect. What had been a category of high status, *nong*, became a far more ambivalently valued mass of peasants, *nongmin*. Chinese peasants could be highly valued as the sources of the tradition that nationalists celebrated. But on the other hand, they could also be valued, if that is the right word, as reactionary and, because less educated, backward (Cohen, 1993).

An anthropological pioneer of 'peasant studies' in the 1950s, Redfield (1956) had established a more analytically ambivalent valuation by setting peasant farmers in relation to the high arts of civilisation as the repositories of 'Little' traditions, which were also named 'popular' and 'folk'. At the same time, he made an important point about peasant farmers, that they worked within family household units and that these units ran a mixed income budget, cultivating the land and raising animals partly — the proportion varies — to feed themselves, but partly also to trade their produce in exchange for what they do not produce but need. In other words, they are parts of a larger, market economy. This is particularly true of the Chinese agrarian empire, which stands out for having had a thriving and continuously growing system of marketing from the Song dynasty onwards (Skinner, 1964). China's monetised market economy was huge and most of it beyond the reach of government monopolies, as Deng has demonstrated (Deng, 2003). Further, the commodities sold by peasant households in the Chinese markets were by no means confined to farm produce. Gates (1996) has called their economy a 'petty commodity mode of production' in which small units of production produced manufactures such as silk thread, silk and cotton cloth, shoes, clothing, and craft products, as well as the raw materials for the artisanal industries of cities.

When agrarian, dynastic empires became republican states in China just as in Europe or Japan, the great majority in their population were of this kind. We have already seen in the comparison of English steam-powered industrialisation with Chinese eventual, later industrialisation (Chapters 3 and 4) that in the economies of Europe agricultural industry of plantations and privatised common lands was the basis of their capitalism and of their war machines by which they imposed their trade and industry on China. There was much more dislocation and enforced migration in England and other European countries as well as in their maritime empires as they became modern states than there ever was in China. But in all cases, including China, large-scale industrialisation and the growth of cities became destinations for increasing numbers of impoverished rural migrants.

This chapter will be about the republican years and in particular the twenty-first century, when the biggest movement of population in the world has occurred in China, out of the countryside and into the cities, newly built and still expanding. It has therefore to be as much about migration and migrants' relationship to their rural homes as about peasant production and rural ways of life.

Attachment to Place of Origin

China was an agrarian country in which high value was attached to belonging to the land that ancestors had farmed and in which they were buried. This was an attachment to locality, not necessarily to farming. For instance, trading and its organisations were typically organised according to place of origin. There was also a long history of rural–rural migration, to frontiers and also to areas of the central provinces of China that had been depopulated by war, famine, or epidemic, hence, frequently heard stories of ancestors having come from another part of China. But cults of first settler ancestors established a close sense of belonging.

From the eighteenth century, an accelerating migration of labour to coastal cities, particularly in the south-eastern provinces of Fujian and Guangdong, extended overseas to what the Chinese called the southern ocean — the Nanyang (Southeast Asia) — and beyond, increasing with foreign steamships to tin mines in Malaya, or to docks in Singapore and London, or to railway construction and the ends of the railway lines in San Francisco and Vancouver. Starting as sojourners many became settlers, creating economic niches in laundering, restaurants, small stores, and from there moving into all other businesses over the generations. They organised themselves through associations based on their home villages, townships, counties or their spoken languages from the places where their ancestors were buried. After many generations, instead of shipping their dead home to China, they began to bury their dead in overseas cemeteries, but still their graves referred back to their ancestral homeland. The Overseas Chinese were funders, supporters and organisers of the Republican movement and Sun Yat-sen: supporters of a modernising project for China and proud, if not politically supportive in all cases, of the Communist revolution and the moment when 'China stood up'.

Migration creates its own dynamic, a chain migration following pioneers from the same place, and involves remittances and savings for the marriage of self and siblings. Most often, migrants aim to return 'home' and to improve home with new businesses and new houses. This point is emphasised by Pieke *et al.* (2004), who write of a 'migration configuration' (pp. 19–20): migrants bring with them an orientation to opportunities elsewhere for earning and advancement. Their information and example infect all the others locally with whom they have contact. Migration flows link all the places to which migrants have gone and had some success. They maintain and extend their networks of contacts themselves with much use of the phone to prospect further opportunities. With the huge increase in internal rural–urban migration, this has become true of all villages. Every village in China includes registered residents who are migrants living and working elsewhere in China and in some cases abroad. As a result,

> 1. The local is rendered incomplete because locals' aspirations for self-realisation are completed elsewhere. They view the local from the perspective of others elsewhere and learn other standards of success and aspiration from their sojourns elsewhere.

"… my dream university … is Fudan University [in Shanghai]… Shanghai is a very beautiful city, where there are many things that we village children have never seen, and … many, many things that we yearn for. I want to leave the mountains to see the life of cities on the outside, and Shanghai is the sacred place I yearn for."

"I hope that in the future, this village can become like those cities with a developed economy and high buildings. I would especially like it to be like Shanghai, which I understand to be an amazing city. Cities outside [the mountains] have many, many shops and supermarkets. Here there aren't many shops and there are no supermarkets. It's not very convenient for people to go shopping."

(From a school essay set by James Johnston, unpublished fieldwork in a mountain village in southern Anhui, 2007).

Johnston (2013) writes of a 'moral geography' of filial duty that draws young adults and their parents downhill to the cities, leaving young children with grandparents, but looking back up in filial duty to their elders and their ancestors, fulfilled in the family gathering at New Year.

Yan Yunxiang (2016) writing about the village in northeastern China where he has been noting changes over three decades and in which, though it is still a farming village, over 70% of the young adults are migrant workers, many of them with homes in the local city, notes a dramatic but complete transformation of the relations among the generations.

Grandparents might have a separate home, usually in the village, but they help look after their grandchildren in the village or go to live with their (usually an only) son and daughter-in-law, both of whom work. Instead of the filial piety of gratitude and obedience that they might once have expected, they now enjoy mutual trust, communication and affection of and with their children and grandchildren. The direction of familial sacrifice is not upward, to elders and ancestors, but downwards to the young children; and daughters are often as important as sons, maintaining relations with their natal, as well as their husband's parents. The downwards orientation to future children is also from village to city.

2. The other way in which this can be viewed is that the local becomes part of a chain of connections, made by the most successful but hoped-for and acted upon by the less successful new migrants.

The chain of connections for those who extend internal to worldwide migration is 'transnational'. The migrants from Fujian studied by Pieke *et al.* (2004, p. 163) are 'tied to a transnational social space that spans the globe, with nodes in Fujian, New York, and, to a lesser extent, other countries and cities in East and Southeast Asia' (the older bases established early in the twentieth century and now renewed), to which they have added Los Angeles, Toronto, London, Budapest and Prato. The social space is established and expands in 'a continuous management of opportunities of geographical and social mobility' (p. 168).

A similar point could be made about migrants within China, creating a chain from the same home area to Guangzhou, Shenzhen, Beijing, Shanghai, and other cities.

Legal and illegal migration is organised through interpersonal networks, by labour gang masters, and for overseas migration by professional smugglers, illegal migration giving rise to extreme exploitation in labour-intensive jobs in or beyond China. The industries in which they work are usually Chinese-owned contractors to local firms, such as the leather and garment factories of Fujianese and Zhejiangese migrants in Beijing, where they form small factories and large markets, and in Prato, Italy, where they have purchased local firms that would otherwise have gone out of business. Abroad, they form trading supply and sales outlets for

China-made goods. Such trade generates rivalry with Chinese from other provinces, often physical, sometimes lethal. There are other dangers from local racist attacks, as well as from the grim conditions of residence and work. Of course, there are also frequent cases of failure to earn or do good business. But migrants learn by phone of other places where earnings are better, police less watchful, trade more hopeful, and they move on.

Now, a new internal migration and a new overseas migration outstrips all previous movements and the investment from overseas Chinese has been the main fuel of China's export industry.

Urbanisation and Internal Migration

The current millennium marks the point when, in terms of population engaged in farming and herding, China ceased to be predominantly agrarian. (Donald and Benewick, 2005 edition of *Atlas of China*, p. 38 top, based on *China Statistical Yearbook*, 2003).

There has been an extensive migration out of agrarian work, or rather from underemployment in agrarian work. 'Since the early 1980s' writes Murphy (2002, p. 1), in less than twenty years 'over 100 million Chinese farmers have left their native villages to work as itinerant labourers and traders in the cities.' The number has more than doubled since she wrote this. They form the largest peacetime movement of people in history. This huge 'floating population', as it is often called, moves more freely, in comparison with the possibility of movement in the Maoist era, for a number of reasons.

One is that despite strenuous and successful creation of rural industries, not only since the reforms, but before, there were still insufficient jobs created to absorb the underemployed rural population and relieve them of poverty. Rural industrialisation had been a policy under Mao as well as post-Mao — starting with the building of small industries closely related to agriculture and housing, brick and tile kilns, fertiliser and cement factories, small food processing plants, agricultural tool factories (enlarged smithies) — plus the larger industries started during the Great Leap Forward, such as the few steel plants that survived, and finally those that were relocated into deep rural China for strategic reasons. Since the post-Mao reforms, there has been a successful creation of new industries, building on traditional sidelines of peasant households. But those that have been successful and grown have become township and county industries, located in small urban centres. Many township capitals have become cities.

A condition enabling rural–urban migration was the free marketing of food products, which meant that what was formerly only available through food ration cards only issued to those with an urban household record was now available to all, including rural migrants in cities.

Third was the extraordinary growth of cities and their industries, especially construction but also the sweated labour factories producing for export, requiring unskilled labour.

But these are general economic reasons. There are other, more personal reasons for migration, to do with the attraction of city life, bare necessity, and continuing links and senses of obligation to the home the migrant leaves.

As Murphy (2002) points out in her study of the villages in the inland province of Jiangxi, much rural migration is what is called circular, migrants returning after a few months or years. In the meantime, they queue at post offices to send remittances home and they crowd trains, including packed extra services, to return at the annual Spring Festival (the traditional lunar New Year). Between 1995 and 2000, a third of rural migrants from China's inner provinces had returned to resettle in their native homes or nearby towns (Murphy, 2002, p. 2).

Initially, the prospects of wage labour in cities, for both girls and boys, led to a lowering of levels of schooling. They left early to go to work and earn. The level of schooling was markedly lower for girls (pp. 92–97). But now the prospects of increased earnings has led to rural migrants taking short courses in requisite skills, such as hairdressing, and their younger siblings stay on at school because of increasing demand for better educated labour.

Maintenance of the household registration system has encouraged return. But the main effect of migration and of the household registration system is temporary accommodation and the segregation of itinerant labour in cities from the registered residents. For the migrant workers, their life in the cities produces an ambivalence that sends them back home, but not to work on the land. Because the migrant is still counted as 'rural', she or he has access to land distributed to households, according to the number of its members, including those presently in cities. This is reckoned by all to be a source of security, but at the same time it is used as a rationale for employers to sack their rural migrant labour first.

They migrated in the first place precisely to escape an existence 'facing the soil, backs to the sky' (Murphy, 2002, p. 197). But in the cities they are a visible 'minority', standing out by their clothes and their accents or their very posture, from longer-standing urban residents who deride and fear them. City governments place prejudicially high conditions of 'quality' (*suzhi*) to deny them urban registration. Back home, however, they feel superior to their country cousins, sporting city clothes and painted nails. Rachel Murphy notes that some young men borrow money to buy motorbikes and attempt to earn some money by using them for above-price passenger transport, but this leaves much idle time together at the roadside where they speculate on further opportunities of enrichment. Their parents and those who have remained say that they are incapable of the hard labour (which is skilled, though not reckoned as being skilled) on the land. This is the story of all rural–urban migrations, in all cultures. They are caught in a space between rural home and hostile city where there are also desirable commodities, life style, and opportunities.

What attracts rural migrants to the hard, often dangerous labour in cities is earned income, as well as adventure and independence, even though the very long hours and therefore lack of sleep and the lack of safety precautions make the possibility of injury great. Their remittances and their periodic returns with gifts from the cities are a performance of what they deem to be success, giving themselves as much face as they can. In other words, migration has its own dynamic, producing further migration.

The possibility of earning wages is itself an attraction compared to the uncertainties of agrarian income. The uncertainty of the crop and the market for it, where it is a cash crop, is anyway income deferred to a time long after the hard work put into it. Wage labour is immediate and a resourceful person can find new work through networking when laid off from one construction site or factory. Wage income is also individuated and remittances to the home household mark the individual source of the needed money, instead of joint farm labour or immediately pooled income in the household budget.

The other attractions are life in the city, the adventure of meeting people from other parts of China, of socialising with people of your own age, possibly of finding your own marriage partner. In other words, the attraction is individual freedom, for both men and women, from the patriarchal rule of family households.

Both poor households and better off households send members to earn. The poor migrate because their families cannot afford to feed all members of the household and they will need the earned income to pay the fees for the schooling of younger siblings and for the rising costs of inputs to agriculture (fertiliser, pesticide, tools) relative to the sale price of the crop. Grain prices fell even more with entry into the World Trade Organization and the ending of government subsidies. For the first time, arable land in the villages Murphy studied was abandoned and left fallow (Murphy, 2002, pp. 78–79).

The better off migrate to diversify income sources for their family-households. Or else they are engaged in industrialising their villages and creating economic links to cities. This process of leaving the land had happened on a large scale in southern Fujian involving better off households, for instance, in the three villages studied by Brandtstädter (2003). In one village, its government developed part of the land for housing and the other part was let to local entrepreneurs for cash-crop farming. In a second village, all the land was turned into shrimp farms by shareholding cooperation among families related by marriage. The third was a fishing village anyway, and both men and women had, as in the other villages, turned entirely to wage earning, on long distance fishing contracts or in factories in southeast Asia and Hong Kong.

Land is still 'collective' but it is let on long leases to registered households of the administrative village. Further, a villager's house and the land on which it is built is indefinitely the property of that household and passed down generations as an inheritance. Land can be sublet to others so that the most enterprising farmers can grow cash-crops (for instances, orchards or shrimp-farms) on more land, using hired labour. But the more the migrants leave the village, the fewer are those left behind to produce the crops.

The greatest need for migrants' remittances is to pay for the earner's own marriage, the bride price to be given by his family and the dowry to be given by her family. Both are a matter of pride, not just for the family but for the bride and groom themselves. Because they earn their own, as well as contribute to siblings' wedding expenses and gifts, migrants have a greater say in negotiating their own wedding arrangements. The biggest expenditure of all is the house or at least separate quarters and their furnishing that a new couple expects from the groom's family. Remember that this is a patrilineal system of descent in which daughters change families to become daughters-in-law in their husbands' fathers' households. But the tendency with individuated earnings and couples having a greater say in their own marriage and residence arrangements is for more emphasis on the conjugal couple and less on inter-generational obedience and respect. And daughters are increasingly appreciated as a lifetime support for parents, as well as for parents-in-law. Some men send remittances to their wives' mothers rather than to their own parents, as a better guarantee that it will be saved for their own use rather than for their siblings and other needs of the paternal household. In sum, remittances, as Murphy concludes, exacerbate inner family tensions (Murphy, 2002, Chapter 4).

The better-off rural households are those at the stage in the cycle of household growth when they have the highest ratio of earners to dependents, or those with least injuries and illnesses (themselves hazards of migrant labour). But there is an extra factor that differentiates richer from poorer households in the villages that Rachel Murphy studied (Murphy, 2002, pp. 58–68). It is the political connections that enable members to acquire local non-farming jobs, as teachers, as state employees, or as workers in local industries and services. Similar connections are necessary to have a bank account, which is the safest way to keep and manage savings yourself.

In general, the most diversified households are the best off. They are also those who have the connections and can afford longer and better schooling. Income differentials have increased in the countryside as well as in the cities. Overall, city incomes are increasing faster than rural incomes. But migrant labour earnings are a way for the more enterprising and adventurous to buck the trend and establish themselves in good positions, as floor managers in factories or in their own small businesses funded by their savings, and thus raise the incomes of their households at the same time, for instance, by paying for a talented sibling to stay on in education.

Policy and the Continuing Importance of Ideology

Government takes a strong hand in encouraging migrants to remain in contact with their homes and eventually to return home and use their savings and the city skills and contacts they had acquired to start small businesses in their home towns, thus increasing jobs there.

It is policy to increase industry in the countryside and its towns, to make towns as entertaining as the cities, and so to retain returning migrants. Local government reorganisation has made the larger newly-grown towns into cities and enlarged their areas of administration so that every village is part of a city-centred periphery. Local government funds, from the fees of local enterprises and households, are spent on improved roads and thus on increased local transport such as minibuses and motorbikes, increasing access to cities. Local government funds have also gone into increasing access to television cable and satellite, and to building entertainment centres in small cities and towns. These and other measures to develop the domestic market for Chinese industries of all kinds has become increasingly urgent because there has to be a way of substituting an internal market for the slowing growth in export-oriented industry. A virtuous cycle is needed of increased earnings and therefore increased local demand.

A major feature of bringing villages into the jurisdiction of a city's hinterland is the urbanisation of villages. This means an increase in the momentum of cash-cropping. All farmers have small plots near or next to their homes on which they produce vegetables and raise poultry or pigs for their own consumption. The main plots of land are now mainly for cash crops. Only the poorest farmers in a remote fringe land still use a portion of their main plots of land for subsistence. Agriculture is now for the market. Further consolidation of land, by leasing it to agrarian entrepreneurs for large-scale agriculture, and consolidating the housing of scattered households or rehousing villages into high-rise apartment blocks, so releasing house land for farming, is now a policy objective for the urbanisation of villages.

Government is equally evident in measures to encourage improvement in household performance, not just economically, but also in all of what is meant by quality (*suzhi*) and civilisation (*wenming*), in both villages and cities.

The Party, in short, still plays an active role in cultivating 'thought', which is political will, though now it is aimed at households and individuals via personal pride in relation to national policy, rather than at collective organisation and mobilisation.

What were collectively organised units of work, teams (*xiaodui*) and brigades (*dadui*) of several teams, have now become units of representation and administration. Teams have become small neighbourhoods or hamlets of households, which are units for the election of one of its residents as a representative in a village assembly. Brigades have become large villages or clusters of villages, with an assembly and an administration by an elected village head, an economic leader and other officials, as well as the Party Secretary. For those who remain in them, the villages are still face-to-face communities, although as always, locally they are part of a marketing system whose node is usually now the town that is also the capital of the lowest level of state governance, the township (*zhen*). Variation in the performance of village elections will be taken up in Chapter 17 on democracy. Here we note the peculiarly Chinese status of an elected 'collective', which is a unit of self-management whose urban equivalent is the residents' 'community' and its representative committee, which like the administrative village is also the lowest level of Party organisation.

Inequality and Redistributive Policies

The first market reform in 1978 was the 'household responsibility system', in which collective land was divided and distributed to the villagers' households along with quotas for planned produce to be sold at a fixed price through the village administration and township warehousing; anything beyond could be sold freely at whatever price the market would bear. Over the years, fixed prices were eliminated altogether. However, the collective, not a state level, but a level of Party organisation, was subject to planning down to the lowest agency in township or county governments, which could through work teams sent to villages enforce changes in cropping. At first, favourable prices for agricultural products brought sharp rises in rural income, but after a few years market prices favouring enterprises, agricultural and industrial, created increasing inequalities. The highest incomes were in the cities, particularly among real estate agents. The most poor were households in the more remote areas of China's economic regions. The extremely poor suffering periodic malnutrition and living shorter lives, numbered, according to the World Bank, 972 million people in 1981. By 2009, it had fallen to 157 million. (Key trends in globalisation ablog.typepad.com accessed fifteenth May 2016). Urban poverty also became an issue with the privatisation of state owned enterprises (SOEs) and consequent unemployment, but even more with the numerous poor rural–urban migrant workers.

Poverty relief was always a government policy, with the designation of 'poor' areas for special measures of development and the enhancing of incomes. But rising inequality posed a danger of disorder, so a number of initiatives, recounted by Wang Shaoguang (2008), successfully reduced the incidence of absolute poverty and also reduced inequality, although the Gini coefficient measuring income inequality still leaves China one of the highest in the world.

Wang Shaoguang places this governmental intervention in the framework of Karl Polanyi's theory of the necessity of embedding market relations in programmes, including state programmes, of sociality and welfare. Left to themselves, free working of market forces will anyway give rise to movements restoring the social relations that they destroy. In China, the place of social movement is taken by numbers of incidents of protest and reports of dire straits suffered because of governmental neglect. To respond to and to pre-empt them, the central government of China has enacted a series of measures, outlined by Wang, first to enforce remittance of taxes from provinces to the centre and then to redistribute that revenue in the form of support for medical insurance and for primary school education in deprived areas.

Conclusion

Rural–urban migration is a worldwide phenomenon. China's is just larger and faster. It shares with all other migration flows the characteristics of the wish to leave agricultural work while maintaining links through circular and chain migration, including the effects on rural bases of remittances, returns home and of extensive linkages to cities. Similarly, rural poverty and growing income inequalities are a global phenomenon, not peculiar to China. Neither are developmental policies, including measures of poverty relief and alleviation, peculiar to China. But it has been argued that since the tax reforms of 1998, the central state's redistributive measures have been outstanding, in global terms, in reducing absolute poverty.

Seminar Questions

Is Chinese rural to urban migration like all rural–urban migration since industrialisation?
How is increased rural to urban migration in China changing villagers' ideas of who they are and what they can be?

Key Readings

Brandtstädter, S. 2003. The moral economy of kinship and property in southern China. In *The Postsocialist Agrarian Question*, C. Hann (ed.). Muenster: LIT, pp. 419–440.

Johnston, J. 2013. Filial paths and the ordinary ethics of movement. In *Ordinary Ethics in China*, C. Stafford (ed.). LSE Monograph in Social Anthropology 79, London: Bloomsbury, pp. 45–65.

Murphy, R. 2002. *How Migrant Labour is Changing Rural China*. Cambridge: Cambridge University Press.

Pieke, F. N., Nyiri, P., Thuno, M., and Ceccagno, A. 2004. *Transnational Chinese: Fujianese Migrants in Europe*. Stanford CA: Stanford University Press.

Wang, S. 2008. The great transformation: The double movement in China. *Boundary* 2, **35**(2), pp. 15–47.

Further Readings

Cohen, M. 1993. Cultural and political inventions in modern china: The case of the Chinese 'Peasant'. *Daedalus,* **122**(2), pp. 151–70.

Deng, K. 2003. Development and its deadlock in imperial China, *Economic Development and Cultural Change*, **51**(2), pp. 479–522.

Gates, H. 1996. *China's Motor: A Thousand Years of Petty Capitalism.* Ithaca: Cornell University Press.

Hemelryk, D., Stephanie, and Benewick, R. 2005. *The State of China Atlas.* Berkeley. University of California Press.

Kearney, M. 1996. *Reconceptualizing the Peasantry. Anthropology in Global Perspective*. Boulder: Westview Press (esp. Chapter 3).

Polanyi, K. 2002. *The Great Transformation: The Political and Economic Origins of Our Time*. New York: Beacon Press.

Redfield, R. 1956. *Peasant Society and Culture: An Anthropological Approach to Civilization*. Chicago, IL: University of Chicago Press.

Skinner, G. W. 1964. Marketing and social structure in rural China, Part 1. *Journal of Asian Studies*, **24**(1), pp. 3–43 (note also parts 2 and 3, *Journal of Asian Studies,* **24**(2), pp. 195–228 and **24**(3), pp. 363–399.

Steinmüller, H. 2009. Chapter 3: Work Through the Food Basket. In his *Communities of Complicity: Everyday Ethics in Rural China.* New York: Berghahn, pp. 98–129.

Yan, Y. 2017. Intergenerational Intimacy and Descending Familism in Rural North China. *American Anthropologist.*

Chapter 12

The City

It was claimed by the famous historian of the working class in England, Thompson (1967) that the chronologically and mechanically disciplined work of the factory replaced the more seasonal and multiple task-oriented temporality of farming. Abstract, chronological and clock time gradually replaced the more local times and times of seasons. In addition, Thompson argued that factory work was increasingly divided from domestic and leisure time. Work as an instrument for wage earning, for income to be spent in leisure time, replaced farming as family labour, that is at once social and instrumental. These contrasts are valid, but they need modification.

Other ways of living and knowing the passing of time co-exist with abstract clock-time, such as the time of life courses or the necessary timing of physical tasks by those who carry them out, distinct from the managerial clock-time that seeks to standardise and control them. Studies of industrial work have in addition shown that work-based friendships go beyond the workplace. They also show that whatever the disciplines of machine-based work standardisation, in practice, work is often sporadic, leaving slack time for socialising. Workers create their own spaces and times for socialising at work, and the extreme of mechanised and intensive work is true only of mass assembly and service lines. What remains true is that the place of wage work and the place of leisure and domestic life are usually separate and also that wage-work-time is regularly divided from leisure and domestic time.

Most of all, studies have shown everywhere that farmers prefer to move out of farming to wage labour to receive more individuated and immediate income.

For instance, Parry (1999, Chapter 4) notes how the highest status work in Bhilai, India, had been agriculture, as in China, but it is now the lowest. What had been the lowest of ranks, to be an employee, is now preferred for the reasons mentioned above as well as because it means getting away from the control of elders and finding opportunities for romance, gambling, and drinking. Parry's study is based in a huge steel-producing town, Bhilai, made up of India's largest steel plant, surrounded by other related businesses, some themselves quite large. The Bhilai Steel Plant was one of the key projects of the newly independent state of India under its Prime Minister Nehru, recruiting workers from all over India as well as giving jobs to the local villagers whose land had been requisitioned to build the Plant. What is peculiar to the Indian situation is the problem of communalism, of caste and religion, and one of the aims of the Plant was to create a sense of cross-communal solidarity, which Parry shows it succeeded in doing. Rivalry for jobs in the Plant does create inter-communal tensions, but at work they are well contained and their boundaries are crossed in work groups that also meet outside work.

The job security, the benefits, which include housing, medical, travel, and other kinds of welfare, are similar to state employment and large-scale private employment in China. Also similar to China is the resentment locals feel when the land requisitioned from them and for which they were paid at a relatively low compensation rate, was not used for the Plant but resold to others at a much higher price.

So, while there are differences in the communal divisions that can be used to exploit and divide a work-force, the reasons for rural–urban migration and the high status, security and welfare that retain workers in large key plants, whether publicly or privately owned, are common to India, China, and much further afield. There is a major economic and social class distance between employees in secure and skilled employment and those employed in the insecure and most menial work. How easy or difficult it is to rise from the latter into the former is a measure of class polarisation.

But that is a description of China since the reforms that included from the 1990s onwards the dismantling of most State-Owned Enterprises (SOEs). Before that, the city of work units was uniquely Chinese.

The *danwei* (Work and Residential Unit)

The Chinese work unit during the Maoist era was a unit of residence as well as work. So, industrialisation under Mao made none of the divisions mentioned above. Domestic life and work took place in the same compound.

Bray (2005) describes the urban work unit (*danwei*) as a uniquely Chinese socialist architectural and social form. It was first conceived in the Yan'an base area, blockaded by the Nationalists, as a cell of production and residence that had to be as self-sufficient as possible and as autonomous as possible, though under the central command of the Party and its armed forces. It was also an organisational and physical form for nurturing a socialist person (as against a liberal individual or the worker-cog in a capitalist work-place such as the Fordist assembly line).

As Chinese cities were gradually, from 1953, turned into cities of work units, rather than centres of services and entertainment with dwellings and work places separated, an interim organisational measure was the formation of Street and Neighbourhood Residents' Committees. They were purely territorial units of collective self-government and Party control. Residents of neighbourhoods were mobilised for voluntary policing and childcare and for factories where wives and mothers of workers could also produce. But by 1978, 95% of urban workers belonged to all-round work units and the residents' committees had become almost entirely redundant (Bray, 2005, p. 182), though in old large cities such as Shanghai and Beijing, the old tenements and courtyards were still separate residential buildings and there were neighbourhood factories for the residents not employed in work units.

The work unit was a shared domestic and work unit, like a college campus. It included not just its workers and managers, but their families, children and retired workers. They differed from traditional Chinese walled compounds architecturally in one significant way. In the socialist work unit, the main building, which is that of the Party and administration, was visible from the entrance and at the centre rather than hidden toward the back wall.

Similarity with and Difference from the Soviet Work Unit

In the Soviet Union, state enterprises were also responsible for the housing of their workers, but domesticity and work were not combined as in China. The workers' housing blocks were near the work place, and as later in China the blocks shared the facilities of heating, storage and entertainment. But they were not in the same architectural unit with their work.

The *mikrorayon* was a neighbourhood of residence in the Soviet urban and industrial planning system. It stressed shared living, reducing inequality and socialising 'private life', but it was part of the urban plan and not inward looking as was the walled work unit in China. It became standardised as did state enterprises in the course of Soviet planning. In the Soviet Union, breaking down time and motion in the measurement of a work process, pioneered in the Ford assembly line and known as Taylorism after its US inventor, was adopted as a part of the system of planning in workplaces that were parts of ministries of the various industries. Top-down planning of this kind was tried in China only at the beginning of the First Five Year Plan before being rejected in 1956 in favour of the dual system of local Party leadership and ministerial planning, stressing mobilisation to produce more and better.

The work unit as a decentralised cell was peculiarly Chinese, suited to the mobilisation politics of Maoism and what Apter and Saich (1994) called the formation of a discursive community of political will and not just a branch of scientific and planning expertise. Leadership of the work unit had to be capable of forming collective selfhood, of acting for the greater good and reminding others to do so, as well as of managing production or administration efficiently — or in simpler terms that were used then, cadres had to be both red and expert (see our discussion in Chapter 8).

So with the turn to the production of commodities for a market rather than for planned prices, what happened to the work unit?

A Case Study of a Work Unit After Mao

Rofel (1999) provides a case study of a large silk-weaving factory, called Zhenfu, in the city of Hangzhou, capital of Zhejiang province. It is not just a case study of factory work and factory workers, but of changing conceptions of modernity and in particular changing senses of gender in the transition from the old work-unit system. Most of the workers in Zhenfu are women. The factory makes exports and luxury items for the home market. Work is managed according to a discipline of efficiency, each work station measured in terms of standard movements and piece-work added up and in rivalry of productivity for bonus wages.

Long passages of her book divide up tellingly descriptive details. In these passages, she interprets 'the state' and the way it tries to have itself and its current modernising project imagined. She argues that workers are thus created as the state's subjects but that at the same time they transgress the roles that the state makes for them and instead make their own senses of what it is to be modern. What she describes is a layering of past generations and the modernising projects of their times. There are three layers, or generations of workers. The two older generations are (1) from 1950s Soviet-influenced privileging of skilled labour and (2) the Maoist political worker-activists who brought domestic tasks into the factory during work-time like washing their bikes or their clothes, as well as attending frequent political meetings. She describes how these two older generations of workers insist on defying orders to stay at their work-places. They come close to each other in order to chat, as a remembered insistence on their former high status and political activities. (3) Post-Mao workers are and know themselves as individuated and instrumental wage labourers.

In this new labour discipline, the workers are in a downgraded status of transnational Asian manufacturing labour, a far cry from workers in the 1960s and 1970s, who were high-status sought-after marriage partners. Other industries (clerical or administrative jobs that allow more flexible working times, or in more high-tech manufacturing) have superseded them in marriage status. In Chapter 7, Rofel describes how the younger, post-Mao workers, consume popular romances, on TV and in print, and the state-published as well as privately published advice on femininity to heighten their attractiveness to boyfriends and to a life of greater fulfilment as wives and mothers. In other words, for them work has become instrumental, a means to ends that are separated from work, away from the workplace and its domination by incentive disciplines. They have moved away from the propaganda of productive efficiency and state-national aims for the economy toward a completely instrumental view of work.

But note how even here the state has 'civilisational' functions. In the same chapter (Chapter 7), she describes how the union representatives and the birth-control cadre between them broker marriage and encourage models of morally upright behaviour, through helpful checking and advice. By the same means of advice, still called by its Maoist term 'thought-work' (*sixiang gongzuo*), they collect details of every menstruating woman worker, who reports her periods and uses the birth-planning office-clinic's facilities for genital hygiene. The birth-control office records her premarital state, or if she is married how the couple are getting on, their sexual activity, their child or children. The office-clinic helps the childless to adopt. It dispenses not just advice on hygiene and appropriate behaviour and marriage guidance, but also birth control devices and menstrual pads. Male workers are not scrutinised in this way at all, even though many are marriage partners of fellow workers.

Note that the labour discipline, the machinery, the technology and indeed the product (sheets of silk for export, printed and dyed silk quilts for the domestic market) are individuated, but the still-lived (and remembered) history, the spatial form and the social functions of the union and the Party (birth-control) in the work-place are still peculiarly Chinese. Note also that this kind of work is still more desirable than farm work.

Post-Mao Changes

There was a gradual turning of state enterprises into capital accounting and profit-making units, which could become bankrupt and have to close, and whose managers have powers to fire and hire workers. In addition, most work units are now separated from domestic units.

From 1978, the standardised and guaranteed wage system became a system in which bonuses were paid out of the retained profits of enterprises. Bonuses increased into ever larger proportions of workers' pay and the amount paid in bonus depended on a manager's unchallengeable counting of points for each worker's productivity and civilisational quality — how well a worker interacted with fellow workers, kept the workplace tidy, and contributed individually to the enterprise. Where there had been a system of model workers for emulation of their collective spirit, there was now rivalry for top points and highest wages in a zero-sum game for winnings from the bonus pool. Self-improvement and material incentives replaced the collective spirit and moral incentives. The shopfloor cadre had been a pastoral carer of the workers and a mobiliser of their political will to produce. Now he or she became a professional, in a bureaucratic structure of managing an enterprise for profit, but still with the responsibility for rewarding 'civilisation' and getting awards for his unit as a 'civilised work unit' (*wenming danwei*).

Most urban housing for the first two decades of the reforms was in fact financed by enterprises, from funds that they raised by loans and from their profits, and from a specific housing fund made from equal contributions by employee and employer. In other words, the huge expansion of cities since the reforms began in 1978 was at first financed by enterprises. The larger privately owned businesses also provided housing and other benefits for their workers as ways of attracting and retaining them or, on the contrary, to trap and exploit them in company dormitories. So the quality of housing varied greatly according to the profitable success of the enterprise or according to the kind of labour it employed. Much of the early enterprise-built housing was sold to tenants, who then sub-let a room to migrant workers.

From the mid-1990s onward, pay has been determined by employers in a segmented labour market, in which there is still some secure employment, with relatively high salaries, including some work units in government apparatuses, state education (including universities) and SOEs. The various gradations into increasingly less secure employment moves down to the least secure and worst paid, zero-hour contracts for piece-work or on building sites for migrant workers. The 1994 Labour Law, a batch of laws in 2008, and their subsequent amendments have been attempts to regulate the labour market, including representation of workers in labour unions affiliated to the All-China Federation of Labour Unions. But they do not include the large proportions of urban workers who are migrants. In some cities, including Beijing and Shanghai, more than half the workforce is made up of migrant workers.

Further, while those with urban registration have guaranteed access at relatively low cost to what had formerly been supplied in urban work units: schooling and medical facilities, plus welfare payments (for periods of unemployment, for injury, and retirement pensions), workers registered as 'agricultural' are not eligible for these, since it was assumed that their 'collective' administrative village of origin would provide them. In the years since 2010, there have been attempts by city governments to include migrant workers if they can show they have worked in the city for a period of time (which varies). But the system of differential registration remains. Work-unit housing was sold off to its tenants and where they could not afford to buy, they continued to rent it but now from a company that is all that remains of the former work unit.

Enterprises can provide subsidised housing, but most housing is provided by municipal authorities or by private development companies. The cheapest housing is that which is let, either by tenants or owners of former work-unit housing or by villagers whose houses have been absorbed by the city. These are where the poorest migrant workers live, in overcrowded accommodation. The most expensive housing is entirely private, such as the spectacularly luxurious compounds in the suburbs of Beijing with special shuttle services to the centre.

Both enterprises and residential compound managements are responsible for policing. Private security forces, in their own uniforms, patrol residential compounds and work places. China's public police forces are among the smallest in the world in ratio to population. But the private security forces are nearly always led by actual or retired police (Public Security) personnel.

Shequ, the New, Elected, Base Unit of a City

The Ministry of Civil Affairs has taken over the welfare functions of the work unit. Its welfare payments and advisory services are administered in the so-called 'communities', which have replaced the old Street and Neighbourhood Committees. Community offices include the desks of fulltime staff administering welfare and advice, as well as representatives of residents who work with local retired women and men volunteers.

The Ministry of Civil Affairs and the Party, working through Street Offices, pursue a policy of social management by generating 'self-governing' communities (*shequ* and their subdivisions, *xiaoshequ*). The task of urban local government, including Residents' Committees, has been to 'build community' (*shequ jianshe*) including a sense of belonging, as a way of containing the disruptions of laying off workers from SOEs and dismantling the work unit. The designation 'community' is therefore a form of involving residents in their own governance. In practice, the Residents' representative Committee is best described as a managerial unit composed out of "two committees and one station" (*liangwei yizhan*), namely a Party Committee, a Residents' Committee (RC) and a Social Work Service Station. They overlap. Indeed, paid staff, who include leading Party members, serve both as the members of the RC and employees of the Station. The RC's role is therefore double, as both a workstation and the grassroots unit of social management (*shehui guanli*) through 'self-government' (*zizhi*).

As Bray (2006) points out, 'community' (*shequ*) and its subdivisions (*xiao shequ*) are planning concepts: spatial planning units of urban housing in which a sense of social responsibility is supposed to occur. It can be a bounded estate or a set of high-rise blocks, or a set of refurbished alleys, or an estate of duplex villas. After a series of experiments with different designs of such housing units in the mid-1980s, the Ministry of Housing promulgated a set of standards for the building of these units, as a technical template that should be repeated in all new urban developments. In fact, there are many variations within and from these standards, but they are still in force, combining rules about uses of space and density of residence with the idea of self-management.

In a case study in the city of Kunming in Yunnan province, Zhang (2010) provides extensive fieldwork material on property developers and housing consumption — marketing ploys and the desires of middle-class homebuyers. In her last chapter, 'Privatising community governing and its limits', she points out that since the issuing by the State Council of a Property Regulation Ruling (Wuye guanli tuanli) in 2003, property developers must establish management agencies in each 'community' (*shequ*, or *xiao shequ*) and residents have the right to organise home-owners' associations. The property management company has the backing of local government authority, but it is a privatised devolution of government responsibility. It charges fees for its staff and functions. Its functions include maintaining peace and order by its security guards, maintenance of public spaces and utilities, waste clearance — including dogshit, a cause of friction among residents — and more. In practice, these management agencies often arrange for the formation of home-owners association committees, so that conflict, for instance, over mismanagement or over broken promises on the extent of open spaces, is kept under control. Nevertheless, Zhang gives instances of serious conflicts between home-owners associations and property management companies, from which local government tries to maintain a convenient distance.

Residents' Committees, their volunteers and other users of its Cultural centre and the planned public spaces, and its Party Committee, mobilise what residents they can to be civilised and to help the old and infirm. But like cities everywhere, Chinese cities are for most of their residents anonymous spaces in which they choose their own networks, form their own associations, and have little or nothing to do with elections to Residents' Committees, the Welfare Station or the Party.

Tomba (2014), based on very close and extended observations and interviews in Beijing, might call this indifference 'consensus'. But the main and a positive consensus of which he writes is the reward to those cadres, officials and others with the connections to make protests effective or with the opportunity to purchase high-grade housing early and for prices before inflation in housing prices occurred.

Are Chinese Cities Becoming Like Cities Everywhere Else? Is There a Universal Form of Modern City?

The modern Chinese city is a sprawl surrounding a number of business districts, the most imposing buildings being those of banks, large municipal offices, corporate headquarters, and the biggest hotels. Shopping malls inside the closer ring roads serve the wealthier residents. Except for spectacular buildings designed by internationally renowned practices as 'icons', all this and the broad avenues of imposing buildings look quite like each other. The avenues of the most imposing buildings of government units and business headquarters are divided from and joined by narrower alleys in which street markets and small stalls cater for the local residents. Intersections and parks are appropriated by locals for their recreation — gossip, exercise, strolls. But the centre-pieces, the malls, avenues and large buildings are spaces with little local character though occasionally they are of architectural interest and in other cases have vernacular add-ons, such as slightly curved eaves, or local-style brickwork and at their entrances stone lion-dogs.

Compared to Mexico, Egypt, France or the UK, China has no dominant city in which most of its wealth and urban population have gathered. Shanghai may be approaching this status, but it is still a regional city with transnational functions, among other similar cities in China, such as Guangzhou and the rest of the Pearl River delta sprawl, including Shenzhen, or such as Chongqing, or Tianjin and Beijing. China has a long-developed system of central places leading up from small to large cities to megacities. Its economy is still divided into regional economies, linked but not integrated into a single economy by the megacities.

All large cities are linked to global consumerism through consumer outlets such as Carrefour and Macdonalds. But megacities are now also linked through certain transnational industries. Sassen (2000) describes those industries and shows how they are linked globally. They are what are classed as financial and producer-service industries: banking, insurance, security and stock trading, accounting, law, consultancy, advertising, research and development, design, transport, communications, maintenance, security, storage — including data storage — cleaning, personnel (including head hunting), and real estate agents.

Megacities tend to grow independently of their immediate territorial hinterland economies and to be more linked to each other at their top ends. As this linkage grows, with the aid of electronic communication, you would have thought that territorial location would become less important. But Sassen shows the opposite to be true. The high-end global managers and directors and their offices prefer to be physically in each other's proximity. In other words, they create their own locations. Their headquarter offices concentrate in a few centres along with the affiliates of other producer service and transnational manufacturing and extraction (oil, mining) corporations.

These transnational industry headquarters and large affiliates offer limited benefits to the local economy: the earnings and expense accounts are locally spent. A portion of the mega-incomes of the top end is spent on less transnational, local industries. States seduce transnational financial and other corporations, as London has, through favourable tax regimes, by deregulation and by contracting government functions and the provision of utilities to them in the expectation of jobs for local employees and for tax revenue and by the brand and buzz of the city as a special place. But this just increases the price of housing in the favoured locales. The trickle down stops quite soon, limited as it was in dynastic China to something like the older court and mercantile global economy, a luxury, except that the transnational set of industries and consumer and service provision is far better linked and far larger than was the old mercantile network. Such centres are often new, some way off the old centres of cities, in areas of spectacular architecture such as La Defense in Paris, Canary Wharf in London, and Pudong in Shanghai. Their differences are not due to vernacular, local styles, but to the character given to them by their transnational architectural firms and, less obviously, by the ambitions and restrictions placed upon them by state planning authorities and the huge private or semi-private developers and consultancies that produce the new centres, including luxury housing and recreation.

Class in the City

In other parts of the same cities are the manufacturing plants, many of them linked to transnational operations or producing directly for export, and then there are the zones where you find manufacturing and service industries that absorb the influx of rural migrants. Such cities are exemplars of the huge social distances within a small geographic space that keeps apart the transnational agents and their huge incomes and enclosures of work, rest and play at one end and the dangerous and low income sweatshops at the other end producing their and others' consumer goods. In between are the factories of manufactured goods that to some extent depend on and are exploited in their financial dealings by the global service industries.

While the poorer migrant workers still live in and work in unsafe environments, it is also true that most urban residents, including those that have been relocated, live in larger and more salubrious accommodation than their parents' former dwellings, with internal lavatories and wash spaces and cooking facilities. It must also be said that labour migration has been one of the chief ways in which absolute poverty has been heavily reduced in China.

But alongside these achievements has been the segregation of housing and socio-economic statuses, making solid the increasing polarisation of incomes in China by the differentiation of housing types topped by the extraordinary proliferation of gated communities that can be afforded by those with mid- to high-incomes, in which residents seek to adapt to their own the visions of lifestyle that property developers offer, usually exotically emulating by pastiche a foreign destination that they can also visit as tourists. The most elaborate and accurate of these pastiches are the most expensive, the least are like those described by Zhang Li in Kunming, but in any case they can be ranked in fine gradations of expense, each guarded by their own property management companies and the migrant workers they employ as gardeners and security patrols. Residents in the most expensive housing are the most secure in the sense that their geographical mobility is their own choice, whereas lower-middle and low-income households are the least secure, subject to dislocation by the planning and development authorities. Tomba (2014, Chapter 1) describes well the process of what he calls 'social clustering' into housing classes in Beijing.

Seminar Questions

Is a Chinese city like a city anywhere else in the world?

What have been the main changes in Chinese cities since the reforms?

What has been the impact of these changes on urban workers?

Readings

Bray, D. 2005. Reforming the Danwei, Chapter 7 of his *Social Space and Governance in Urban China: The Danwei System from Origins to Reform*. Stanford, CA: Stanford University Press.

Parry, J., Bremen J., and Kapadia K. (eds.) 1999. *The Worlds of Indian Industrial labour* (Chapter 4 by Parry).

Rofel, L. 1999. *Other Modernities: Gendered Yearnings in China after Socialism*. Berkeley: University of California Press (Chapters 7 and 8).

Tomba, L. 2014. *The Government Next Door: Neighbourhood Politics in Urban China*. Ithaca and London: Cornell University Press (Chapters 1 and 4).

Zhang, Li 2010. *In Search of Paradise: Middle-class Living in a Chinese Metropolis*. Ithaca: Cornell University Press (Chapter 1).

Further Readings

Apter, D. and Saich, T. 1994. *Revolutionary Discourse in Mao's Republic*. Cambridge: Harvard College.

Bray, D. 2006. Building community: New strategies of governance in urban China. *Economy and Society*, **35**(4), pp. 530–549.

Feuchtwang, Stephan, Zhang, Hui, and Morais, Paula. 2015. The formation of governmental community and the closure of housing classes. In *China's Urban Century: Governance, Environment and Socio-Economic Imperatives*, F. Gipouloux (ed.). London: Edward Elgar, pp. 195–212.

Friedmann, J. 2005. *China's Urban Transition*. Minneapolis: University of Minnesota Press.

Lee, Chang Kwan (ed.) 2006. *Working in China: Ethnographies of Labour and Workplace Transformation*. London: Routledge.

Sassen, S. 2000. *Cities in a World Economy*. London and Pine Forge: Sage.

Smith, S. 2008. *Revolution and the People in Russia and China*. Cambridge: Cambridge University Press (Chapter 1).

Thompson, E. P. 1967. *Time, Work-Discipline, and Industrial Capitalism*. Past and Present, **38**(1), pp. 56–97.

Wang Mingming 2009. *Empire and Local Worlds: A Chinese Model for Long-Term Historical Anthropology*. Walnut Creek, CA: Leftcoast Press.

Wu, Fulong (ed.) 2007. *China's Emerging Cities: The Making of New Urbanism*. London: Routledge.

USSR Comparison

Buchli, V. 1999. The Narkomfin Communal House and Marxist Domesticity. In *Archeology of Socialism*. Oxford: Berg, pp. 99–135.

Humphrey, C. 2002. The Villas of New Russians, A sketch of consumption and cultural identity in post-Soviet landscapes. In *The Unmaking of Soviet Life, Everyday Economies after Socialism*, pp. 175–201.

Smith, D. 1996. The socialist city. In *Cities after Socialism. Urban and Regional Change and Conflict in Post-Socialist Societies*, Andrusz, Gregory, Michael Harloe, Ivan Szelenyi (eds.). Cambridge: Blackwell Publishers, pp. 70–99.

Chapter 13

The Family and Gender

It has long been a sociological tenet that with industrial capitalism and urbanisation comes a new sense of self, often described as individualism. The modern individual is self-conscious (or reflexive), nurtured in the intimacy of family relations that are no longer related to production but whose emphatic function is emotional and the nurturing of a sense of identity. Bodily appearance to others is a vital manifestation of this self-identity. Anthony Giddens' *Modernity and self-identity; self and society in the late modern age* (1991) is a classical text summing up these conclusions. And like many sociologists, Giddens' examples are all based on Europe and North-America.

Rationalism and Enlightenment moral philosophy posits an individual acting on her desires but also according to a moral conscience, judging in a way that justifies action — the famous self-interested individual formulated as a central figure in the classical sociology of Max Weber. The implicit idea (never realised) is that all individuals acting for their well-being are equivalent to each other and have equal rights. The capitalist market and consumerism breed social imaginaries in which a narcissistic self is defined according to the senses of display to imagined significant others who are the mirrors of the self, that is to say, self-identity is a result of being sensed by others. The philosopher Charles Taylor describes the modern 'Sense of Self' (2000) and the corollary Social Imaginaries (2004) as rooted both in the social and intellectual transformations that took place in modern Europe. And you can add to this the more psychoanalytic teaching that all humans through attachment to others also negotiate and reflect the underlying gap or abyss of alterity and live with the accompanying anxiety and uncertainty between an undefined self and a differentiated other. So, the question is whether this is universal and if so, does it have a particular narcissistic flowering in modern Euro-America and then everywhere else in consumerist cultures. Certainly, the languages of the world all have first person positions and personal pronouns. As Lydia Liu elaborates in her book *Translingual Practices* (Liu, 1995) 'individualism' and first person narrative were adopted in Chinese literature in the course of Chinese intellectuals' nationalist campaigns and contests. She shows that claims for and counterclaims against (materialist) individualism, as strength or weakness, both had to address 'individualism', and the Chinese literary idiom began to use the first person pronoun '*wo*' and the third person pronoun '*ta*' (with different written forms for masculine, feminine and neutral persons) in the new narratives of story, essay, and novel.

The first attempt at an empirical world survey that linked family change, individualism, and industrialisation had already been published in 1963 before Giddens and Taylor had their influential say (Goode, 1963). William J. Goode's *World Revolution and Family Patterns* survey of every statistical study of the family in the context of industrialisation that he could find posited a number of crucial correlations (leaving aside what caused what) between family formation and industrialisation. One was the formation of independent conjugal families. Another was that parents' authority over children was diminished. A third was that greater autonomy of the individual went with reduction of extensive kinship obligations, such as dowries and bride-wealth. So it appears that there is empirical support for what might appear to be Eurocentric conclusions.

Others after Goode have added the importance of romance in choice of marriage partner and the ideal of love as a transport beyond self that some say derives from Christian love of God (Lindholm, 1995).

Much of this is summarised in the introduction by Yan Yunxiang (2003) in his book *Private Life under Socialism*, in which he argues that the above is largely coming about in China. But we do need to check, to see what qualifications he and others make to the general tendencies that seem to confirm Goode's findings in China.

Ideal and Reality of 'Family' in China

Chinese and non-Chinese sociologists and social psychologists often contrast Confucian values with Western individualism, or Chinese 'collectivism' with individualism. But it is possible to argue along the lines of Fei Xiaotong (1992) that the traditional Chinese individual is a self who is not individualist but also not subsumed within a collective, a self defined in relations of uneven reciprocity. It is also without doubt that classical Chinese texts of Confucianism, Daoism and Buddhism all refer to an inner and an outer self whether it is named *ji*, *zi*, *xing* (personality or character) or *nei*. But the disciplining of the self or inner circuits of energy, breath and feeling is always with the aim of resonating with a larger external and encompassing set of relations, starting with the family, and bringing it within so that inner be integrated with outer. We should therefore ask whether this self has been transformed.

The ideals to which both urban and rural Chinese used to aspire were the three good fortunes named *fu lu shou*, prosperity, high office, and long life. Underlying them all was another. This was the ideal of an extended family so that in old age, a family of several sons and their wives, their own sons and wives and a further generation of children would be living together in a large courtyard house of several wings, over which the oldest ruled or were at least deferred to in decisions actually taken by the most capable son. The old would be cared for with love. After they died that care would continue in respect for their graves and their names on the family altar shelf, by which through offerings of food they would continue to be part of a familiar social life, rather than an orphan soul. From at least the Song dynasty, becoming an ancestor was the most common form of achieving immortality in China.

On the way to this ideal, the proper form of marriage was an arrangement with the acquiescence of the couple, in which their families were matched in respectability and wealth or if not exactly matched, the bride's family would be of slightly lesser status. Marriage in this long transmitted norm was a form of death for the daughter as bride to be marked by laments as she left her beloved parental home to join that of her husband, where eventually, starting from the lowest position in the family hierarchy she would move up by becoming the mother of sons and end in the husband's family tomb and altar as a much respected ancestor. That was the desired norm. The achieved reality was different.

Very few families actually grew and stayed together to become an extended family of several branches living together. Those that did were invariably those with sufficient property or sufficient wealth from diversified sources of income (from land, from trade, from official position) to make it good economic sense not to divide. The rest divided and never achieved the ideal. But families moved towards that ideal. They could, for instance, divide domestically but maintain economic links of interdependence.

According to surveys conducted in the first half of the twentieth century, most actual families, in both urban and rural China, were in fact nuclear — a parental couple and their children — or stem, one or both paternal grandparents living with the nuclear family of one of their sons or married-in sons-in-law.

Calculating ancestry in a male line of descent and a norm of marriage that is virilocal, the bride moving into the groom's father's household, is patriarchy. But relations within a family conveyed a very different reality, one that Stafford (2008) has called 'actually existing Chinese matriarchy'. Recounting his own field researches in Taiwan and two mainland locations and reviewing Yan Yunxiang's and others' too, he suggests that there are some conditions in which women take prominent public roles. But he emphasises the importance of women in managing domestic affairs throughout the various conditions before the PRC's policies made households more secluded and private in the course of bringing women into active if less valued positions in the economy, with the results that Yan Yunxiang has demonstrated in rural Northeastern China.

Ongoing Changes in the PRC

These changes are tendencies. They are not sudden or complete.

- Reproduction is still under surveillance in the longest campaign of the PRC, the control of population quantity and quality.
- Change in the relation between generations in favour of the young. Due to the law on the collective and state ownership of land and the severe reduction of heritable property, the old who had been adults

during the Mao era had little property to pass on. In the same period, politics gave the young leading roles as activists. Now technological knowledge, education and acquaintance with new consumer products, mean the young have little to learn from the older generation. But the home, a house or an apartment, is heritable property.

- Change in the position of the elderly and care for them.
  Care for the aged is still the responsibility of the family, in cities too now that the welfare responsibilities of work units have been reduced or annulled. But so is care for grandchildren often the responsibility of the aged. When the younger couple has a child or children, both of the young parents need to continue to earn because the state welfare system is insufficient to provide for the old and sick and the costs of a child's education add more, so the older generation is loaded with domestic chores and childcare and, in the countryside, with farm labour. Young parents migrate to earn an income. This is not a new phenomenon. Even during the late 1950s, old people complained of having to look after grandchildren and do heavy domestic chores and of being neglected as both sons and daughters-in-law were at work (Diamant, 2000, pp. 252–253). But, such instances have increased.
- Change in the relation between marriage partners, such that they are more egalitarian and conjugal.
  The young earn their own income. Even more dramatic, women have been earners of individual income not only in urban China but also in most of rural China since collectivisation and payment by work points. They insist on being respected as providers of income instead of immediately pooling their income as domestic commodity producers and traders.

  There is still gender stereotyping in what are considered women's and what men's work: e.g., women for medicine, accountancy, the caring professions; men for computing, engineering, top management. But women are now preferred by top managers for the patient skills of middle management and of course personal relations in the newly expanding service and light industries (Fong, 2004, pp. 108).
- Change in the status of daughters, such that they are now often favoured as much as sons in urban and many parts of rural China.
  Because of changes in marriage practice, daughters remain near their own parents, even marrying in the same village or urban

neighbourhood. So they can be relied upon to help look after their own parents.

Marriage is still the norm. It is very rare even in a city like Dalian for a woman to remain single, and even rarer for a woman to give birth outside wedlock (Fong, 2004, pp. 137). But there have been changes in what was considered to be a desirable marriage partner, in what constituted high status and in what constituted income security. Under the socialist *danwei* system, high status consisted of being from good classes (children of cadres, workers, or poor peasants) and from employment in a state enterprise or government unit or in education. Now it is a job in one of the new industries or wealth made in whichever way possible.

There has also been a change in the desirable qualities of a marriage partner, from hard worker to social know-how and adventurousness.

- Change in the status of wives.
  The marriage law (1950) allowed women the right to divorce, as well as men, and women the right to inherit as well as men. The new law was implemented by a mass campaign publicising and implementing it and resulted in a great number of divorces. But after 1953, until the reforms after 1978, the divorce rate declined. Courts became very reluctant to grant divorce, emphasising reconciliation. What the 1950 law established was the threat of divorce as a bargaining tool, according to the detailed study of records, including court records, by Diamant (2000). The threat of divorce by women, the main initiators of divorce proceedings, could be used to make demands on husbands and their families (pp. 260–261).

  The revised and strengthened Marriage Law of 1980 heralded another increase in the rate of divorce. But the more general effects of the reforms, the increased capacity of the young to earn their own living and to choose their own lifestyle, played a greater role in increasing the status of wives.
- Sex.
  Revolutionary (sexual) virtue was practiced by intellectuals, but not by the revolutionary classes of workers and peasants themselves. This led to their being denounced as 'backward' by judges and Party writers. Diamant (2000) shows that among peasants and workers there

was far less political calculation about marriage partners and far less sexual asceticism than among cadres and intellectuals. Among cadres, the asceticism demanded by revolutionary virtue was anyway often a cover beneath which was use of their power to seduce and have affairs in semi secret. Among peasants, after collectivisation brought women into the fields and other workplaces, and always among factory workers and small traders and retailers, marriage remained a matter of seeking partners that could provide income rather than just matching with appropriate political status. Sex was also always much more open. Sexual attraction, banter, affairs, and the use of seduction and serial divorce to make a better life, denounced as 'chaotic' by the courts, were and remained normal among workers and peasants, even during the Cultural Revolution.

The effect of the reforms was to generalise sexual attraction, in advertising, in television serials, in print fiction, in celebrity culture, and among the formerly ascetic category of intellectuals, the rates of divorce increased and so did cases of adultery. Many successful male rural–urban migrants went further and set up concubinages, separate urban households with a second partner. So did Taiwanese business immigrants.

Case Studies: Urban

Yan Yunxiang combined surveys and direct observation of family life in a rural location of north-eastern China. Another, urban study is set in Dalian, the fourteenth largest city in China, which had been one of the main centres of heavy industry in the Maoist industrialisation. Let us start with the urban study, before turning to the more thorough rural study.

Vanessa Fong (2004) points out that at least a third of city residents at any one time are migrants with a rural household registration. They are not included in her survey. But, as she says, nearly all urban residents in Dalian were rural within the past one or two generations, their grandparents or parents came to the city from rural parts of the north-eastern provinces or they were absorbed into the city as it expanded, to make up its growing industrial workforce.

In the three schools in which she in 1999 conducted her surveys of entire classes (taking as her base what she calls 'home rooms', which are the classrooms in which school students sit all day and have their lessons) and which recruited exclusively from urban areas, 94% (of 2167) were single children, or singletons as Fong calls them, while over 80% of their parents had siblings (p. 4). So unlike their experience of their own parents, the young parents of single children devoted all their love and attention and hopes on their one and only child. Two thirds of the mothers of the students in the survey had done paid work, and they lived in apartments with their husband and single children, without parent or parent-in-law.

Since the early 1980s, income had risen for everyone in Dalian and the availability of a growing variety and range of consumer goods had grown even more. Yet, Vanessa Fong met a striking response to this prosperity among some of the parents of the late adolescent school students she surveyed. They would say they are poorer now than they were in Mao's time. Although they have more than their parents did in Mao's time, and they only have one child to feed, the costs of having, feeding and educating their single child are so high that they both have to work. Their work is insecure, a third of them had been laid off, and they resorted to peddling goods in open markets to a falling clientele who are themselves poorer than they were a few years before. If shoppers have a good income they prefer to shop in the newly opened Carrefour or Walmart, not from street traders. Starting one's own small business is in any case to be under the pressure of being out-competed by rural migrants, who are hardier and willing to work for less (p. 88). A small business can often be a shop (for sale or craft, repair skill) the premises of which is also the dwelling of the couple, so there are still domestic work units in cities. But most domestic units in cities are quite separate from work and earning income.

The children are at once nurtured to the point of being spoilt and pressured into doing nothing but schoolwork, with extra tutoring outside school hours and long hours of homework. Students do get sullen and rebel. For instance, one boy was beaten by his father for not listening while Vanessa Fong was tutoring him in English at home. The boy then threatened his father that he would give him a much worse beating when he grew old. Both father and son in their rage threatened to kill each other and the mother wished she had never borne the son. (Fong, 2004, pp. 146–148). But more often, especially as their parents make themselves ill by going without food in order to save money or suffer extreme cold by peddling goods in the deep north-eastern winter, their children vowed to themselves and privately to Vanessa Fong that they will work extra hard to get a place in college, a good degree, a good job and earn a lot of money, so that they can look after their parents. One boy who with his father was an enthusiast of car magazines, though they had no hope of buying a car, worked hard so that in the future, he could buy his father a BMW that he could drive around and boast to his friends what a good son he has.

Parents not spending enough on their children risked shame in the eyes of other parents. For instance, a richer parent met a poorer parent and admonished her: surely, you can spend more on clothing your child better. She offered to give her some clothes her son had hardly worn because he did not like the style. The infuriated poorer parent was forced to say that her son does have nicer clothes, but doesn't want to get them dirty, and felt obliged to go out and buy him the branded Adidas outfit he had been craving (Fong, 2004, pp. 84–85).

The pressure increases in a vicious circle because all children are aiming for a secure well-paid job and of course there are far fewer such jobs than there are applicants with the qualifications required at any one time, so there is qualification inflation, the threshold rising all the time. As the teenagers said to Fong (p. 29) 'society is a contest where people eat people' — the jibe about traditional China made by the great twentieth-century Chinese writer Lu Xun in one of his most famous stories 'Diary of a Madman'.

What they want is a job that gives them self-respect and is satisfying. In very many cases, their parents have not had that satisfaction and the status of their jobs in manufacturing industry has decreased and become less secure. So school children work incredibly hard at schoolwork and grandparents and parents clothe and feed them and demand of them nothing but hard schoolwork.

All this is an application of the old saying, which is on their own tongues: *yang er, fang lao* (nurture the young to make old age comfortable). This is a sentiment in what Stafford (2000) in his pioneering study of Chinese relatedness calls the nurture cycle of reciprocity between the generations. It has just become more pressurised when the single child is the sole object of parental devotion and has the prospect of two sets of grandparents to look after.

The expression makes the investment in children sound calculated, but the calculating rationality is often exceeded in the parent's present willingness to risk health and even life for their child. The child is an extension of the parental self and her or his sense of accomplishment into the next generation. And these hopes are scaled up into wishing their child's quality to be, as some of the parents said to Vanessa Fong, 'a contribution to the motherland' (pp. 140–141). More immediately, they still wish to become cared-for ancestors. A great many of them perform rites for their ancestors, only now they perform them for ancestors on both sides of their marriage (Fong, 2004, pp. 130–133).

The result is that school students spend longer in education, retaking examinations, getting into vocational or better colleges, and incidentally postponing entry into the job market and so increasing the strain on their parents' earnings. Parents usually acknowledge the near impossibility of one person having to look after four old people and are determined to do what they can to stay healthy, by taking exercise and eating properly. They dread the prospect of illness and fear their children will not be able to look after them, or that they will not be filial, and they have begun without much trust to put some savings into insurance schemes.

They express the fear that their children will not be filial, and that they will be victims of neglect. This expression of fear is often a ploy to bind their children to them (Fong, 2004, p. 151). But their fears of insecurity are justified on many counts: the unreliability of the insurance schemes offered so far, the possibility that their child will not earn enough, however filial, and that in their disappointment they will be harsh to their parents.

Inevitably, there are losers in the race to pass the exams and get the jobs that they and their parents had been striving for. They have to resign themselves to the jobs available to lesser high school graduates. But another result is unwillingness to accept the menial jobs, without prospects, which are below their expected dignity. Instead, they try to go abroad or to start their own business with loans, or they turn to crime. In starting a business and anyway in lowering their expectations and seeking a menial job, they are now in competition with rural migrants.

In this urban setting, the new phenomenon of the single child family and the costs of schooling have not changed the family as an intergenerational aspiration for a better future. But it has added enormous pressure on the school qualifications of the child.

Rural Family and Gender in Northern China

Many of the changes observed by Yan Yunxiang have been noted in villages in other parts of China. One of these is the great transformation that began during the collective era: the earning of individual incomes, male and female, in the form of work points, and then cash incomes in separate occupations, jobs or self-employment since the reforms began in 1978.

Another is the reduction in the number of children. In this village, the care for parents will increasingly fall on a single child, just as in the city, because by 1998, 91% of all births were to parents without another child and all births of second children were allowed, rather than happening without permission. The policy did not have to be enforced by sterilisations or other coercive means. It was now voluntary. (In other parts of China the number of singletons may be much lower.) The reforms and rising incomes have had five notable results in Xiajia:

1. A process of housebuilding which is also a process of increasing spaces of privacy for couples, from sharing a *kang* (the heated platform on which people are entertained and on which the household sleeps) with the man's parents and only having separate bedclothes, to having a separate room, to having a separate house.
2. Brides themselves negotiate their bridewealth (what their families are given by the groom's family as a contribution to their dowry and as a contribution to the conjugal couple, in particular their housing), instead of just their parents, the result of having their own earning capacity.
3. A process of breaking the taboo on pre-marital sex. This goes together with increasing stress on romance and its more open expression about desirability in a mate. Engaged women would go to the city to buy their own trousseau. In later years, the couple would go together to do the same, get photographed and stay overnight in town and sleep

together thus declaring that 'the rice is cooked'. This is spoken about as stealing her or his heart. Even in visits to future in-laws, now that houses have separate rooms it was possible by the 1990s for intending couples to sleep together before marriage. But note that this is sex before marriage; it is not casual sex.

4. Fluency in words of love, including the lines of pop lyrics, is becoming a criterion of choice of mate among young women. Romance is no longer distinct from the criteria of choice of mate. It is more emphatically one of the woman's criteria; women take the initiative more than men in breaking up engagements.

   Yan also notes that the principle of matching gates (finding a partner from a family of similar status) in brokering marriages has been replaced by *duipiqi* — temperamental matching. Official discourse also stresses this in the context of the importance of a permanent bond that holds the family together.

   In short, romance and romantic passion are no longer set aside from marriage and marriage choice. One of the themes of Chinese novels and poems was the frustration of a love match by having to marry someone else. Now romance is associated with individualism and with conjugal bonding.

5. Emphasis on the conjugal couple has led to a change in the balance of reciprocity of care. Yan Yunxiang (Chapter 7) describes a change over the generations. The older parents expect care and love from their children and daughters-in-law as well as respect on the grounds that they have given their children life, an unreciprocable gift. But the younger parents consider that they are just doing what is natural and proper in giving life and bringing up their children. They acknowledge an obligation to look after their aged parents, but not necessarily to respect their words. They have an expectation of reciprocal balance; their parents should help them set up independent lives and they in return will look after their parents. For the middle-aged parents, it means putting a lot of effort and finances into pleasing their children when they reach adulthood and get married.

The conjugal couple are now more independent and matched by mutual choice. But often they do not live together, because both need to earn for the same reasons as urban couples, to afford the education and other costs of their child or children. So, quite often the father's parents (sometimes the mother's parents) look after children for their children who are absent migrant parents, increasing the bond across the generations and the debt of gratitude to old parents in their children.

The emergent pattern is for grandparents to live separately, in the old house, until they cannot look after themselves, when they join their married son or daughter and risk the inevitable clashes and the humiliations of being a dependent.

From subsequent returns to Xiajia, Yan (2016) has confirmed these three-generational familial arrangements. In different homes, one in the village and another in the local city, families maintain earning and the care of children. He has also noticed that the older generations no longer expect the gratitude and submission of their children. Instead, all three generations enjoy each other's affectionate communication and trust. And as noted by Fong, the conjugal couple look after both sets of their parents. Relying on both means their looks backward are becoming bilateral in any one family, up the mother's as well as the father's line.

Individualism and Familism

What have these changes in family and gender relations done to Chinese, especially young people's senses of self? On the one hand, there is the common appeal to Confucian values. Instead of the common analogy drawn in the dynastic official propaganda between filial duty and loyalty to the emperor, it is now common to think of patriotism by analogy with belonging to a family, as the word for the state implies — *guojia*, a state-family. And it is remarkable how reliant on daughters-in-law older couples are still, and how daughters-in-law pride themselves on working hard for their parents-in-law as well as for their children (an observation made in Moonshadow, a village in the Pearl River Delta by Ellen Oxfeld, 2010, Chapter 3). Just as remarkable is the way in which bosses in the factories in which migrant workers are employed expect the same virtues of loyalty and the biting back of personal feelings of humiliation and resentment. Bosses demand anticipation of their wishes without their need to state them, and they expect gratitude just as parents did of their children within families (Fang I-chieh, *Growing up and becoming independent; an ethnographic study of new generation migrant workers in China.* 2012 PhD LSE). In other words, the personal self is there, as it was within kinship and other relations in the dynastic era, for self-discipline and self-cultivation, along with its internal resentments. It was subordinated into a collective 'we' only in Maoist campaigns and then not entirely successfully. But it is a self that still negotiates its way through constraints and obligations.

On the other hand, the aim of that self is to choose a marriage partner and to earn enough to set up in business on their own or to acquire knowledge, skill and a profession that requires self-reliance, creativity and autonomy. The ideal of gender equality enshrined in the Marriage Laws has suffered as a result. Male demands of femininity, or rather feminine cuteness, derived from and reinforced by marketing images, and not to be a challenge in terms of carer and educational qualifications, coexist with stories of women business leaders and women becoming the breadwinners in their families.

Individualistic and with greater privacy, in terms of property and intimacy, the new self does seem to have become like that of the rest of the capitalist, industrialised world, though possibly with more gendered inequalities. But it is combined with two qualifying additions, noted by Yan Yunxiang (2016). Intimacy is the new bond between the three generations of a child-rearing family, as already noted. In addition, the private self still pursues the traditional sense of self first theorised by Fei Xiaotong. It is a self defined by its communicative obligations to others, both within family relations and within reciprocal, more associative relations among friends and interpersonal contacts of establishing trust. Familial relations highlight the further characteristic of a continuing Chinese self, namely that it is a project, something fashioned over a lifetime making relationships, in particular in becoming a grandparent.

Seminar Question

Have filial love and duty been reduced and are 'Chinese' values what they were?

Key Readings

Fong, Vanessa L. 2004. *Only Hope: Coming of Age under China's One-Child Policy*. C. A., Stanford: Stanford University Press (Introduction and Chapter 4).

Stafford, C. 2008. Actually existing Chinese matriarchy. In *Chinese Kinship: Contemporary Anthropological perspectives*, Brandtstädter, Susanne and Santos, Gonçalo D. (eds.). Routledge Contemporary China Series . Routledge, Taylor & Francis Group, Abingdon, UK, pp. 137–153.

Yan Yunxiang 2003. *Private Life under Socialism: Love, Intimacy, and Family Change in a Chinese Village 1949–1999*. Stanford: Stanford University Press.

Yan Yunxiang 2016. '*Egoist Individual, Moralist Self, and Relational Person: A Tripartite Approach to the Changing Chinese Subjectivities' The Marilyn Strathern Lecture*. University of Cambridge, Department of Social Anthropology.

Further Readings

Diamant, N. 2000. *Revolutionising the Family: Politics, Love and Divorce in Urban and Rural China, 1949–1968*. Berkeley: University of California Press (Chapters 5, 6, and afterword).

Fei Xiaotong (tr Gary G. Hamilton and Wang Zheng) 1992. *From the Soil, The Foundations of Chinese Society: A translation of Fei Xiaotong's Xiangtu Zhongguo*. Berkeley, Los Angeles and London: University of California Press.

Fong, V. 2002. China's One-Child Policy and the empowerment of urban daughters, *American Anthropologist*, **104**(4), pp. 1098–1109.

Gal, S. and Kligman, G. 2000. *The Politics of Gender after Socialism: A Comparative-historical essay*. Princeton, NJ: Princeton University Press.

Giddens, A. 1991. *Modernity and Self-identity: Self and Society in the Late Modern Age*. CA, Stanford: Stanford University Press.

Goode, W. 1963. *World Revolution and Family Patterns*. New York: Free Press.

Hsu, F. L. K. 1943. The Myth of Chinese Family Size, *American Journal of Sociology*, **48**(5), pp. 555–562.

Lindholm, C. (1995). Love as an Experience of Transcendence. In *Romantic Passion: A Universal Experience?*, William Jankowiak (ed.). New York: Columbia University Press, pp. 57–71.

Liu, L. 1995. *Translingual Practices*. CA, Stanford: Stanford University Press.

Oxfeld, E. 2010. *Drink Water, But Remember the Source: Moral Discourse in a Chinese Village*, Berkeley: University of California Press.

Rofel, L. 1999. *Other Modernities: Gendered Yearnings in China after Socialism.* Berkeley: University of California Press.

Stafford, C. 2000. Chinese patriliny and the cycles of *yang* and *laiwang*. In *Cultures of Relatedness: New Approaches to the Study of Kinship*, J. Carsten (ed.). Cambridge: Cambridge University Press.

Taylor, C. 2003. *Modern Social Imaginaries*. Durham: Duke University Press.

Chapter 14
Schooling

Since the inventions of writing in various parts of the world, about 5,000 years ago, the ability to write and read was the privilege of a small minority until state nationalism instituted mass schooling only a century ago. In China, mass literacy, the expectation that all children should learn to read and write, has been realised only in the last 60 years. One of the standard institutions is the school system, which is compulsory in most contemporary states.

For most of the history of writing, the small classes of the literate were the epitome of civilisation, but not of political rule; rulers were often illiterate and were served by a clerical elite, where 'clerical' has the two senses of being custodians of a textual, often religious, tradition on the one hand, and on the other hand, recorders and keepers of an archive and scribes of political decisions and laws and their administration.

There is a parallel between classical Chinese and classical European ideas of education, that schooling and further education are a way of cultivating a potential human (considered to be universal in both traditions). The conception of what is 'human' has changed over the centuries in both traditions. And they have lasting differences. In Hellenic Greece, the idea of becoming human was one of becoming capable of participation in the public sphere of the Athenian city, with its exchange of ideas and the cultivation of rhetorical arts of persuasion, for a citizen minority of the population. From this classical ideal, Europeans arrived at the modern idea of mass learning to be a subject and citizen who is self-regulating. Classical

Chinese, Confucian self-cultivation of the educated minority referred to as *junzi*, distinct from the small or common people, was also a project for the maturation of the human being and its chief accomplishment of *ren* — responsive harmonisation with all things including other humans. Literate accomplishment was the life work of the fashioning of self, through the learning of *li* — proper conduct of hierarchical and responsive relations for rule through the imperial civil service and the education needed to qualify for entry into it, and by exemplary conduct to influence others through interpersonal relations and the high arts of writing. From these ideals, via republicanism, the politics of self-strengthening to recover from weakness and humiliation, Chinese governments arrived at the current ideals of mass literacy and schooling for quality, science, and the capacity to contribute to the economy and to public good.

Teaching the Nation

'Civilisation' transmits a sense of the world and of a centre from which that sense is most powerfully or authoritatively made. Every civilisation is universal in its reach, about the whole world and of the place of humanity in it. If history is taught in religious and civilisational schools, it is a history of mystery, of transcendental truth, of myth and of moral lessons, of ideals and heroes, on a world scale that is a cosmology. This is very different from the teaching of history in modern schools. This history is a story of the nation, its emergence, its liberation, and its future in a project of modernisation, among and in rivalry with other nations, though it usually also retains the universal claims of a civilisation. In addition, there is a stress on documentation and evidence, on finding out about the events of that history, and often there are arguments about what has been marginalised or excluded from school history based on empirical research.

As the anthropologist Gellner (1983) argued, the new kind of social solidarity needed and promoted by modern industrialising states is a shared history, geography and language within the territory of the state conveyed to its whole population through mass schooling (see Chapter 6 on nationalism). Every modern state system of schooling, particularly through its teaching of language, geography and history and the moral education taught as such, but also in sport, ritual, and classroom conduct, teaches a national belonging.

Nationalism, which confines civilisation to one of many other civilisations, is about a political centre and its past-future narrative in a world of many such centres, a multi-centred world of humanity that each centre acknowledges. It is a world of humanity and therefore has a distinctively secular, historical narrative, however much the particular centrality of the nation in question is also coloured by one religion or one civilisation among many. In other words, the system of modern states has as its basic premise a political and historical world of multi-centred humanity.

But something remains from the earlier, civilisational centricity, namely that each nation-centre in one way or another goes beyond claiming a place for itself in a world of many centres. It also claims to be a centre of universal humanity. This claim varies enormously. For instance, the justifications of nations that colonised or imposed trade and indentured or enslaved labour in large parts of the world were usually derived from the European humanist enlightenment, or an elaborate conception of Roman law of humanity (the law applying to non-Romans is called, in Latin, *jus gentium*) as well as evolutionary and Christian conceptions of human origins and progress. As against these, the nationalism of movements of liberation from such imperial exploitation and imposition was often couched in terms of human freedom and emancipation, taking up the eighteenth-century European philosophy of emancipation but knowing it to have been betrayed by the European conquerors. Exclusion from the high culture of empires in Europe had the same effect in the European continent, fostering new identities and histories of their emergence into nations, such as those of Estonia, or Hungary, or Czechoslovakia in the nineteenth century (Vickers and Jones, 2005, p. 10).

Now, we have even more stress on rights, democracy and the United Nations (UN) conventions on human rights and genocide to justify intervention by one state against the tyranny of another. The standards and discourses of universal human rights have become the sites of sharp conflict, of armed intervention, and of International Non-Governmental Organisations (INGOs) and local Non-Governmental Organisations (NGOs). What is more, every religion claims to be universal in its prospect of salvation and/or of the good life, not excepting the newly encouraged Confucianism in China, Korea, and Taiwan.

So in every school history or religious, moral and civic education, and in the rituals of saluting its national icons — founders of the nation and liberators of the nation, great leaders, flags, national anthems, and other songs and ceremonials in the school calendar — there is the same balancing between a distinctive history and a universalising message.

The big issue, as Etienne Balibar says in Chapter 2 of Benei (ed.) (2005) with reference to schooling about the European Union, is whether that balance is outward-opening or inward-closing: whether it is an opening to further redefinition of the national identity or European identity and of what it is to be human in the world, or an exclusive sense of belonging that at the same time has pretensions to a strong and high place in the world, excluding others, or a third view that sees itself as the model for the world so that its national interests coincide with what is good for the rest of the world. All three views may well be held in any one country and the tensions between them generate controversies over the school curriculum.

Probably, the most important events in the teaching of history are wars: wars among alliances of nations, wars of liberation, and civil wars. The threat of war, international tensions and insecurities, and wars themselves are the greatest generators of nationalism. And the events of wars, key battles and war leaders, are at the same time historical and mythologised — memorialised, celebrated, put on postage stamps — alongside the great artists and monuments of national historical pride. So, you would expect that school history and geography would be more tightly controlled and nationalistic in conditions of regional international tension and ambition, as they were between Japan and China in the 1920s and 1930s, when Japanese officials criticised Chinese school textbooks for their xenophobic attacks on Japan (Vickers and Jones, 2005, p. 7).

Modern Schooling and its Variation

Beside the spectrum of open to closed, there are different methods of teaching and a spectrum of centralisation as opposed to school and local autonomy. Schooling involves a timetable and a curriculum, a particular method of teaching, distinct from older forms of teaching and learning, such as apprenticeship and learning from a guru — or master — and learning through ritual, as in rites of passage. They continue alongside school learning.

Varying pedagogy: Within school learning, there are different methods and philosophies of teaching and learning. They range between rote learning (teaching through memorisation) and child-centred learning (facilitation of a child's ability to learn on its own initiative). Memorisation of poetry, arithmetic tables, dates of events and names of people and places, is the learning of things that will later acquire significance as more is added to what has been committed to memory. Large school classes are most effectively taught by the maintenance of strict discipline and teacher-centred attention, in which school students acquire knowledge by listening, reading and passive absorption followed by exercise of what has been absorbed. This kind of teaching depends much on rote learning. From traditional schooling, whether it be in Chinese village schools, or religious schools in Christian, Jewish or Muslim traditions, this extends to the method continued in more secular schooling because of lack of finance for more teachers, for teacher training, and/or lack of books and other facilities. With growing wealth and with the needs of a knowledge-based economy and the premium on inventiveness in the design of production and of product, there may be a turn to more child-centred enhancement of creativity. Such a turn is presently advocated in China.

Varying local and teacher autonomy: Under a state system of schooling, there has to be some standardisation, but there is great variation. On one extreme is a strict setting of the content of the curriculum and its examination, so that wherever a child is at school the same timetable, subjects and textbooks are used. On the other extreme is setting a broad curricular outline allowing great autonomy to local education authorities and to schools to find their own teaching materials, governed only by an inspectorate of books and other materials for use in schools and an examination system that maintains parity of assessment. An important element in this is not only the materials chosen by teachers but also the school as a building and a resource for local residents. Is it strictly controlled from above or is it part of a more autonomous locality with its own traditions? China may be moving from a strict, centrally controlled standardisation toward greater local autonomy.

The Hidden Curriculum Within the School System

Mass schooling implies everywhere a cultivation of talent and an opportunity for the talented to rise, whatever their class or culture. But at the same time, mass schooling establishes a hierarchy of qualifications and of merit, the academic above the vocational. One of the main issues in all school systems is its inclusiveness and exclusiveness. Schooling excludes even as it includes, just as citizenship does (Benei, 2005) — so you have to ask this question: What religious traditions does school include more than others, what historical narratives does it include and what it excludes, what cultural capital, including the language of tuition, is central and what does it marginalise?

Much of this inclusion and marginalisation is conveyed implicitly. The French sociologist and anthropologist Pierre Bourdieu wrote extensively about the importance of what is learned incidentally, in experiencing these inclusions and exclusions, through formal schooling and what is learned anyway, out of school as well as in school. We all pick up habitual ways of acting and treating others, and learn without thinking about them senses of success and failure, of what is realistic, or simply of what is real and what is possible. He calls this '*habitus*'. The *habitus* we learn forms and limits our perceptions so that even when we think we are going against the stream, rebelling, scorning academic learning for instance, we are likely to be reinforcing an accepted hierarchy of values and of what reality has to be — the nature of things. It takes personal or social crisis to question *habitus* and the reality that we are taught to take for granted as the only and necessary reality. Willis (1977) is a classic study of how this works in an English working-class school.

One hierarchy we reinforce even when we say we reject it, or find school boring, is a hierarchy of cultural capital and of *distinction*, the title of one of Bourdieu's later books (Bourdieu, 1984). We learn without thinking to place things in a status hierarchy, whether it is an accent — such as received English or northern Chinese Putonghua — or distinguishing fine from popular arts. Even when the distinction is crossed and questioned by musicians and artists, we nevertheless know of the distinction between refined and vulgar or pop taste. The acquisition of cultural capital, what is acceptable at the top of these hierarchies of distinction, and whether one feels at ease with them has to be learned in order to move up a social hierarchy.

There can be several such hierarchies. The main hierarchy is the reproduction of economic capital, and of the class that manages and controls it. Bourdieu's French surveys and fieldwork, and the theory he elucidates from them with his colleague Passeron (Bourdieu, 1977), says there are three other hierarchies: (1) of cultural capital (or distinction); (2) of social capital (of connections and access to people with authority, often acquired in the higher reaches of education); and (3) of symbolic capital (the authority with which you speak and do things, your eloquence and manipulation of rhetoric and symbols). They are analytically separable, but they reinforce each other and the reproduction of economic capital, even while there is some mobility up and down these hierarchies. His conclusion does not exclude change, a transformation of hierarchies of cultural, social, symbolic, political and economic capital. But he strongly suggests how difficult it is to bring about radical change.

Republican, Nationalist and Communist China

The new, post-dynastic, republican ministry of education in the 1910s and early 1920s in the main cities promoted a child-centred, humanities-based curriculum, putting world history first, and placing China within it. From 1927, the time that Jiang Jieshi (Chiang Kai-shek) took over the leadership of the Guomindang (Nationalist) Party and established its capital in Nanjing, this was radically changed. China's anti-imperialist self-defence and self-strengthening was put first, world history second, science first, humanities second. The Guomindang exerted a strict and centralised control over the curriculum and kept uniformity of textbooks, with the Party controlling civic and patriotic schooling based on the Three Principles of the Founder of the Nation, Sun Zhongshan (Sun Yat-sen) and Chiang Kai-shek's own highly selective version of Confucian virtues in his doctrine of the New Life. Four virtues were stressed: decorum (*li*), righteousness (*yi*), integrity (*lian*), and a sense of shame (*chi*). In addition were the civic virtues that were all emphatically nationalist: saving the state (*jiuguo*), loyal service to the nation, serving the masses (*renqun*), liberation from imperialists, nationalist revolution, and the nation (*minzu*). They were promoted as the key to history and to becoming great again (Jones, 2005, pp. 59 and 68–70). The same strict central control of schooling continued until the 1990s in Taiwan under the same regime (see Stafford (1995) and the chapter by Allen Chun in Benei (ed.) (2005)).

Alisa Jones (Vickers and Jones (ed.) (2005) Chapter 2) remarks on similarities of the Nationalist (Chiang Kai-shek) and the Communist school systems. Both were highly centralised, with strong single-Party rule and involvement in schooling. Only recently in Taiwan and in the PRC, in fact since 2000, has there been encouragement of primary and junior middle schools to produce their own materials for teaching local history and geography.

Despite her stress on continuity and similarity, Jones also describes what is specific to the PRC school system. History teaching as a separate lesson comes up first in junior school, the last few years of compulsory schooling. Under the system established in 1953, there was just one publisher of textbooks (the People's Education Press), itself a subsidiary of the Ministry of Education. History was the history of class struggle, in the world and in China, where peasant uprising rather than dynastic rule was stressed. Civic virtue was to be learned through simple texts expounding Marxism, Leninism and the Thought of Mao, promoting the virtue of being willing to engage in revolutionary struggle for world peace. After that universal struggle came love of the motherland. But even there, what was stressed were the virtues of class struggle, people's labour, protection of public property, the learning of science, and the maintenance of health, creativity and self-consciousness (*zijue*) (Jones, 2005, pp. 73–75). In short, in history teaching and moral education, a universalising revolutionary struggle and people's labour, rather than Confucian virtue, accompanied love of motherland. Modern history (from the Opium wars onward) portrayed the Nationalists as corrupt and in league with the imperialists, contrasting them with the Chinese Communist Party (CCP) as the spearhead of liberation.

The two school systems were closer in their definitions of the Chinese nation: the Nationalist Party condoned Chinese inclusion of weaker peoples (*minzu*) into the Chinese empire-nation. CCP nationalism included the national minorities in the same race-nation (*minzu*), all descended from Peking Man, who was also 'the ancestor of all humanity'. But the

CCP's stress on world history and the evolutionary Marxism in which it was framed is quite different from the Guomindang's New Life self-strengthening. The CCP stresses state patriotism (*aiguozhuyi*), rather than nationalism (*minzuzhuyi*) in schools.

Until 1957, the top subjects in terms of the timetable were Chinese, maths and history. Then, during the Great Leap Forward (1957–1960) and again in the years of the Socialist Education and the Cultural Revolution mass mobilisations 1965–1976, the teaching of history was reduced to make room for part-work, part-study, and for political education through mass meetings, in which internal and external enemies and friends, their identification and the struggles between them and the need to take sides was the principle.

People's Republic of China — Recent Changes

Since the opening and reform instituted by Deng Xiaoping, there has been a return to the school syllabus of the years before 1957, reinstating the teaching of the history of the hundred years of humiliation 1839–1949, from which China was liberated and stood up under the leadership of Mao, but now with the gradually increasing addition of other great men, including Confucius and Genghis Khan, and stressing the leadership of the Communist Party rather than the genius of Mao.

Promoting the quality of the nation (*tigao minzu suzhi*) has meant that from 1996, central control of textbooks has been loosened. A guiding outline for schools and a teaching inspectorate now allows for the publication of history textbooks by many publishers, and for movement toward devolution of decisions on what books to use and what and how to teach. History teaching now includes visits to museums and to sites of the events taught (see the chapter by Rana Mitter in Benei (ed.), 2005), and other attempts to make the teaching of history and geography stimulating, vivid and with more stress on teaching to enable learning. This is part of the project to bring about the so-called 'generation of new people' (*yidai xinren*) in all four dimensions: moral (*de*), intellectual (*zhi*), physical (*ti*) and aesthetic (*mei*), balancing practical with abstract knowledge.

Continued from the Maoist mobilisation phase of schooling, mass gymnastics still forms part of the morning timetable, and at least once a week a raising of the flag and a patriotic salutation heralds the announcement of winners in class competitions (Kipnis, 2011, p. 46). Running through from primary to higher education are compulsory classes in 'moral character' (*sixiang pinde*) and then 'political economy' (*zhengzhi jingji xue*) which can be summarised as the learning of loyalty and attachment to a history of the Party-state and its scientific ideology of the moment. Of course, the attachment can only be partial. Teachers are themselves often partly detached, teaching pupils and students what they need to know just to pass the exam.

There has also been governmental approval of the building of private schools for the children of better off middle class parents, and along with this has come approval of a new civilising mission to teach the classics of Confucianism in many of these private schools and some state schools (Billioud and Thoraval, 2015).

School Hierarchy

In recent years, there have been repeated calls in China to reduce examination-oriented teaching and pressure. The Ministry of Education has tried to deflect educators from teaching exam-taking skills, toward learning what is more appropriate to real life situations and to more innovative thinking. But the examination system has not been reformed, so the real-life situation is still to be skilled at passing examinations at every stage.

Fong (2004, p. 122) gives a good outline of the school hierarchy: The valuing of university entrance and so academic teaching over vocational qualifications persists, as it does in most other school systems, maybe least so in Germany. Urban children have better access to the higher ranked schools. The school system is still dominated by competition for entry to the schools that are the ones with access to the best high schools because of locality and household registration, or are best at training the student to take the examinations for the best high schools, and then for these to train the student through examinations to enter the best universities. The ranking of school categories is as follows:

1. keypoint college preparation high schools (*zhongdian gaozhong*),
2. ordinary college preparation high schools (*putong gaozhong*),

3. private college preparation high schools (*minban gaozhong*),
4. profession-training high schools (*zhongdeng zhuanye xuexiao*),
5. vocation-training high schools and adult education schools and technical high schools (*zhiye gaozhong, zhiye zhongzhuan, chengren zhongzhuan, jigong xue xiao*).

For college entrance, it is the same again in a ranking of colleges. And at each stage, parents use whatever connections they have available, and whatever gifts they can afford to give in order to get over the threshold under which their child has performed.

In his chapter on the schools he observed and the pupils and parents he interviewed in Zouping county, Shandong province, in 2005, Kipnis (2011) writes of parents and pupils both wanting the children to become what they still called 'work-unit people' (*danweiren*). The parent generation self-disparagingly called itself just ordinary people (*laobaixing*). The way to become a work-unit person was to get a job in town and city through educational qualification.

Zouping county prides itself on a long tradition of producing scholars, from the Song dynasty onwards. Statues of its most eminent scholars are meant to inspire local school children. Lists of university entrance exam successes are displayed on a bulletin prominently placed on the busiest street of Zouping county city. Most parents cannot in fact afford the university fees. Yet, even those who cannot hope to find the money for fees, even with great effort, still wish they could. Kipnis points out that this cannot be for the sake of a job in which their children could become wealthy and look after them, because there are too many known cases of university graduates who don't get any better paying jobs than do vocational college graduates. It is simply the local tradition and the esteem that drives the aspiration for academic success, a form of symbolic capital to use Bourdieu's term.

Kipnis remarks on the rural–urban divide and a division between homes of parents that graduated from senior middle school and beyond and parents with lower school leaving standards of education. The better educated live in towns and cities and can help their children with homework better. So rural parents are pleased at the building of new schools outside villages, in towns, where their children stay longer hours, or, at senior middle school, where they board during the week. The teachers have longer to supervise their children and the parents have longer to work to pay for the fees.

Children in junior school learn by rote to recite a Tang poem about a mother mending the clothes for her son to wear as he prepares to leave her to become an official. Parents in interviews repeated the motif that they willingly sacrificed themselves (*xisheng*) through hard work for their children to stay on at school and that the children study hard in reciprocity for their parents' sacrifice. At school, the teacher knows that she or he is expected to be a model (*weiren shibiao*) for pupils and to help them personally as well as didactically.

These are ways of travelling up the school and 'quality' hierarchy that describe a 'moral geography'. A study of a poorer, mountainous place by Johnston (2013) shows that schooling is a way of moving away from home, stretching the distance and the yearning of aspiration from remote to central places. The movement away from home, Johnston points out, is combined with moral ambiguities: children are supposed to leave their parents and the security of places for ever more distant and anonymous cities. These distant places are both higher up on the hierarchies of place and progress, but also potentially dangerous.

Non-School Learning and Influence

Plainly, domestic and school environments reinforce each other according to both Fong and Kipnis. But Fong has also given us another perspective, which is what the children want as they work hard to pass examinations. They are the experts, as are children in many other parts of the world, in the latest brands of clothes, of music, of food and drink, and exert peer pressure on each other to keep up with what is fashionable. Some lead, others follow, others still resist the pressure and go their own way. But the overwhelming point is that television and pop — and video games in internet cafes — exercise a largely felt attraction, heavily influenced by Hong Kong, South Korean, Japanese and Taiwanese media. This peer-group knowledge of trends marks off the younger generations in all their gradations of age and youth from each other and from older generations. The fashion for foreign brands influences aspirations and senses of self, at variance with the school taught patriotism. Local senses of history are learned at home, in parallel to school learning (Stafford, 2000).

Other kinds of non-curricular, non-school learning, from parents' religion, for instance, the Hui sense of Islamic civilisation (Gillette, 2000), or the enjoyment of local festivals and other rituals (see Stafford, 1995) or of Christian church services, can be added, transmitting alternative senses of self and of aspiration to those taught in school.

Failure as a Product of Schooling

Sociologists of schooling have for a long time pointed out that the main product of schooling is failure, failure to reach higher in the hierarchy of aspiration. This failure, as one of Fong's students said to her, is a spur to finding other ways of getting on, such as going into business or finding a way to go abroad and eventually reach tertiary education there.

The most obvious sense of failure and being marginalised is in the hundred or more million migrant workers and their children in segregated schools, contrasting with the urban schools and urban registered residents who look down on them. They are negatively recognised as lacking in education and in quality, for which it is little compensation that in 2009, the celebrations of the Sixtieth anniversary of the PRC included the singing of The Proud Builders, a song composed just about them and their building dreams out of their sweat. They could well have commented that the dreams were those of the consumers of their products and the residents in the buildings they constructed, whereas their own dreams were a good deal more modest and more frequently postponed. Nevertheless, the sense of being negatively categorised in the hierarchy generated by schooling comes first, before such reactions. The centralisation of schooling and of further and higher education and its own hidden curriculum is a structured hierarchy of cultural and symbolic capital.

Now, instead of a privileged literate elite of imperial China, we have the new elite of those who have scaled the upper reaches of mass schooling and tertiary education and an identification with a national civilisation. But we should also note that this new elite is also often outward-looking, while others are more inward-looking and patriotic in the way Balibar has described the project of European education for citizenship.

Seminar Questions

What if anything is distinctive about mass schooling in China?

Is it possible for Chinese school leavers to question governmental versions of merit and quality?

Key Readings

Benei, V. (ed.) 2005. *Manufacturing Citizenship: Education and Nationalism in Europe, South Asia and China*. London: Routledge (Introduction and chapters by Balibar, Chun and Mitter).

Jones, A. 2005. Changing the past to serve the present: History education in mainland China. In Vickers, Edward and Alisa Jones (eds.). *History Education and National Identity in East Asia*. London: Routledge, pp. 65–100.

Kipnis, A. 2011. *Governing Educational Desire: Culture, Politics, and Schooling in China*. Chicago: University of Chicago Press (Chapter 3).

Further Readings

Billioud, S., and Thoraval, J. 2015. *The Sage and the People: The Confucian revival in China*. Oxford: Oxford University Press.

Bourdieu, P. 1984. *Distinction: A Social Critique of the Judgement of Taste*. Cambridge, MA.: Harvard University Press.

Bourdieu, P., and Passeron, J.-C. (1977) *Reproduction in Education, Society and Culture*. London: Sage Publications.

Fong, V. L. 2004 *Only Hope: Coming of Age under China's One-Child Policy*, Stanford CA: Stanford University Press.

Fong, V. L. 2011. *Paradise Redefined: Transnational Chinese Students and the Quest for Flexible Citizenship in the Developed World*. Stanford, CA: Stanford University Press.

Gellner, E. 1983. *Nations and Nationalism*. Ithaca, NY: Cornell University Press.

Gillette, M. B. 2000. *Between Mecca and Beijing: Modernisation and consumption among urban Chinese Muslims*. Stanford, CA: Stanford University Press.

Johnston, J. 2013. Filial Paths and the Ordinary Ethics of Movement. In Stafford, Charles (ed.), *Ordinary Ethics in China*. London: Bloomsbury.

Hau, Kit-Tai, and Ho, Irene T. 2010. Chinese Students' Motivation and Achievement. In Bond, Michael H. (ed.) *Oxford Handbook of Chinese Psychology*, Oxford: Oxford University Press.

Stafford, C. 1995. *The Roads of Chinese Childhood.* Cambridge: Cambridge University Press (esp. pp. 166–185).

Stafford, C. 2000. Developing a sense of history. In *Separation and Reunion in Modern China* Cambridge: Cambridge University Press, pp. 127–143.

Vickers, E. and Jones, A. (eds.). *History Education and National Identity in East Asia.* London: Routledge.

Willis, P. 1977. *Learning to Labour: How Working Class Kids Get Working Class Jobs.* Farnborough, Hants.: Saxon House.

Chapter 15

Civil Society and Political Society

1989 was the year of civil society, the fall of the Berlin Wall and the year of the most recent grassroots social movement in China. And as it happens, 1989 was also the year of publication of the English translation of Jürgen Habermas' *The Structural Transformation of the Public Sphere*, possibly the most influential elaboration of the idea of civil society.

The concept of civil society is indissolubly linked with the idea and the institution of the modern state. Both, state and civil society, begin life as the ideals of European political philosophers and the revolutionaries of what they themselves called the Enlightenment of reason against absolute monarchies, feudal nobility, and religious mystification. Eventually, similar ideals fuelled struggles against colonial rule. Civil society is whatever exists as a public field of mass and personal communication and of organisation against tyranny. In the politics of modern states, civil society is the formation of opinion and organisation that can check the overweening use of the state's executive powers.

The peculiarity of the concept 'civil society' is that it is active, it is a category that inspires political action in the same way that 'emancipation' does and 'revolution' did and might possibly do again and, in a less overtly political and a more pretentiously 'scientific' way 'free market' is. It is something people think with but also something people fight for. Any such active category is at the same time both normative — a set of ideals and criteria of judgement of reality — and empirically descriptive. The descriptive task it sets is to identify what are the groups, associations, institutions and bonds of affection, obligation and loyalty that since the eighteenth-century emergence of the human sciences in Europe have been called simply 'society' and its relation to the states that govern society, including the protection of human rights, even while admitting that a state is part of 'society'.

Civil Society and the State: Private and Public

Among the ways to define this political relationship, the most common is through the distinction between private and public. But there are different ways in which this distinction is used and at the same time questioned.

Private can be defined in two different ways. One is the personal conscience of the citizen voter. This is a secularised version of the personal conscience of the Christian moral subject of God who exercises free will to do good or evil, in particular the Protestant subject equal with all others before God and, in the most radical kinds of Protestantism, in a direct relationship with God. Another, closely linked to it, is private property in a capitalist market economy with its exclusive rights of decision-making: the consumer (individual or household) as sovereign chooser and the firm as consumer in order to produce, including the production of services. In this sense, the units of the private sphere are economic actors. In each case, the modern state can be said to guarantee their privacy as well as to be dependent on them. The state is dependent on the first, treated as a sovereign voter and holder of legitimating or delegitimating opinion and on the second as buyer or as producer in a domestic market that is the basis for a state's revenues. Performance in the separate sphere of economic activity and its growth also constitute the source of the global power of the state. In these senses, private citizens and private property are civil society.

Hegel's classic *The Philosophy of Right* first theorised this interrelation between civil society and state as mediation, law and legitimation, publicity, and forms of association. Karl Marx's critique of Hegel reformulated civil society, which in German translates as 'bourgeois society' (*bürgerliche Gesellschaft*), as the class of economic actors, namely capitalists, that exists by the exploitation of the proletariat, namely those who sell their capacity for work for a price called a wage. The state is a servant of the bourgeoisie and of a capitalist economy and its class relations.

Emancipation is a philosophical ideal for humanity, for Hegel epitomised by the state, for Marx only to be achieved by the working classes and their victory through the abolition of private property.

When we turn to the definition of 'public' we come to a quite different way of conceiving civil society. The state itself is public. But between the state and the private citizen is a conceivably distinct public sphere, its spaces and its organisations. The space of the state is literally a sovereign territory, over which the state's governments rule. The public spaces of civil society are within that territory, but not of the state, not one of its instruments of rule, but rather where opinion is formed and governments legitimised or delegitimised. These are actual spaces, places where people gather, organise, or demonstrate. Or they are virtual spaces, provided by media of various kinds — print, broadcast or web.

One of the classical theorists of such public spaces of civil society was the German sociologist and philosopher, Jürgen Habermas. His book entitled (in English translation) *The Structural Transformation of the Public Sphere*, first published in German in 1962 and published in English in 1989. It was at the same time one of the most important readings among intellectuals in China in the 1990s. In this book, Habermas noted how in circles of skilled workers, business people, and intelligentsia, independent of court life a new public life of meetings, for instance in coffee houses and printed magazines, flourished. Habermas' later volumes on *Communicative Action* based his concept of the public sphere on a universal human condition upon which a normative ideal can be built. The condition is that the human species depends upon and is defined by language. Human language is peculiar because through it every human being is conscious and knows her- or himself by communication with (and dependence on) others. By self-identification through communicative action with others, we build what he calls our life-worlds. At the same time, we also build social systems, and system integration, which is social structure, economies, and states. Life-worlds can be blocked by state or other systemic forces. The ideologies of the dominant forces of system integration can segregate life-worlds, blocking them off or marginalising them in the system.

The ideal and the possibility of communicative action and of the public sphere is openness to the persuasion of others and to agreement following reasoned and rational debate. The most insidious closing down of that possibility is through (1) self-centred consumerism, which is subjection to the practices of the market, (2) the formation of mass opinion by political party organisation and governments' legal-bureaucratic regulation, and (3) an assumed identification of a national or cultural essence, a race or ethnicity. Against all this, Habermas proposes the alternative notion of constitutional patriotism, the always moving agreement to abide by procedures that link us and our life-worlds in a civil society under a state, extending into a global civil society. Such procedures include the manners of civil conduct, or 'civility'. The sociologist Norbert Elias (1982) described at length the bourgeois cultivation of civility in relation to the court of the absolute monarchs of Europe and then to the power of the modern state created by bourgeois revolutions.

This conception of civil society is on the side of the life-world and of communicative action, against their restriction and marginalisation although it is impossible to do without regulation and system integration. So it is a descriptive norm, pressing for the most open possible communicative action and the negotiation of realisable life-worlds in communication with each other, given the necessity of systems and their forces of integration.

Public Good and Social Justice

Another strand of political philosophy is about the closely linked ideas of public good and social justice. Among these ideas are concepts of the commons, the environmental and other conditions that we all need, but for whose maintenance the private — in the economic sense — is incapable of doing a good job.

Concepts of social justice and public good as well as ideas of responsive government and the legitimacy of protest are also based in religious traditions. Any and all of them, not just Christianity, contain ideas of what it is to be and what it is to act as a proper human being. Nevertheless, the conceptions of justice stemming from secularised Christianity are foundations for the concept of human rights whose main secular institutions are the United Nations, international courts of justice and international non-governmental organisations. They come out of the same European tradition that also, paradoxically, produced or continued and justified abominations of its own ideals (slavery and colonisation) in the name of bringing human civilisation to the world.

It is no accident that, along with the formation of national movements and the establishment of modern states, the role and position (including class position) of those who bring and carry out these normative concepts and categories are intellectuals and political elites. They usually act as representative elites, rather than in service to and respect for the citizens of other class positions. There is already something questionable about this elitism by the very ideals of human universality, of equal humanity, that elites promote and use to justify their actions. Even more, the ideals of universal humanity and justice can be and are used to question the justifications of European and North American colonists, imperialists and slaveholders. So, European humanist categories have in fact become universal, in that in every country in the world they have been assimilated to the local categories — in particular through the inclusive category of 'the people' — that are used to question as hypocritical the ideologies and self-justifications of politicians and governments.

India

An appropriate place to begin a more distinctly comparative approach to civil society in China is the colonial situation in India out of which its local tradition of civil society developed, combining the British European normative concepts with Indian civilisational and religious concepts. Out of this colonial situation, the world's largest democracy was established at independence in 1947.

As part of the Constitution of India, an Electoral Commission was founded that would be and is in fact above electoral politics. It organises every election. Every election is an exception to the rest of the year, an occasion that is exceptionally punctual and well organised, in which participation increased over the years in its rate and its enthusiasm and in which the least educationally qualified are the most participant and are as well informed and subtle as the best educated in their responses to the normal corruption and unfulfilled promises of politicians. But the fact that the poor and less qualified participate more than the more qualified and wealthy may well be because this is their only chance to influence what is discussed and decided elsewhere through the power of control over economic resources and through personal connection (Banerjee, 2014).

The chapter in Kaviraj and Khilnani (eds.) (2001) by Partha Chatterjee argues forcefully that civil society in India started as a minority pursuit and became hugely effective in achieving independence from Britain. But it has remained a small part of political life and governance in India, compared to the governmentality of the Indian state and what he calls the political society of electoral mobilisation. He starts from the fact that civil society came to India as European secularised Christianity, a civilising, pedagogic project for a colonial Indian intelligentsia. The British colonial state sought to legislate for all economy and society, by direct or indirect rule, and through a civil service in whose upper reaches English was the required language.

The Indian, English-speaking intelligentsia that this colonial state cultivated, created secular institutions of public association and organisation. Chatterjee in fact starts his chapter with a discussion of a public meeting to mourn the death of a great Bengali poet, a meeting of a literary society that was among the first in this new world of 'the public', for which there was no word in Hindu. Rabindranath Tagore, another writer of poems, essays and much else, revered in both the English and the Indian worlds, was a witness to this public meeting. In an essay published in 1894, from which Chatterjee quotes, Tagore observed that there had recently been 'changes in this society of households. A new flood has swept into its domain. Its name is the public…..The word 'public' and its opposite 'private' have now come into use in Bengali' (Chatterjee, 2001, p. 167). Tagore defended what others attacked as the artificiality of public association and meetings. In the same way, a century earlier in Europe artifice was not just defended, but celebrated against the so-called 'natural' organic growth of social custom through which people were held and were supposed to accept their inherited positions in feudal relations. Public life and the regulation of social life were, Tagore said, for the benefit of all. This is one instance of the much more general fact that rule of law and democracy is a result of social and political movements, then of the construction of states. Such states pursue a project of modernity (aka artificiality) and their extension is the result of further political movements, both in the Euro-American West and everywhere else in the world.

In India, both those like Tagore who supported and others like Nabinchandra, another writer cited by Chatterjee, who attacked this artifice in defence of Hindu traditions (where mourning is an intimate act not a public show) did so with pride in being Bengali or some other language and tradition that makes up India. Both sides were part of the growing movement for independence from the British. That movement included the popular, village-based participation in a non-violent movement for independence led by Gandhi, a lawyer from South Africa. He was able to mobilise into a movement for independence and a modern secular state, religious ideas of the ascetic life. It was a public movement of highly successful boycotts of British goods and institutions that he could then represent to the point of conducting negotiations in London for independence.

Chatterjee's view of the resulting, post-colonial state and its politics is that civil society, as public association and interpersonal political discussion with influence, is confined to a political elite, the elite that created the modern state of independent India. The rest of the population is mobilised to participate in something else, which he calls 'political society'. This distinction is elaborated in the first three chapters of his book *The Politics of the Governed* (2004).

Civil society is based on established and sovereign law, the basis of which is property and rights, and the community of the nation. Citizens are bearers of rights and have the capacity to make policy, forming parties and civic organisations of the nation. In reality, it amounts to a hierarchy of restricted social mobility by means of education and wealth, maintained by inheritance. Political society is mediated through a number of other institutions, over which the multi-religious secular state governs. In particular, it is mediated through governmental (in Foucault's sense) institutions and the formation of population groups by self-organisation, through mediating leaders who have the required education and political connections that can mobilise votes and politicians to gain entitlements. Other intermediate institutions organise religious and domestic life, constantly changing and being changed by their involvement through the parties and their organisations of political society. They exist for the mobilisation of votes and between elections to demonstrate or otherwise make demands for recognition for themselves as 'communities' by the state and the disposition of the resources that the local or the federal state controls. Each such 'community' also claims to be central to a larger community, which is that of the nation.

This is not the politics of civil society and its public spaces, rather it is the creation of what can be called public constituencies through a politics of communal identity. The state of India, whatever party is in power, governs the whole territory and the whole of social life within it, as a developmental state. On the one hand, it reproduces the political elite through which it governs. On the other hand, it pursues policies of economic growth, the alleviation of poverty and some positive action to counter caste hierarchy. It is through such political mediation and organisation that changes in the law, and thus changes in civil society, are achieved. Indeed, it is often by the organisation of semi-legal subjects of the state, such as squatters or the small traders and criminals of the so-called informal economy, and by creating disorder or by civil disobedience, that political society works and brings about changes to law, property rights, and recognition of who belongs to the national community. Much of this politics is clientilist, politicians in personal deals with other members of the elite and with the wealthy, doing corrupt deals, avoiding tax, using their positions for personal gain, but also using these gains and their positions to benefit their lower-level supporters as patrons.

Chatterjee's distinction between civil society and political society may well be, as he intends, applicable as a description of all politics in the global system of states. At the same time, as he points out, the political issue raised by this distinction between civil society and political society is whether political society is actually democratic. Democracy remains a normative and active category and so through it there is a constant demand to know whether India's political society is a full, or just a diminished democracy.

One major point to be drawn from Chatterjee is that what bore up the anti-colonial civil society and became a national political society in India was a transformation of the civilisation of Hindu and other ritual traditions, and the result was communal politics.

China

Now let us turn to the chapter in the same book (Kaviraj and Khilnani, 2001) written by Thomas Metzger on how the introduction of civil society in China feeds on and transforms Chinese civilisational tradition — which, in his treatment, is Confucian and not religious.

He takes a very different angle of view on civil society from that of Chatterjee. Where Chatterjee is a critical political analyst, determined to test the normative categories against empirical description, Metzger is much more a political philosopher comparing normative categories. But they both end up with a historically informed commentary on the nature of the two (Indian, Chinese) political societies, societies of elites.

Metzger starts with what he thinks are the constituent elements of a political culture that is the condition for the existence of a modern democratic state. On pages 207–208, he lists eight elements, derived from a number of theorists, and looks for their possibility in China. They all converge on the requirement of 'civility', which in turn depends on a minimum amount of trust between fellow citizens, which is on the one hand willingness to abide by morally neutral rules of the game of politics and, on the other hand, trust in the resulting government because it can be held accountable. This is his version of civil society: the culture by which the game of politics can be played. It is fostered by the idea of sharing a common nationality, its history of suffering, its emergence and its achievement of a modern state, and its future. Metzger posits as a precondition for all this a considerable degree of cultural homogeneity, which he treats as an objective historical condition. Like the theorists of civil society and the public good, he stresses the abstract unifying principle of a normative ideal, but insists it is an ideal inherited and adapted from and within a long history.

Here he begins to make distinctions between the Chinese and the European traditions from which such an ideal is derived. In the European traditions, the ideal is one of justice, rights and legal procedure. In the Chinese it is the Confucian ideal of *ren*, which is responsiveness to others and to all things through a sense of the world as a set of relations, not an association of individuals, a world that is balanceable (out of balance, needing to be brought into balance). Trust in government in the European tradition is based on its being accountable by reference to laws that previous governments have passed, the most important of which are enshrined in a Constitution, a code of procedural rules of governance, or a common law set of precedents, for appeal against misgovernment. But in the equivalent Chinese tradition, this was and is not deemed to be sufficient. In the Chinese tradition, above procedures come guidance by moral rules, rules of interpersonal conduct, and a consensus of their acceptance.

Leadership is first of all moral example and moral prescription by a literate elite of public intellectuals.

Then he turns to a ninth condition posited in the European ideal of the public sphere, which he thinks is absent from the Chinese, even from Chinese democracies, namely those of Hong Kong and Taiwan. He calls this condition 'perspicacity'. We can also call it competence to discuss and make policy. It has to be learned by practice, and that practice is cumulative. That is, the practice of discussing political issues. Metzger argues that this practice is against the Chinese tradition. Instead, Chinese citizens expect governments to act according to their ideas of a leadership's responsibility and can condemn them for not doing so. Rather than discuss political issues and exercise empathy with others' views through abstract categories and the rules of the game of politics and international affairs, which is rare among the Chinese intellectuals he has met and the reports and writings he has read, Chinese intellectuals in his experience either condemn government for insufficient morality or work out the moral stance that they prescribe to both government and people. They don't discuss policy. Protest and condemnation can challenge legitimacy on moral grounds rather than legitimate government coming from and being checked by a civil society of dispute and discussion of policies.

He contrasts European intellectuals' individual autonomy with Chinese intellectuals' heteronomy, dependence on others. Note that civil society is in his version everywhere led by intellectuals, which is to say the influence of ideas produced by a minority and becoming, as they filter down, citizens' political persuasions and their differing voices. But in the European tradition these voices and the intellectuals and ideas that influence them are, ideally, autonomous. In China, he argues, the tradition of deference to an enlightened elite working alongside the state, idealised as sages, still holds. Modern literati, those with the best educational qualifications, are expected and are left to give a moral lead to state governance. This is another aspect of heteronomy — deference to what should be sage leadership.

In Chatterjee's terms, Metzger could be saying that in China there is no civil society, but there is a newly educated elite of a political society of mediators and self-organisation that can establish entitlements to whatever government provides and administers and that can question the legitimacy — the moral quality — of government.

The great Chinese anthropologist and sociologist, Fei Xiaotong, in his part-academic and part-campaigning analysis of what needs to happen in the China of the 1940s, Reconstructing Rural China (*Xiangtu Chongjian*), also advocated a new class of literati. Fei hoped that the local self-regulation of agrarian China, which was the politics of rule by elders and local gentry, and which was indispensable to the central rule of official bureaucracy from the emperor downwards, could become a new kind of elite including local elites of local autonomy based on rural industry. Assemblies of elected representatives would replace local gentry. The national government would then have to be a public administration of the central state responsive to such local assemblies (Fei, 1992, pp. 143–145).

Returning to Metzger, where other historians have seen an emergent civil society in dynastic China, from the Song dynasty onwards but in particular under the Qing, he sees simply indirect and autonomous realms of self-government under the central state, which was what he calls an 'inhibited centre'. It was 'unable to stretch its organisational capacities beyond a limited scope … leaving the bulk of the economy in the private sector' — a point Metzger makes based on his study of the salt monopoly under the Qing and similar to the argument of Kent Deng (see Chapter 3). The gentry looked to this inhibited state and to each other for the organisation of public works, including militia, water distribution, and the resolving of disputes, deploring the moral decay of both state and society. They did not look down for guidance. Instead, their ideal, which Metzger says persists, is that of their own moral responsibility, the responsiveness of the good moral state (if it *was* good) and their own leadership (replacing government where it is found *not* to be good).

The ideal is contained in the phrase that he quotes: a sage within and a monarch facing outward (*neisheng waiwang*). Sage leadership is used by the people, but does not depend on or use the people. It is an ideal, but it is posited historically and therefore it is considered to be a practical ideal, because it had once existed. Moral leadership could be attained because it once had been there; so it could be again, through a remaking of a great togetherness or harmony (*datong*). It is the moral way of accordance with universal principles (the *dao*) of responsiveness (*ren*), in which the only hierarchy is that of age, gender, and merit.

Its contemporary version, after the republican revolution, would have to cut out deference to age and the privileging of male authority that republican governments have eroded, leaving only a hierarchy of merit — but Metzger doesn't spell this out.

In sum, Metzger distinguishes the tradition of moral leadership and consensus that Chinese elites bring to the European tradition and institutions of civil society, introduced by the republican revolutions and reforms. It is a tradition of what he calls 'epistemological optimism', namely that we can and must reach human unity and rely on a real possibility of ending corruption and establishing good conduct. To this he contrasts the European tradition of 'epistemological pessimism', in which civil society and democracy can correct human propensities to harm and can correct the state's inherent fallibility, by reaching the current best knowledge through reason and debate.

The European tradition is as much a moral tradition as the Chinese, both in the notion of civilisation — stemming from Adam Smith and others — and in the philosophical current stemming from Immanuel Kant's categorical imperatives, inherent in the state of human being, through Rousseau's conception of the premise of human nature that has everywhere been enslaved and corrupted by private property and its states. But where the European tradition places the possibility of reaching a right, both moral and rational, decision in the institutional protection of minority opposition and continued discussion, the Chinese sage tradition places it in an elite duty within a state and the possibility of deposing a state that has gone morally wrong. But note in addition that ideas of democracy and of civil society, of anarchism, communism, republic and revolution have been introduced into China and become part of Chinese normative discourse for more than a century.

In Metzger's view, Chinese civil society turns all these into a popular expectation of sage rule, and of public intellectuals working out a code of morals for the conduct of government and living together. Listening to urban and rural residents discussing what political leaders and local officials have done or not done, you may find grounds to disagree. But are they expecting to be heard as politically competent critics or as people expecting responsive leaders? Certainly, the Chinese equivalent to Indian political society is the mobilisation of good conduct through the single Party.

Here is one illustration of how translation into Chinese has inflected the main theory of what Metzger calls perspicacity.

Habermas in China

Habermas' works, translated into and discussed in Chinese, followed by his visits and lectures in 2001 and after, had an impact similar to the visits and lectures of the British philosopher Bertrand Russell in the 1920s.

Metzger's view, contrasting Chinese propensity to seek a didactic moral example for all seems to be borne out in the way Habermas' ideas of the public sphere were received and used in China. Davies (2007) in fact relies on Metzger to describe the ways in which Habermas' conception of communicative action and acceptance of the other was received in China. She says in China it has been turned into a search for moral prescription or into problem-solving and dispute-resolving agreement. For instance, one writer interprets the public sphere as the Chinese historical and cultural self that has been preserved as a life-world, even while using the means of practical technology and the construction of state systems. The terms used for this sinification of Habermas are *ti* and *yong*, themselves a prescription of how to oppose and at the same time learn from Western knowledge and invention: preserve Chinese substance (*ti*) by using Western technology and practical knowledge (*yong*). This pairing is recommended to the world as a better formula for modernisation than that pursued by the West itself. Note how nationalistic it is, and so against the grain of Habermas' conceptualisation of human being.

Another way in which Habermas has been appropriated in China is as a critique of capitalism by supporters of the Chinese Communist Party (CCP). But at the same time, non-government intellectuals also use Habermas to oppose the Chinese Party-state in its headlong pursuit of capitalist development. So, all sides use Habermas as an authority in factional dispute over what each side seeks to establish: norms of conduct for a public sphere of academic and intellectual debate, disagreement and its resolution, in moral leadership and the setting of examples of high standards and the denunciation of negative examples — in ways reminiscent of Maoist leadership.

Thus, Habermas became popular with the rising number of intellectuals — university students and teachers and their friends in other walks of life — organising discussion groups outside Party control.

Withdrawal of the Party-State in Contemporary China

Finally, we come away from the normative to the descriptive. Take Howell's (2004) book about 'governance', which focuses on organisations that are not those of state administration. Governance is defined on page 2 as 'processes and arrangements, both formal and informal, by which power and public authority are distributed and regulated' — a descriptive, not a prescriptive definition, and one that can embrace both state and non-state 'processes and arrangements'. Indeed, the book is entirely about linkages between political society, civil society and the state in China.

All writers on current political tendencies in China, whether they are writing about censorship or the economy, property rights or religion, agree that the Party-state has withdrawn from direct administrative controls, while retaining powerful means of selective intervention. One withdrawal is in favour of regulation by reference to laws and judicial procedures. Another is by reliance on professionalism, which is to say a high degree of training and self-regulation by experts, be they lawyers, academics, architects, engineers, doctors, managers, or public administrators, or by business-people in organisations such as chambers of commerce. The Party in broadening to make sure it represents all three of the most advanced forces (scientific, cultural, and economically productive), endorses and absorbs this professionalisation of expertise.

Interpersonal linkage between the Party-state and the economy or for educational opportunity and access to state-controlled opportunities and other kinds of resource continues. This is China's version of clientilism. It may be based on the morality of reciprocity or on sheer instrumental gain, condemned politically, legally and morally as corruption. Clientalism of this kind is both prevalent and at the same time politically questioned and challenged. Corruption of politicians was one of the main issues that protestors raised in the student and citizen demonstrations that occurred in the months up to their military suppression on June 4, 1989 and the next few days in many cities as well as Beijing. Since then it has been a prominent topic of both investigative journalism and the Party-controlled media and of political action by the Party-state.

There had already been well-publicised trials and dismissals of corrupt officials and entrepreneurs, for instance, for smuggling automobiles into China. But since 1989, the number and the seniority of those disciplined and tried have increased. Much else has likewise been spurred by response to the 1989 protests, including the institution of village elections, which as Howell points out have generated their own dynamic of demands for greater accountability and increased airing of protests against unjust local government officials. But the powers of the Party to absorb and curb professional and non-governmental association is unabated despite the loosening of its controls.

There has been a loosening of controls over the formation of Non-Governmental Organisations (NGOs). Howell divides them into three kinds. One kind of NGO is also called a Civil Society Organisation (CSO). It is perceived by Party leaders and policy advisors to be necessary, since the CSO are pioneers, serving the poor, the disabled, or the diseased, drawing attention to new welfare issues and responding to them, locally, in ways that state agencies cannot or have not. CSOs have also been valued for their fund-raising and for getting their finances from International Non-Governmental Organisations (INGOs), from foreign states and non-state funds. Another kind is the self-organisation of professions and of business. The Party-state encourages their formation as a bridge between state agencies and the population in governance. There is also a third kind of NGO, which is a non-profit-making economic enterprise, providing a service for fees though started from donations.

More recently, Howell (2015) has identified a fourth kind of NGO, which acts for and organises labour and raises welfare and safety issues in work places, alongside but carefully not in confrontation with the official Federation of Trades Unions. All four kinds are closely linked to governmental institutions and we must ask how restrictive these links are.

Regulations on registration of NGOs were promulgated in October 1989. At first, they were strictly enforced. Every NGO had to have a supervisory body in a state agency, its so-called 'anchor unit' (*guakao danwei*). And there could be no more than one NGO for its stated purpose in the locality governed by its supervisory unit. But in the years since then conformity with the regulations has been loosened considerably, partly by the ingenuity of NGO organisers and partly by increasing laxity of supervisory bodies themselves. So the number of NGOs has grown. Anyone seeking to organise seeks official advice and Howell gives some revealing examples of such advice. It is that formal registration under the regulations is too cumbersome. Advisors say it is simpler to affiliate to an already registered NGO or to register with a university as a research organisation. This is not hiding behind a lie because much of the work of NGOs is to advise and inform those it seeks to serve and in the other direction to gather evidence and be an advocate in a cause for concern.

Many NGOs are started by Party-state agencies, such as the educational charity for schools in poor areas, Operation Hope, started by the national China Youth League. And in the other direction, NGOs organised by people outside the government and Party still need continuing advice and support from someone inside. Both kinds form networks with each other, but the networks do not turn into a large organisational extension or federation of NGOs. That could only take place if it were organised by the state. But NGOs and their networks can influence policy-making. For instance, the network of research organisations funded by foreign aid donors on the treatment of people with HIV/Aids, according to Howell, fed into provincial and central Party policies in removing the taboos on admitting the existence of the problem and on the necessity for education to remove the stigma on those who have contracted HIV. Other research networks or networks of so-called 'document handling service centres' inform each other in giving legal advice to migrant workers, or to women on issues of reproductive health.

All this has grown into a large number of semi-autonomous organisations that do their work of service, advocacy and advice more effectively than the Party-organised mass organisations: the Youth League, the All-China Womens Federation, and the All-China Federation of Unions. But each of these mass organisations, though probably least of all the official workers' Unions, themselves sponsor NGOs (Pringle and Clarke, 2011).

Religious Civic Organisations

Religious and ritual organisations and meetings for dance and exercise, gatherings for festivals and for playing music, are civic though none is explicitly political. They rehearse moral standards that are used to judge the actions of individuals, including local officials (Feuchtwang, 2001, last chapter). Ku Hok-bun (2004) describes the case of an unpopular Party secretary replaced in the village elections by a village head who had shown himself to be properly responsive to fellow villagers by his work in organising and finding finances for the rebuilding of the local lineage ancestral hall.

Very few of the 10s of 1000s of temples and their festival organisations or of house meeting places for Christians are registered, in the way the official religions and their main organisations and institutions (churches, monasteries, mosques) are. But they are the main ways in which people meet and informally rehearse and discuss standards of moral conduct.

What Does All This Amount To?

Plainly none of this amounts to a public sphere, nor a political society of mobilisations of votes as in India. So what is the right term? Jude Howell's 'governance' crosses the opposed ideas of corporatism and autonomy. Corporatism means Party-state-organised and state-dependent NGOs. Lu Yiyi (2008) points out that registered NGOs *are* dependent. And in addition to them, there are countless more unregistered organisations. The capacity of the Party-state to intervene prevents the linking of such organisations into a nation-wide association, as it did against the Falun'gong religious organisation from 1999 onward. But they do have some autonomy, a dependent autonomy as Lu names it.

Political differences are aired on blogs, and in small personally organised meetings such as the salons (*shalong*) and academic workshops of intellectuals. This is something like a public sphere, though not one of registered organisations. Environmental issues are raised and published, reaching across national borders (Mertha, 2011; Duara, 2015, pp. 260–273). Websites and publications do push the boundaries of possibility. So,

Howell (2004) concludes, 'There is a multiplicity of proto public spheres that are occupied by technical and intellectual elites, that are.... both transient and episodic' (p. 161). On the other hand, she also concludes that the Chinese version of political society, of registered and unregistered non-governmental organisation and association, is a 'depoliticised pubic sphere' that can influence policy.

Questions of Perspicacity, Trust and Respect

Lastly, consider another local study by Isabelle Thireau and Hua Linshan (2002), which seriously challenges but does not entirely refute Metzger's claim of a common Chinese reluctance to discuss policy but to rely instead on the demand for morally good leaders. In their study of several villages in the Pearl River Delta near Guangzhou (Canton), they find what they call the opening of 'local mediation spaces' 'where different ways to identify and manage common issues can be mobilised, confronted, and eventually combined, diverse links being established between the spaces coexisting in a single locality' (p. 159). In these spaces, issues are discussed and trustworthy leadership is negotiated. They include spaces between the official institutions of the Party-state and other non-state locally maintained institutions such as temples, festivals and lineages. Within them, villagers have created officially recognised mediating organisations such as an elderly people's association and a cultural association. In the leadership of these organisations, there is usually a retired cadre or official or an army veteran, a fellow-villager who has shown that their co-residents could trust them, based on their past record. Thireau and Hua point out that such people would anyway be consulted by the appointed and elected village leaders to make sure that their decisions will not be opposed.

One villager told Thireau and Hua that:

> Since the reforms, officials care about their reputation, they care about what people say about them. This is a great reform. And when they don't care about villagers' opinions, they care about what others outside the village will think about them. This is why it is sometimes so effective to write to the media (p. 180).

Thireau and Hua observe that 'One cannot actually spend a few days in a given locality without witnessing discussions evaluating and often criticising officials' actions' (p. 179). These are the spaces that allow for the identification of morally trustworthy leadership and for discussing local policy issues and the public good.

But do they amount to a local public sphere or political society?

Seminar Question

Is a Chinese version of civil society and/or political society emerging?

Key Readings

Chatterjee, P. 2004. *The Politics of the Governed: Reflections on Popular Politics in Most of the World*. New York: Columbia University Press (Chapter 2).

Howell, J. (ed.) 2004. *Governance in China*. Lanham MD: Rowman and Littlefield (by Howell, Chapters 1 and 8)

Howell, J. 2015. Shall we dance? Welfarist incorporation and the politics of state-labour NGO relations in China. *The China Quarterly* pp. 702–723.

Kaviraj, S., and Sunil K. (eds.) 2001. *Civil Society: History and Possibilities*. Cambridge: Cambridge University Press. (chapters by Chaterjee and Metzger).

Thireau, I. and Hua L. 2002. Power beyond instituted power: Forms of mediation spaces in the Chinese countryside. In Mengin, F. and Rocca, J., (eds.) *Politics in China: Moving Frontiers*. New York: Palgrave Macmillan.

Further Readings

Banerjee, M. 2014. *Why India Votes?* London and New York: Routledge.

Brook, T., and Frolic, M. B. (eds.), 1997. *Civil Society in China*. Armonk, NY: M. E. Sharpe (chapters by Brook and Dean — to give city and rural, long-term perspectives).

Cai, Y. 2010. *Collective Resistance in China: Why Protests Succeed or Fail*. Stanford, CA: Stanford University Press.

Davies, G. 2007. Habermas in China: theory as catalyst. In *The China Journal* 57, pp. 61–85.

Duara, P. 2015. *The Crisis of Global Modernity: Asian traditions and a sustainable future*. Cambridge: Cambridge University Press.

Elias, N. 1982. *The Civilising Process* (2 volumes), Pantheon.

Fei Xiaotong (1992) (tr Hamilton, Gary G. and Wang Zheng) *From the Soil, The Foundations of Chinese Society*: A translation of Fei Xiaotong's *Xiangtu Zhongguo*. Berkeley, Los Angeles and London, University of California Press, pp. 144–145.

Feuchtwang, S. 2001. *Popular Religion in China*. London: Routledge Curzon. (last chapter).

Hildebrandt, T. 2013. *Social Organizations and the Authoritarian State in China*. Cambridge: Cambridge University Press.

Ku Hok-Bun, 2004. *Moral Politics in a South China Village: Responsibility, Reciprocity, and Resistance*. Lanham, Md: Rowman & Littlefield.

Lu Yiyi, 2008. *Non-governmental Organizations in China: The Rise of Dependent Autonomy*. London: Routledge.

Mertha, A. 2011. *China's Water Warriors: Citizen action and Policy Change*. Ithaca: Cornell University Press.

Metzger, T. A. 2004. *A Cloud Across the Pacific: Essays on the Clash between Chinese and Western Political Theories Today*. Hong Kong.

Pringle, T., and Simon C. 2011. *The Challenge of Transition: Trade Unions in Russia, China and Vietnam*. Basingstoke: Palgrave Macmillan.

Pringle, T. 2011. *Trade Unions in China : The Challenge of Labour Unrest*. Abingdon ; New York: Routledge.

Shils, E. 1996. Reflections on Civil Society and Civility in the Chinese Intellectual Tradition. In Tu Wei-Ming (ed.) *Confucian Traditions in East Asian Modernity: Moral Education and Economic Culture in Japan and the Four Mini-Dragons*. Boston, MA: Harvard University Press.

Simon, K. W. 2013. *Civil Society in China: The Legal Framework from Ancient Times to the "New Reform Era."* Oxford: Oxford University Press.

Wang, H. 2001. Contemporary Chinese thought and the question of modernity. In Zhang Xudong (ed.) *Whither China? Intellectual Politics in Contemporary China*. Duke UP.

Weller, R. 2001. *Alternate Civilities: Democracy and Culture in China and Taiwan*. Boulder: Westview Press.

Chapter 16

Rule of Law

> The Duke of She informed Confucius, saying, "Among us here there are those who may be styled upright in their conduct. If their father has stolen a sheep, they will bear witness to the fact." Confucius said, "Among us, in our part of the country, those who are upright are different from this. The father conceals the misconduct of the son, and the son conceals the misconduct of the father. Uprightness is to be found in this."
>
> James Legge's translation of *The Analects*, *Zilu*, 13:18

> If a son reports his father's crime and the accusation is proven wrong, that is, if the father has not committed the crime the son reported, the son shall be executed. If a son reports his father's crime and it is found out that it is true and the father has indeed committed the crime the son reported, the son shall receive 100 blows with a stick and shall spend three years in prison.
>
> The Law Code of the Qing Dynasty, our translation

These two quotes, from the Analects of Confucius, and from the Law Code of the Qing dynasty, are both about the 'principle of concealing one's relatives'. The popular saying 'The father conceals the misconduct of the son, and the son conceals the misconduct of the father' (*fu wei zi yin, zi wei fu yin*) is still widely known in China, as is the shorter form 'relatives mutually conceal their misconduct' (*qin qin xiang yin*). These principles of 'concealing ones relatives' nicely embodies the potential conflict between Confucian morality and the law in China. In the first section of this chapter, we will deal with the opposition between Confucianism and Legalism. This will be followed by a discussion of the introduction of modern 'rule of law' in China, which will be compared with developments in India. The last sections deal with questions of the law in contemporary China and a brief outlook on contemporary and future developments.

From Confucianism and Legalism to the Rule of Law and of Men

The opposition between Confucianism and Legalism is perhaps the most important debate in the history of Chinese governance and law. The followers of Han Fei and Lord Shang directly opposed the Confucian ideals of governing by virtue and propriety, and proposed to govern by law, order, and surveillance instead. The core ideas of both doctrines can be opposed in the following way:

	Confucianism	Legalism
Core principle	Li 礼 ritual, propriety, etiquette	Fa 法 Law, order, obedience
Representatives	Kongzi, Mengzi	Shang Yang, Han Fei
Rules and standards	Differentiated different rules for different people	Absolute same rules apply to everyone
Family-state	Family above state	State above family
Govern	By virtue moral exemplars reward virtuous people look for virtue	By power reward and punishment punish wrongdoing look for offence
Human nature	Fundamentally good	Fundamentally evil
History and poetry	Useful for self-cultivation	Useless for governance
In local society	Inspire others	Spy on others
Society as a whole should be like	A school	A barrack

Source: Adapted from Qu (1961, pp. 226–226).

Some regimes in Chinese history were more obviously one or the other: The first Emperor Qin Shi Huang's regime, for instance, was founded on the legalist ideas of his advisor Li Si. Later emperors would accord primacy to Confucianism. But in between Chinese politics were often "ornamentally Confucian and functionally Legalist" (*rubiaofa li*): rulers pretended to be good-willed Confucians and moral exemplars, whereas in reality they were cold-blooded and power-hungry Legalists.

Even if the rulers and the political system were often "ornamentally Confucian and functionally Legalist", this was so not only to deceive the governed. Surely both in Confucianist- and Legalist-inspired political systems — just like in any system of political order and hierarchy — obedience to rules and the contingencies of human action and thought must be reconciled. One way to do so this is by 'pretended following' and 'pretended rule', or 'hypocrisy'. In a Confucian-inspired political order, for instance, it is vital that people pretend they are good, well-meaning and polite. Only then can rituals be completed and social order maintained. By the same token, it can be argued that in a legalist political order, it is necessary that people admit they are evil (*wei'e*).

Rulers on the one hand 'pretended' to be Confucian, on the other hand they also sometimes demanded absolute obedience and punished their subjects. This was seen as necessary for cases of grave deviance and offence; but often it was also invoked against the ordinary unruliness of the 'small people'. As Confucian ritual was interlinked with literacy and the art of writing (Zito, 1993), the illiterate peasants were incapable of this kind of ethical governance and hence in need of a strong and unrelenting rule. But if this was a common elite description of ritual and law, the realities were often exactly the other way around: commoners managed their deals according to Confucian propriety, whereas rulers schemed and ruled according to legalist principles.

While contemporary legal practices in China cannot be described in terms of some unchanging essences of Confucianism or Legalism, the opposition of 'Confucian outside' and 'Legalist inside' still has important implications now. Philip Huang, in a recent overview article on Chinese legal practices (2015), identifies a long-lasting preference of substantive over procedural justice, concrete over abstract reasoning, and altogether emphasises the influence of what he calls 'Confucian familism' and 'practical moralism' in Chinese law. Huang also makes the points that the history of the relationship between Confucianism and Legalism in Chinese thinking and practice should not be seen as a binary opposition, but rather as a symbiotic and corollary relationship (2015, p. 28). So 'Confucianism outside, Legalism inside' does not have to mean that both frameworks exclude each other, but rather have to be constantly related. By concealing and revealing either framework in ordinary social action, people relate to and recreate 'judging publics'.

It is clear that both Confucianism and Legalism are very different from a modern 'rule of law'. Implying that no one is above the law, modern rule of law opposes the arbitrariness of personal rule. Confucianism and Legalism both represent a 'rule of men', be it virtuous philosopher-kings or brutal autocrats. Modern rule of law requires that the law is certain, equal, and known by everyone. The classical texts of the Confucian and Legalist traditions are however more dialogical commentary and mirror-for-princes than scripted 'law'. Hence, the modern opposition between rule of law and rule of men — *fazhi* and *renzhi* in Chinese — is of a rather different nature than the opposition between Confucianism and Legalism.[1]

In China, just like elsewhere, the rule of law is cause and consequence of political representation, universal citizenship and nation-state sovereignty. At the same time, 'rule of law' implies independence of the law from state power and social convention. Ideally, law should be separate from both state and society, but obviously it has to emerge from somewhere and be embedded in state and society. This leads to a series of contradictions, which are fundamental to modern sovereignty. Gilmartin and Ocko (2009) frame their very insightful comparison of the rule of law in China and India exactly along these contradictions.

The 'Rule of Law' in British India and Qing China

The independence of the law from state power and social convention implies a number of contradictions. The modern discourses that opposed

[1] For an overview of early debates about the 'rule of law' and the 'rule of men' in Early Republican China, see Jenco (2010).

the rule of law and the rule of men to each other always had to deal with such contradictions — even though the law is supposed to be independent, equal, and transparent, it needs to be created by someone and its force needs to be guaranteed by someone. Ocko and Gilmartin list the following contradictions:

1. The discourse of law both legitimises and constrains the political authority of the state.
2. Law and legal procedures define and shape society, while at the same time being themselves confined to their social environment.
3. The law defines an economic and social order based on contract, property, and rights.

Ocko and Gilmartin proceed to compare British India and Qing Dynasty China along those lines.

The law legitimised and constrained the political authority of the state in different ways. In the China of the Qing, most law was particularistic, that is, tailored and different for different subjects. The law's ultimate authority rested on the power of the emperor, who was himself also exempt from 'legal authority'. But this was balanced by the opposite idea that rule was given by heavenly fate (*Tianming*), and that the law as well as the emperor's legitimacy derived, ultimately, from the moral sovereignty of *Tian* (heaven). In British India, on the contrary, discourses opposing the 'rule of law' to the 'rule of man' emerged earlier. They often put the civilising force of the law against 'oriental despotism'. The 'rule of law' should limit the (irrational and ruthless) power of local rulers. But the rule of law was ultimately guaranteed by the Raj; and together with the objective of education and civilisation, from the beginning it drew differences between colonials and natives, and between different groups in Indian society.

While being shaped by its social surroundings and context, the law (legal codes and procedures) also embodied official visions of society and normative assumptions about social relations — which in turn shaped society. In India, as in other British colonies, this meant fundamentally the separation of procedural law for the colonial state and the assimilated native elites, and substantive law for Indian communities. Whereas the former was modelled on modern contract and rationality, the latter was basically customary law, and jurisdiction was left to local communities.[2] In India, this separation played a crucial role in the reshaping and reinforcement of caste (Dirks, 2001), communal identity, and in particular the Hindu–Muslim divide. Surely, the Great Legal Code of the Qing Dynasty (like any other book of law) also dealt with social convention, that is, its object was society. But a core difference was that the Qing Code and the Qing legal profession were not seen as completely separate from society. In India, an opposition emerged between the (procedural) state and (substantive) society. This explains also the emergence and growth of the legal profession in India at the same time; the task of this profession was basically to mediate between state and society. In China, the boundaries between the procedure and the substance of the law were not as clear because the law continued to embody universal morality. In other words, the Confucian moral order (*li jiao*) was substantially articulated and fused with the law. Accordingly, substantive justice — in particular the principle that punishment should fit the crime — had priority. At the same time, there was also a large group of litigation masters and petition writers. But they had stayed out of the courts of the county (*xian*) magistrates, unlike the lawyers who attended the courts of the Indian Raj. Similarly, in China, most contracts of land sale and agreement were registered by the parties and their mediators or arbiters. Only when disputes became violent or threatened violence did the magistrates investigate and intervene, often in order to amend the outdated records for taxation. By contrast, in India, a complete cadastre of land holdings by the colonial state was kept up-to-date, and courts were much taken up with disputes over land on the principle that land ownership was a contract between the individual and the state. But these disputes were in practice ways of establishing the rival statuses of the land-holders in terms of their customary communities.

In India, communal statuses and a universal procedural law and electoral suffrage based on individual property rights prevailed.

[2] The historian Mahmood Mamdani (1996) describes the same bifurcation in southern Africa, and argues that the split between citizen and subject it implied ultimately created and entrenched authoritarian rule and violence, and that this legacy is the core obstacle to democratisation in the former British colonies of southern Africa.

It transmuted into a mixture of a universal moral sovereignty of self-restraint and self-determination in Ghandi's anti-colonial campaigns and the constitution of independent India proclaiming individual freedom and the rule of law.

In China, there was no conception of individual property rights under the Qing, just the obligations of contracted agreements and 'one's due' (*fen*), which is closely tied to the ideas of destiny and a social relationship that is fated. This idea of due and of obligation is still strong in China. But it now coexists with a republican constitution that places high emphasis on a definition of an independent people's definition by loyalty to the ruling party to which it owes its independence, be it the Guomindang or the Communist Party.

The Qing emperor's rule of man (*renzhi*) was tempered by the universal moral sovereignty of *Tian* and transcendent Confucian ideals of sage rule. The People's Republic is ruled by a tension between rule by law in which the Party is law and policy maker, and the constraints on both state and Party that the appeal to the law and the constitution affords to local activists claiming the need for a rule of law (*fazhi*).

In comparing India and China, Ocko and Gilmartin have resorted to a useful concept of 'moral sovereignty' that is a claim to a universal civilisation, which is both within and above the rule of law.

The sinification (*bentuhua*) of the Law?

A very important book about the legal landscape in contemporary China was Zhu Suli's Sending the Law to the Countryside (*song fa xia xiang*) (2000).[3]

Zhu starts out with a case of a local judge visiting a village to mediate in a local conflict (Zhu, 2000, pp. 27–53). He is a judge in the image of the popular fictional hero of dynastic China, Judge Bao, a trustworthy county magistrate who is the subject of many stories and plays. In the Chinese countryside, judges sometimes instead of summoning parties to court, visit the locality and try the case there. Why is this, Zhu asks.

[3] The book hasn't been translated into English, but there are good summaries available in Upham (2005) and Chen (2004).

Basically, because state power is weak, and government offices just like legal offices need to be strategic in such 'peripheral zones' of power. Historically, the law has been part of state building, and hence the 'law' was 'brought' to the countryside, just like technology, culture and education. It was part of a system of distributive power, yet such relationships of distribution remained partial and temporary (*jubu fenpeixing quanli guanxi*). Local officials, therefore, operate according to local conventions and local knowledge to mediate and guarantee the implementation of higher level doctrine and order, to the best of their capability. For all these reasons, the 'rule of law' in China has not only to do with the professionalisation of the judicial system, but most importantly, it has to be based on a thorough acquaintance with the local conditions. The legal profession, Zhu argues, should understand rural realities and use the 'local resources' (*bentu ziyuan*) available, and build a legal system on this basis. With these arguments, Zhu also strongly opposes those who would argue that China should introduce Western 'rule of law' and emulate Western legal arrangements.

Zhu then suggests looking at local communities and courts at the lowest level of the legal system. This is, first of all, because the majority of the population (in 2000) was still in the countryside, and because here the task of modernisation was most pressing (in Zhu's formulation). The basic-level courts also constitute the largest component of China's judicial system. It is also, secondly, because modern ('Western') law is adapted to urban conditions, and much ('Western') legal research neglects social conditions of the countryside. And in the countryside, legal arrangements have to be thoroughly embedded in local social conditions, and this poses particular challenges for the rule of law (Zhu, 2000, Introduction).

Zhu makes arguments in favour of collective judgement. He defends the employment of military personnel as judges and warns against the dangers of professionalisation of the law in the countryside, not so much because of the lack of well-educated legal professionals but more because of the inappropriateness of book-knowledge acquired in law schools. Zhu shows how ordinary people and legal practitioners bridge formal rules of law and social norms of the countryside. This might happen, for instance, when there are informal local agreements about using draught animals together, or when dealing with compensations for extra-marital affairs.

Zhu provides a hypothetical case comparison to illustrate his arguments (Zhu, 2000, pp. 216–219): the conflict over the purchase of steel products in the city versus an argument over the use of field oxen in a village. In the first case, the relationship between buyers and sellers is purely commercial, and all parties have alternatives. Property rights are relatively clear, and backed up by legal deeds. The interests involved are prospective, unrelated to daily necessities, and relatively easy to quantify. Such commercial activities are specialised and standardised, and dispute resolution can rely on this. Related to this, urban Chinese are used to deal with legal documents. None of these things are true for the second case, the disagreement over the use of field oxen. When mediating such a conflict, judges have to use particular techniques to address what matters to the parties in their everyday life (many elements of which might not have a direct legal manifestation). Good mediators will minimise the formal fact-finding and procedure, because this itself can alienate parties to the conflict. And ultimately, it can be expected that judges themselves will use the system to protect themselves.

Zhu Suli is not arguing that these features of informal semi-legal arrangements in the countryside are a mere survival of Chinese tradition. Instead, in his view, they represent a transitional stage, in which historical practices have been partly transformed with the arrival of a formal legal system. His main recommendation is to appreciate such Chinese realities, rather than blindly introducing a 'western' and 'liberal' legal system (which might include, for instance, the professionalisation of judges).

The American legal scholar Upham (2005) has reviewed Zhu Suli's work, and criticises it for one mean weakness, which is that Zhu fails directly to address the role of political power in China's legal system. Party and Government obviously have the ultimate say in every legal decision; and it is impossible to speak of a separation of powers in China's one-party state. Upham points out an inherent contradiction in Zhu's work: Zhu argues for an appreciation of local practices, yet also, ultimately, expects that formal and procedural law will grow stronger. But he fails to suggest how these two arguments could be linked, and on which basis formal law should develop. Hence, there is no reason to believe in the rule of law, other than a vague belief in modernisation, which is not justified. Related to this, then, Zhu never deals with the role of the communist party in the legal system (neither at the local level, nor at the national level), and he omits the various possibilities of popular resistance against party and state (which might happen even with the support or tacit acknowledgement of local courts).

Upham further points out that Zhu constantly writes against the 'Western' concepts of the law, but fails to take account of alternative comparators and alternative views of the 'law' in legal history and in other developing countries. In this sense, his anti-Western stance might be described as a kind of self-orientalism. Alternative views, Upham points out, might be found in law-and-development theory. If Zhu argues that judges in China are strongly connected to local society and do not always operate according to intelligible and universal rules, then this is not fundamentally different to what has been pointed out for different contexts, including the United States.

Such an understanding (including a further institutionalisation of legal rules) might also help to prevent unnecessary destruction of local norms. Hence, according to Upham, the solution may be to institutionalise the dialectic which Zhu describes, between formal and informal, modern and customary, central and peripheral.

The Future?

Various observers point out that China's current regime operates according to a principle of 'rule by law', rather than 'role of law' (Diamant, Lubman and O'Brien, 2005). This implies that law is used as an instrument for conflict management and for rule by state agencies; yet state and party remain in various ways fundamentally exempt from legal control. Such an arrangement had been used by other late developers, such as Germany in Bismarck's time, Meiji Japan, and Turkey in Ataturk's time (*ibid.*, p. 6). In contemporary China, 'rule by law' is based on the lack of consistency between different legislative entities (for instance, between local, provincial, and national levels). Because of one-party-rule, there is also no clear separation between executive, legislative, and judiciary, and party organs are often exempted from legal challenge. Policy campaigns and propaganda efforts generally promote the principle of 'rule by law', according to which the political leadership of the party stands above legal principles. At the local level, judges depend on local party institutions for promotion and pay. The decisions of local agencies sometimes contradict what is declared by higher levels; and local government might sometimes actively block knowledge of the law.

Yet, at the same time, there is official encouragement to use law to check government officials. And a new law is often accompanied by a campaign to spread 'legal awareness' and knowledge of the law (*pufa*) (O'Brien and Li, 2006, pp. 31, 34–35). This forms a basis for petitions and protests, which are partly encouraged by higher levels of government to check on lower levels. O'Brien and Li (2006) draw particular attention to the laws on village elections, instituted to curb self-serving Party members and the1990 Administration Litigation Law capacitating citizens to sue government officials in breach of the law.

Clarke (2007a), for another instance, points out that there is an increasing professionalisation of judges, including a tendency to watch each other's judgements, rather than to obey the authorities who appoint them. In commercial law, standards have been strengthened by China's entry into the World Trade Organization. In family law, the rights to marry, divorce, and to be protected from domestic violence are all clearly established in law, setting standards of the abstract citizen as bearer of rights.

We are left with an ongoing conflict. On the one hand, there is the reluctance of the central state to let independent litigants and the media check local Party and state authorities and local police who act arbitrarily or bring about distortions and inconsistencies of law and regulation. On the other hand, 'decentralised legal authoritarianism' can be challenged by citizens. They can charge that officials/government act 'against the law' (Lee, 2007) or against the moral sovereignty of human good civilised conduct (Huang, 2015).

Seminar Questions

Should the Chinese government 'sinify' the law?

Can you see the development of a new 'rule of law' in contemporary China?

Key Readings

Ocko, J., and Gilmartin, D. 2009. State, sovereignty, and the people: A comparison of the "Rule of Law" in Qing China and British India. *Journal of Asian Studies*, **68**(1), pp. 55–100.

Qu Tongzu 1961. Li versus Law, Chapter 6 of *Law and Society in Traditional China*. The Hague: Mouton, pp. 226–246.

Upham, F. K. 2005. Who will find the defendant if he stays with his sheep? Justice in Rural China. *Yale Law Journal*, **114**, pp. 1675–1718.

Further Readings

Bodde, D. 1981. Basic concepts of Chinese law: The genesis and evolution of legal thought in traditional China, *Essays on Chinese Civilisation*, Charles Le Blanc and Dorothy Borei (ed.), Princeton: Princeton University Press.

Brandtstädter, S. 2011. The law cuts both ways: Rural legal activism and citizenship struggles in neosocialist China. *Economy and Society*, **40**(2), pp. 266–289.

Chen, A. H. Y. 2004. Socio-legal Thought and Legal modernization in Contemporary China. A Case Study of the Jurisprudence of Zhu Suli. In *Law, Legal Culture and Politics in the Twenty First Century*, Guenther Doeker-Mach and Klaus A. Ziegert (eds.), Stuttgart: Franz Steiner Verlag, pp. 227–249.

Clarke, D. C. 2007a. The Chinese legal system since 1995: Steady Development and striking continuities. *China Quarterly*, **191**, pp. 555–566.

Clarke, D. C. 2007b. Legislating for a Market Economy in China. *China Quarterly*, **191**, pp. 567–585.

Diamant, N., Tubman, S. B. and O'Brien, K. (eds.) 2005. *Engaging the Law in China: State, Society and the Possibilities for Justice*. Stanford, CA: Stanford University Press (esp. Introduction).

Dirks, N. B. 2001. *Castes of Mind*; *Colonialism and the Making of Modern India*. Princeton and Oxford: Princeton University Press.

Haley, J. 2006. Law and Culture in China and Japan: A Framework for Analysis. *Michigan Journal of International Law,* **27**(3), pp. 895–915.

Howson, N. C., and Mark D. W. 2006. Law, norms, and legal change: Global and local in China and Japan. *Michigan Journal of International Law,* **27**(3), pp. 687–693.

Huang, P. 1996. *Civil Justice in China: Representation and Practice in the Qing*. Stanford, CA: Stanford University Press.

Huang, P. C. C. 2015. Morality and law in China, past and present. *Modern China*, **41**(1), pp. 3–39.

Jayasuriya, K. (ed.) 1998. *Law, Capitalism and Power in Asia: The Rule of Law and Legal Institutions*, London: Routledge.

Jenco, L. K. 2010. "Rule by Man" and "Rule by Law" in Early Republican China: Contributions to a Theoretical Debate. *The Journal of Asian Studies*, **69**(1), pp. 181–203.

Katz, P. 2008. *Divine Justice: Religion and the Development of Chinese Legal Culture*. London: Routledge.

Kaufman, W. J. 1994. Relational practices and the marginalization of law: Informal financial practices of small businesses in Taiwan. *Law & Society Review*, **28**(2), pp. 193–232.

Keith, R. C. 1994. *China's Struggle for the Rule of Law*. Basingstoke: Macmillan (esp. Chapter 2).

Lee, Ching Kwan 2007. *Against the Law. Labor Protests in China's Rustbelt and Sunbelt*, Berkeley CA: University of California Press (esp Chapter 7 and conclusion).

Mansfield Centre for Pacific Affairs (ed.) 2000. *The Rule of Law. Perspectives from the Pacific Rim*, Online publication. http://www.mansfieldfdn.org/backup/programs/program_pdfs/compendium.pdf. [Accessed 27 February 2012].

Mamdani, M. 1996. *Citizen and Subject: Contemporary Africa and the Legacy of Late Colonialism*. Princeton: Princeton University Press.

Michelson, E. 2007. Lawyers, political embeddedness, and institutional continuity in China's transition from socialism. *American Journal of Sociology*, **113**(2), pp. 352–414.

O'Brien, K., and Lianjiang, L. 2006. *Rightful Resistance in Rural China*. Cambridge: Cambridge University Press.

Peerenboom, R. (ed.) 2003. *Asian Discourses of Rule of Law*, London: Routledge.

Peerenboom, R. 2007. *China's Long March Toward Rule of Law*. Cambridge: Cambridge University Press.

Zhu Suli. 2000. *Song Fa Xia Xiang* (Bringing the Law to the Countryside). Beijing: Zhongguo Zhengfa Daxue Chubanshe.

Zhu Suli 2006. Political parties in China's judiciary. *Duke Journal of Comparative and International Law,* **17**, pp. 533–560. Available online at http://www.law.duke.edu/shell/cite.pl?17+Duke+J.+Comp.+&+Int%27l+L.+533. [Accessed 16 February 2012].

Chapter 17

Democracy

In a series of three blog entries posted in late December 2011, the blogger and author Han Han expressed a series of opinions that are common statements to refuse the applicability of Western theories of liberal democracy to China. He wrote that China does not need a revolution, be it a 'velvet revolution' (Czech Republic) or a 'green revolution' (Egypt). The 'quality' (*suzhi*) of the Chinese people is too low to have a democracy now. The only possibility is small-scale, slow reform. One point to start with is increased freedom in culture, publishing, press and cinema (Han, 2011a–c).

At the same time, there is a long history of democracy (*minzhu*) in China, which includes numerous engagements with Western theories of democracy. This chapter first sets out different theories and concepts of democracy, and then provides some suggestions about a comparison of Chinese democracy with Indian democracy. Further topics are the historical relationship of democracy and economic development, and how it applies to contemporary China. Theories of liberal democracy are then contrasted with the Maoist theory of 'people's' democracy. The last section deals with the possibilities of procedural democracy, and alternative concepts of democracy in contemporary China.

Different Concepts of Civil Society and Democracy

A classic distinction in political thought is the distinction between liberal and republican concepts of democracy. Liberal models, championed by theorists such as Adam Smith, John Locke, Jeremy Bentham and John Stuart Mill, emphasise 'negative freedoms'; i.e., 'freedoms from' state control, oppression, and force in general. Citizens are then free to participate in the public realm. The role of the state in such conceptualisations is a regulator and a peace-keeper, which maintains minimal standards of social security. Democracy then is mainly the contest of interests, which are often represented by political elites.

Republican conceptualisations, on the contrary, emphasise 'positive freedoms', i.e., 'freedoms to' participate. Theorists in mainland Europe, such as Rousseau and — perhaps most importantly — Hegel put emphasis on the continuous and positive participation of citizens in the public realm. Beyond freedom from control, this requires a certain measure of social equality and guaranteed livelihoods. The role of the state here is further inclusion and participation; in fact, these definitions often imply a critique of the liberal and utilitarian state, of private property and capitalism, inasmuch as they limit democratic participation. Democracy, in this tradition, is the continuous and widening participation of all citizens in the public realm.

Within the basic 'freedom to' tradition, there is 'associative democracy', whose founders are GDH Cole in England and Marcel Mauss in France, which emphasises means of representation and accountability based on local solidarity and associations (Hirst, 1994). It includes syndicalism and workers' control, in which the workers control their own workplace and these productive units of self-government are the cells of a cooperative society and its state, or without a state altogether: socialist anarchism (for anarchism in China, see Bernal, 1976). A more Marxist version of workers' occupations and management of their work places informed the socialism of the Italian Communist leader Antonio Gramsci and his conception of 'hegemony', which is the prevailing common sense of reality and possibility that serves the capitalist economic order and the states that support it, but that can be challenged by a counter-hegemonic movement of workers' democracy. Laclau and Mouffe (2011) have recalled and re-thought this idea of democracy.

Less radical — in the sense of aiming at a fundamental change of social conditions and the political system — in the republican tradition are theories of 'deliberative democracy', which emphasise the continued participation of citizens in the democratic process. Jürgen Habermas' work is the most prominent in this tradition, stressing the importance of participation through the channels of civil society. Civil society works through procedures guaranteed by a state, but they are always subject to change because active opinion is never fixed, so the procedures by which rational debate occurs are themselves open to being the subject of debate and to being recast.

We conclude from this very brief summary of different definitions of democracy that the mechanism of registering public approval for a government or for replacing it by elections is simply one among many possible procedures of representation and accountability. (For a very influential theory that provides more general concepts of the possibilities of democratic action of giving or denying support, see Hirschman, 1970).

All of the above are Euro-North-American conceptions of democracy. Other civilisations have their own conceptions of responsive government and of humanity. But the European conceptions of democracy (including liberal democracy, anarchism, workers' cooperatives, and socialist versions of republican participatory democracy) have entered China, and have become part of China's history. Before we specifically deal with Chinese adaptations of European ideals, we will have a look at two broad comparative frameworks.

India's Democracy in Comparison with China's

India is a federation with a strong central government. Since independence, the country has frequently been governed by coalitions (both national and provincial governments). Nehru's long rule (17 years as the head of the Congress Party and then first prime minister) resulted in strong attachment to procedures of electoral democracy. The combination of relatively fair elections and oppositional politics (checks and balances) lasted, even though challenged in the emergency under Indira Gandhi, communal unrest, and autocratic tendencies in federal states. Desai (2007, 35ff) describes how two constitutional features continuously reinforced electoral politics:

- The independence of the judiciary from the executive — such that acts of government can be challenged in court.

- The electoral commission that organises elections and is equal to and independent from all other branches of government.

Democratic procedures are further strengthened by affirmative action and universal suffrage. Affirmative action guarantees reserved places in electoral chambers and in higher education for members of the untouchable castes (*dalits*) and the scheduled tribes (*adivasi*). Universal adult suffrage ensures that all parties must court the votes of the entire population, including the poor masses, lower castes, minorities, and women.

Chatterjee (2004) characterises the courting of votes in India as 'political society', in which the universalising conceptions of electoral democracy and of civil society are in the power of political elites who canvass votes through much more particularising appeals to communal identities. The result is a coalition politics of Indian society, differentiated into constituencies of interest, which are often religious (Sikh, Muslim, Christian, Buddhist) or caste-based (Hindu) as well as political (Communist, Congress). In Chapter 15 on civil society, we asked whether we can describe another 'political society' in China.

The government of these electoral coalitions is clearly different from the centralised, non-federal, and non-electoral rule of the Communist Party in China. Yet, provincial leaders and governments also enjoy substantial autonomy and independent bargaining positions in China (even though their loyalties might not necessarily be attached to locality). Negotiations between provincial governments and the centre generally take place behind the scenes and not in open elections.

Compared to India, few substantial minorities of religion or ethnicity are present in China (aside from the provinces of Tibet, Xinjiang, Qinghai, and Inner Mongolia). There is no divide based on religion and nationalism as between Hindu and Muslim populations of India exacerbated by communalist political mobilisation.

Hence, even if open elections for leaders were held, it is not likely that similar religious/ethnic political mobilisation comparable to India would occur.

In China, there is a history of breaking up into warlord domains (1919–1927). There is a constant fear of division; and the leadership of the Communist Party refuses to consider more federal government (the variously relative autonomies of Hongkong, Taiwan, Tibet, Xinjiang, and Inner Mongolia, are a constant problem, for instance).

Democracy and Development

Peerenboom (2007) restates a classical argument that there has to be economic development first, before deeper processes of democratisation will be possible in China. The sociologist Seymour Martin Lipset had formulated the following sequence: sufficient general prosperity will lead to a powerful middle class; only such a middle class can meaningfully participate in civil society and demand a say in government; and only with such a civil society will there be a meaningful democracy.

Peerenboom relies mainly on two historical facts: First, what he calls the 'East Asian Model' of development. This includes Japan, and the 'four dragons' of newly industrialised countries, that is, Hong Kong, Singapore, Taiwan and South Korea. Second, the record of waves of developing countries that introduced electoral means of selecting their governments, in Africa, Latin America, and Southeast Asia. In most of these cases, there was prosperity before democracy. Peerenboom also refers to indices and opinion polls, from China and elsewhere, which show that people give priority to well-being over democracy.

He contrasts this with the failures of countries that are officially democracies, but have only low levels of economic development (measured in income per capita). These countries often fail in terms of politics: elected leaders turn into autocrats; political instabilities sometimes lead to civil war. These countries are also relative failures in terms of further economic development: they remained poor, and wealth remained confined to a privileged elite (note that Peerenboom counts India among these countries, pointing out high levels of corruption and civil-war-like conditions of many northern states). Peerenboom concludes that the Chinese Communist Party (CCP) is right to give priority to prosperity over democracy. Unless an economic crisis becomes a political crisis and there is a sudden transition to multi-party or factional politics, there will be managed economic growth and managed gradual transition to increasing electoral democracy. This will be brought about by the already apparent formation of a technocratic elite.

There is some similarity between Peerenboom's argument and Chatterjee's description of elitist civil society and guided 'political society'. Mobilisation and technocratic governance in both arguments correspond to relatively limited political participation. But the concept of democracy that both Chatterjee and Peerenboom use is a liberal one. And there is, in fact, a very different tradition of thinking about democracy in modern China, namely the Maoist concept of 'people's democratic dictatorship' based on mass participation and the mass line.

People's Democracy in China

In her work on the *Transformations of Chinese Socialism*, Lin Chun (2006) considers in detail the intellectual history of (Maoist) democracy in China. Mao's 'people's democracy' is based on Marx's and Lenin's criticism of liberal democracy; they had pointed out that liberal democracy was distorted and limited by class and colonial oppression of capitalist imperialism. Lenin, instead, suggested 'democratic centralism', that is, participation under an authoritarian state that, through the Party, mobilises participation. One important source for Lenin were Marx's writings about the 1871 Paris Commune. During the siege of the city by the Prussian army, the people of Paris had created a popular government formed of delegates of workers and residents. The Paris Commune became a model for the 'Soviet' councils in urban Russia, which formed a basis for the Russian Revolution in 1917.

But for Lenin, the leadership was still clearly with the avant-garde party. Mao, on the contrary, further emphasised the role of society, and participation. As Lin writes (2006, p. 137, citing Blecher, 1997, p. 220): 'while most authoritarian states seek to insulate themselves from society by repressing it into quiescence the Maoist state chose instead to rule by activating society ... It wanted believers, not subjects'.

Maoist democracy also, to some extent, took up elements of Confucian traditions, such as the 'people-rooteness' (*minben*) about which thinkers such as Mencius had written. The latter had interpreted the people's well-being as the heavenly mandate of rule: 'heaven sees as the people see, heaven hears as the people hear', (Lin, 2006, p. 140). In these formulations, the people are the 'root of government', and rulers are required to be responsive to the people's will (*minyi*). Lin Chun contrasts this with the more exclusive direct democracy of educated political citizens in the European traditions stemming from the city-state of Athens (pp. 189–190). The people's will in China, on the contrary, originated from the people unified by a government responsive to petition and to the sanction that it can be overthrown when it is seen to have lost the mandate of heaven, which — again — is linked to the people's will symptomatically.

The people's democracy of Mao Zedong is then a radicalisation of Mencius: it makes the people themselves into Heaven, instead of a people owing deference to Heaven. 'Democratic citizenship …. and revolutionary mobilisation fundamentally contradict "patrimonial rulership with a human face"' (Lin, p. 142, quoting McCormick, 1990, pp. 195–196).

In these radical conceptions of popular sovereignty, the state and the system of exploitation are both to be overthrown in order to achieve a fuller, people's democracy. But 'people' must therefore exclude or at least disempower those who want to continue with the old system. How that problem of exclusion is dealt with is one of the fundamental problems of socialist democracy.

Mass Line and the Inherent Contradictions of People's Democracy

This radical notion of democracy faces a series of internal contradictions. Perhaps, the most fundamental one is how to combine direct and representative democracy? Even though Maoists emphasise the former, some kind of representation and leadership through party and state remained necessary, hence the formulation of the 'dictatorship of the unified people' — or 'people's democratic dictatorship' in China.

Mao himself suggested the concept of the 'mass line' (*qunzhong luxian*), to deal with this fundamental problem. Party cadres had to always stand on the 'mass line', that means, they had to live with the people and 'serve the people'; yet, they also had to represent, unite, and supervise the people.

Concretely, this continuing engagement between cadres and people took place in the organisation of mass meetings, in which criticism and complaint were encouraged. Party officials had to continuously investigate the conditions and the grievances of the population. The results of mass meetings and investigations then had to be fed upwards, and meetings at higher levels would pool knowledge and formulate new policies and directives. A further institutionalisation of this engagement were the recurrent campaigns (*yundong*) (Bennett, 1976).

Another tradition from dynastic China that continues into republican China is the popular conception and hope that although the local officials are corrupt scourges, the higher levels, and especially the top of the government is virtuous and responsive to appeals. The person of the ultimate leader, especially Mao, figures as a sage ruler and Mao and his prime minister Zhou Enlai are now often enshrined on domestic altars and as door guardian gods. The Cultural Revolution can be seen as a battle over views of sage rulers and who was 'the people', who their enemy. Democratic deliberation and opposition among the people would on the other hand occur without the warlike structure.

Bureaucracy was, ideally, institutionalised as 'reciprocal accountability' (Lin, p. 145). Yet, this accountability could also become subject to abuse: cadres might turn responsiveness and accountability into dictatorial commands, which could lead to an emphasis on the dichotomy of friends and enemies, rather than further working on resolvable differences.

'People's democracy' therefore carried within itself 'insurmountable contradictions' (p. 140). It could easily be manipulated and turned into a personality cult (p. 167). It lacked laws and sanctions that could prevent participative democracy turning into cruel and vengeful criminality. Lin Chun calls it a 'totalitarian democracy' which 'emphasises elite idealism and popular enthusiasm mediated by ideological messianism' (p. 177).

Maoism was very contradictory in its encouragement of criticism, rebellion and opposition. Therefore, the label 'totalitarian' maybe too monolithic to describe Mao's government, which was much more flexible and self-adjustive. Indeed, it was this very quality which brought about the adjustments by Deng Xiaoping: rejection of people's democracy in favour of administrative efficiency and rule by law.

Lin Chun concludes that Deng's project of efficiency and legal regulation is itself a utopia betrayed by corruption and illegality, leaving the former participatory ideal of people's democracy as a potential alternative.

Procedural Democracy and 'Rule of Law' in China Now?

How does 'rule of law' relate to democracy? Liberal writers argue they are linked. Radical critics (including Lin Chun) would argue that it is more important to look at changing power relations, control of resources, and the representation of people than 'just' the making of the law.

People's congresses at every level of government consist in indirectly elected members who are delegates, not just representatives. They are not professional politicians, but go back to jobs when the congresses are not in session. Their selection as nominees for election is meant to reflect the range of age, religion, nationality and occupation in their region and to have some gender balance. But there is a built-in bias against rural residents. And the congresses have as yet not been able to assert much autonomous power in relation to the executive and the Party.

Even if the People's Congresses were to become more open to debate and differences of view, this would be an increase in democracy but not in the rule of law, because as they stand, there is a great imbalance of powers between the congresses and the courts of law. The congresses supervise the courts of law, all the way up to the Supreme Court and the courts of law do not check the statutes that are passed by the People's Congresses, though formally citizens can appeal for judicial review of official decisions through the Administration Litigation Law. So there is no effective check on the legislature by the judiciary.

Village Elections and Informal Politics

Lin Chun is quite dismissive about village elections and the current state of the law in the PRC. Others, such as Kevin O'Brien and Li Lianjiang (2000) see more potential in them than she does. Village elections were introduced in the early 1980s (He, 2006). Single-candidate, Party selected names of leaders of production teams were submitted for approval by elections in the Mao era. But in 1981, local governments experimented with multi-candidate direct elections every three years to the headship of the village committee, as well as elections of the chairs of villager representative assemblies. First test cases were later taken up by national levels and spread via the Ministry of Civil Affairs.

There are a number of sources of political power in administrative villages (*xingzheng cun*). Each section, or small group (*xiaozu*) of the neighbourhood elects a representative onto the *villager representative assembly*. The villager representative assembly also includes the following officers, selected by the township government: the village treasurer, village secretary, village women's officer, militia head, and others. They form the 'village committee', which leads the assembly. The assembly meets three or four times a year (Oi and Rozelle, 2000, p. 519). The representative assembly is a mix of elected and appointed members. The party secretary is appointed by the next higher level (mostly township) of the Party, and approved by village Party members. The Party Secretary is both the lowest policy-making and influencing cadre, and the main executive officer of the village administration. In more industrialised villages, there is sometimes a special *village economic committee or board of directors* consisting of the managers of the village enterprises, sometimes including the village head.

Kevin O'Brien and Li Lianjiang (2000) describe the political controversy surrounding village elections of the head of the committee. Support for village elections came from senior members of the Party, who argued that they were the only way to maintain supervision over local cadres, the Party disciplinary organs being unable to do so at the base level because there are just too many base level officials and cadres. Peng Zhen, one of the main supporters of village head elections, recalled his long advocacy of the mass line, from Yan'an onwards. The proponents of village elections encountered strong opposition from ministries and different levels of government, particularly the township level above the village, fearing that village electoral self-government would bring about chaos, disobedience to state policies and refusals to pay tax. Another source of opposition came from within the Party, fearing a pole of opposition to the authority of the Party Secretary. Those in favour said that, on the contrary, elected leaders could test the legitimacy of Party Secretaries and effectively discipline them, so improving the quality of Party members, and that reminders to pay taxes would be obeyed more readily if they came from elected heads of villages. The proponents won, but implementation of the law finally promulgated in 1989 that there should be elections in every village has frequently been avoided.

Findings from a survey in 1999, by a US–China studies team (Oi and Rozelle, 2000), show where elections were implemented most thoroughly, village administration (by Party secretary and others) has become more transparent (as measured by open publication of village accounts) and taxes have been more willingly paid in those villages as opposed to villages where elections had been avoided. There is also evidence that the elections had already by 1999 induced villagers to become more aware of laws in general and the law on village elections in particular as grounds for protesting against overweening officials and corrupt cadres (O'Brien and Li, 2000, pp. 481–483).

Village elections do set up two poles of official authority in a village, the Party branch whose secretary is nominated by the upper level of the Party and approved by village branch members, and the village committee whose head is elected by all the villagers.

While it seems that village elections in many places are well run according to standards such as strict registration of those eligible to vote, having more than one candidate, an open system of nomination, secret ballots and forbidding proxy voting, in many other places these standards are not applied. There are strong indicators that in villages where substantial economic gains are at stake, village elections become less important (Oi and Rozelle (2000) point out that this happens where village enterprises became share-holding companies).

On the basis of a survey of over 300 villages, Tsai (2007) shows that provision of public goods in the countryside depended on informal, non-governmental institutions of accountability, such as local temples and lineages, that included village leaders. Village elections properly conducted may have provided greater willingness to pay taxes, but it was not the main factor inducing the spending of funds on public goods such as roads and schools. Nor was the average income of villagers a good predictor of the provision of public goods. That depended strikingly on whether village Party Secretaries and elected leaders were also in the same non-governmental local organisations with fellow villagers. Through these non-governmental organisations, villagers could hold their leaders to account.

Feuchtwang (2003) also draws attention to the neglect of informal institutions in the Chinese countryside and their democratic potential. Writing about anthropologists in particular, his argument can be extended to many other intellectual observers of rural China (both Chinese and non-Chinese): elitism of intellectuals makes them blind to the democratic potential of informal rural institutions. But can such institutions (including, for instance, local leaders elected by divination) be justifiably called 'democratic'?

Since 2008, as we pointed out in Chapter 12, formal electoral democracy has been extended to city neighbourhoods' 'small communities' (*xiaoqu*). But as we also pointed out there, compared with village elections, the residents' participation in elections of their representatives has so far been very restricted. Small community representatives' offices are dominated by local Party members who seek to mobilise fellow residents to take part, with little success, and by the welfare officials of the Ministry of Civil Affairs. There is, of course, potential for fuller participation, particularly when residents have issues that they want to raise. But it is limited by the enjoyment of 'freedom from' by urban residents, as everywhere in the world, who form their own associations, work-based, family-based, or activity based, and take far less interest in urban representative assembly elections than villagers in their face-to-face neighbourhood social relations (see Feuchtwang, Morais and Zhang, 2015; Tomba, 2015).

Seminar Questions

Is people's democracy a legacy for a Chinese future?

Compare Chinese and Indian democracy (based on Desai, Chatterjee, Peerenboom and Lin).

If there are more village elections, petitions, and general knowledge of the law in China, does this imply there will be more democratic procedures and accountability?

Key Readings

Peerenboom, R. 2007. What if China democratizes? What if it doesn't?. Chapter 8 in his *China Modernizes: Threat to the West or Model for the Rest?* Oxford: Oxford University Press, pp. 257–281.

Lin Chun 2006. People's democracy? Chapter 3 of her *The Transformation of Chinese Socialism*. Durham: Duke University Press, pp. 132–204.

O'Brien, K. and Li Lianjiang 2000. Accommodating "democracy" in a one-party state: Introducing village elections in China. *China Quarterly* **162**, pp. 465–489.

Further Readings

Blecher, M. 1997, *China Against the Tides*. London: Pinter.

Bennett, G. 1976. *Yundong: Mass campaigns in Chinese Communist leadership*. China Research Monograph No. 12, Berkeley: University of California Centre for Chinese Studies.

Bernal, M. 1976. *Chinese Socialism to 1907*. Ithaca: Cornell University Press.

Bernstein, T., and Lu Xiaobo 2003. *Taxation without Representation in Contemporary Rural China*. Cambridge: Cambridge University Press.

Chatterjee, P. 2004. *The Politics of the Governed: Popular politics in Most of the World*. New York and London: Columbia University Press.

Chung Jaeho, Hongyi Lai and Ming Xia 2006. Mounting challenges to governance in China; surveying collective protestors, religious sects and criminal organisations. *The China Journal*, **56**, pp. 1–32.

Clarke, D. C. 2007a. The Chinese legal system since 1995: Steady development and striking continuities. *China Quarterly*, **191**, pp. 555–566.

Clarke, D. C. 2007b. Legislating for a market economy in China. *China Quarterly*, **191**, pp. 567–585.

Desai, M., and Ahsan A. (eds.) 2007. *Divided by Democracy*. Lotus Roli (Chapter by Desai).

Feuchtwang, S. 2003. Peasants, democracy and anthropology: Questions of local loyalty. *Critique of Anthropology*, **23**(1), pp. 93–120.

Feuchtwang, S., Zhang Hui and Morais, Paula. 2015. The formation of governmental community and the closure of housing classes. In Francois Gipouloux (ed.) *China's Urban Century: Governance, Environment and Socio-economic Imperatives*. London: Edward Elgar, pp. 195–212.

Fincher, J. 1981. *Chinese Democracy*. London: Croom Helm (Chapter 9 Differentiating democracy in twentieth-century China and Asia).

Guha, R. 2007. *India After Gandhi: The History of the World's Largest Democracy*, Basingstoke: Macmillan.

He Baogang 2007. *Rural Democracy in China*. Basingstoke: Palgrave Macmillan.

Hirschman, A. O. 1970. *Exit, Voice and Loyalty: Responses to Decline in Firms, Organisations and States*. Boston: Harvard University Press.

Hirst, P. 1994. *Associative Democracy*. Cambridge: Polity Press.

Laclau, E., and Chantal Mouffe. 2001. *Hegemony and Socialist Strategy: Towards a Radical Democratic Politics*. London: Verso.

Li Lianjiang 2008. Political trust and petitioning in the Chinese countryside. *Comparative Politics*, **40**(2) pp. 209–226.

Lieb, E. J., and He Baogang (eds.) 2006. *The Search for Deliberative Democracy in China*. Basingstoke: Palgrave Macmillan.

McCormick, B. 1990. *Political Reform in Post-Mao China: Democracy and Bureaucracy in a Leninist State*. Berkeley: University of California Press.

O'Brien, K. 2004. Neither transgressive nor contained: Boundary-spanning contention in China. In Peter. Gries, and Stanley Rosen (eds.) *State and Society in Twenty-first-century China*. London: Routledge/Curzon, pp. 105–122.

Oi, J. C., and Rozelle, S. 2000. Elections and power: The locus of decision making in Chinese Villages. *The China Quarterly*, **162**, pp. 513–539.

Tilly, C. 2007. *Democracy*. Cambridge: Cambridge University Press (Chapters 1 and 7).

Thogersen, Stig, Jorgen Elklit and Dang Lisheng 2008. Consultative elections of Chinese township leaders: the case of an experiment in Ya'an, Sichuan' *China Information* XXII:1, pp. 67–90.

Tomba, Luigi 2014. *The Government Next Door. Neighbourhood Politics in Urban China*. Ithaca and London: Cornell University Press.

Tsai, Lily 2007. *Accountability without Democracy: Solidary groups and public Goods Provision in Rural China*. Cambridge: Cambridge University Press.

Han Han 2011(a,b,c).

http://www.zonaeuropa.com/201112a.brief.htm#008.

http://www.zonaeuropa.com/201112a.brief.htm#009.

http://www.zonaeuropa.com/201112a.brief.htm#011.

http://blog.sina.com.cn/s/blog_4701280b0102dz9f.html.

http://blog.sina.com.cn/s/blog_4701280b0102dz84.html.

http://www.wenxuecity.com/news/2011/12/22/1576946.html.

Chapter 18

Conclusion

For every topic in which we put China into comparative perspective, from empire to democracy, we have asked whether China is an exception. And every time, the answer is mainly 'no' but also 'yes'. That is itself no exception. Whichever history and country we might have considered in depth, as we have China, the answer would have been the same. But the 'yes' is also what is most interesting because it forces us to review the ways those topics have been treated. It forces us to pay them critical attention. This book has provided the means for a critical review of the various social sciences we have covered and brought Chinese history and current realities to bear on them.

How We Have Proceeded

We started this book with a warning against the Eurocentrism of most concepts and theories in social sciences. Instead, we recommended looking at the ways in which *centrisms* work, including Sinocentrism, as well as orientalism and occidentalism. Now, in conclusion, we can see that every universalising claim can harbour useful conceptions, but must also be seen to bear a bias and a project of the country in which the claim is made. Universal truths are proclaimed as part of a country's being in the world of states. Many of the universalising ideas of humanity, individualism, rule of law, civil society and democracy come as part and parcel of

European imperialism and the spread of nation-states in revolutionary liberation from it. But, when we see how these ideas have been adopted and adapted in China and its relevant comparators, such as India, Russia or Japan, we can see that not only do they come head to head with other universalising conceptions of humanity and moral sovereignty in their own and regional histories. These other conceptions also challenge the basic concepts of the individual, of the state, or of rights. Each has to be reconceived in order to accommodate the other and the practical realities that pretend to endorse them.

Observing these mutual adaptations and making comparisons, as we have, does not force us to substitute the Indocentric or the Sinocentric for each other or for the Eurocentric. Instead, they force us to find bases for rethinking them so that all these centrisms can be accommodated. One such basis is a resort to middle-level theory, for instance, on what are the common characteristics of all modern states and nationalisms or what are the common characteristics of all rural–urban migration. Another is to look for more basic theories of, for instance, the human self, to say that all humans act both as individual and as social beings. And then see how different historically transmitted social formations of a reasoning and moral self fare under the common conditions of modern states and city residential conditions. Or we see how democracy can be reconceived in several different variants on the more basic criteria of accountability and responsiveness, or exit and voice. Or how dichotomies such as patriarchy and matriarchy, hierarchy and equality are in practice combined in the way families and gender relations work, business relations and trust established, indeed how everywhere and not just in China, contractual and maximising economic conduct is mixed with personalising, emotionally loaded and lasting relationships.

In support of these conceptual explorations, we have offered extended empirical comparisons with China. Some have been with Europe, but many have been with India and the Soviet Union and the Russian Federation. One of the advantages of such comparisons in detail is that it trains us to avoid dichotomies, China and the rest, or the West and the rest. But the main advantage is that we select the comparators according to a number of explicit and obvious similarities with China and then drive toward specifying how exactly they differ on this common ground of similarity, be it the project of socialism or the rule of law in conditions of anti-colonialism or of development.

Chinese Peculiarities? The Self

Readers will have made up their own minds about the ways in which China in comparison has shown you in what ways China is peculiar, if not exceptional. We will not come to any firm conclusions, but instead expound two that may have occurred to you.

One is the familial sense of self that carries the label 'Confucianism'. In Chapter 1, we introduced the great Chinese anthropologist Fei Xiaotong's concept of Chinese acting on the basis of an other-oriented, or differentiated self. This sense of self is a life project, a project of maturing if possible to a person respected for their responsiveness to others. Anthropologists have observed this in everyday practice. Philosophers have elaborated it as a system of role ethics based on close reading of a wide range of classical Chinese texts. There is nothing peculiarly Chinese about the self being differentiated. Indeed, this is the common condition of all peoples, but just as the social self was ideologically contained in England by an historically developed individualism of yeoman farmer freedom of property owners, Chinese history produced a deferential individual and an ethics of responsiveness (*ren* and *renqing*) as the basis for acting in capitalist economic orders of private property and competitive calculation of interests. The Chinese differentiated and deferential self and the self-discipline that is required and expected in order to maintain what we have heard Chinese people call 'social capacity' (*shehui nengli*), mediations between third parties and the making of interpersonal networks of relationships can be counted as a central characteristic of civilisation in China.

It is the Chinese version of the universally human social, differentiated and divided and other-oriented social being. And Yan Yunxiang's studies (2003) show how it has been changed by absorption of the individualism and independence that young people in China now also aspire to.

This differential and networking self and the role ethics it obeys is the basis of a great deal of business practice in China. But again we should not mistake its peculiarity to China to mean that Chinese business is peculiarly prone to networking and establishing interpersonal, as well as or as part and parcel of contractual relationships. It just consists in the particularly Chinese way of all business social relationships. One of the reasons that global finance and its headquarters staff enjoy the zones of the so-called global cities between which they travel (see Chapter 12) is precisely the expensive venues where they can establish interpersonal relations, each in their own way and in each other's ways.

Chinese Peculiarities? The Party

Our second example of a way in which contemporary China may be peculiar is far less old. It is the great importance of its central institution, a single ruling party.

As we mentioned in Chapter 6, Henrietta Harrison, the acute political and social historian of republican China, has characterised the ideology of Chinese nation formation as 'state patriotism' — the demand for loyalty to the ruling party that has liberated its people — be it the Guomindang (the Nationalist Party) or the Communist Party. Being ruled by means of a single party is not in itself peculiar, of course. The Soviet Union was ruled through a single Leninist party and Russia is a close approximation under Putin, although not with the same ideology. Japan's Liberal Democratic Party has ruled since its foundation in 1955 for all but three years. The common ground of 'single-party rule' demands greater specificity of us: in what way is the rule of the Chinese Communist Party (CCP) peculiarly different from both the Guomindang and the other one-party ruling states?

Chapters 7–9 spelled out the differences of the CCP from the Bolshevik Party and their respective states and the successors to those states. Among these are the legacy of the Maoist mass line and people's democracy: what remains is unrest as backing for appeals to higher levels to right the wrongs committed by lower; there has been abatement but not abandonment of its mobilisation politics — for instance, the mobilisation of residents to vote for their representatives in Residents' Committees; there has been separation of Party from state bureaucracies, but still with Party Committees at their every level.

Another of its differences from other single parties of government is that it has a presence in every large firm, private and state-owned, as well as every state, including educational, work unit. The Party's own policy-making hierarchy of Party Congresses, culminating in the top-level Politbureau, still dominates the People's Congresses of civic delegates. In addition, it exists as a branch and its committee at all units of the so-called 'collective' and 'community' governance, below that of the lowest level of state.

There is within it an electoral mechanism by which its committee members are chosen by branches and congresses, but always subject to higher-level approval of candidates. So, it looks like a huge autocracy and the means of maintaining autocratic rule. Its own disciplinary policing works without recourse to judicial courts, even while it encourages the people of China, who according to its ideology the Party serves, to have recourse to the law. As discussed in Chapter 16, this is rule by law more than rule of law. In every other topic we have covered, including fertility control in work units or property rights and the controls over strategic economic sectors, we have had to mention the CCP as a key institution.

There are other Communist Parties with the same powers, in North Korea and in Vietnam and Laos. The CCP has ruled over the radical loosening of state controls over the economy, just as the Vietnamese equivalent has, the Laotian less, and the North Korean even less. So, it is not unique. But in one respect it might be. Since it adopted the so-called theory of representing the most advanced forces of production (science and technology of production, enterprise and management), the highest culture (education and civilisation), and the broadest interests of the majority of the population, the Party has expanded to include everyone except those declared as treasonous enemies of the people and state as a means of furthering their career. Though by no means everyone in research, in business, or in cultural production does choose to seek nomination to become a Party member, the inclusive policy has made the Party one of the largest organisations in the world. With around 90 million members, it organises more than 40 times the number of employees of the world's largest employers such as Walmart or the British National Health Service. The chief executive officers of the largest global agglomerate corporations, such as the banks, were shown by revelations following the

2008 crash not to know well how the organisations under their formal command, which includes the making and implementation of strategic planning, work.

Looking at the top, it is possible to think of the leadership of the CCP as political strategists with an ideology of Chinese civilisation (its having re-found a powerful place in the world) and Party control. But networks and client-patron factions exist at all levels (as found in Pieke, 2015). Control is at best more like guidance from the top, commanding a performance of loyalty and obedience that allows for much leeway and reinterpretation, differences with and dilutions of what the next higher level of state officialdom and of Party hierarchy inspects as compliance with performance targets (Birney, 2014). Seen from the grassroots, Party members, retired members, officials and veterans of the armed forces are coordinators and improvisers of local variations in the imperfect and fragmented policy that the Party makes, as Thireau and Hua (2002), Steinmuller (2013, pp. 217–222) and Pia (2016) found in villages and Feuchtwang, Morais and Zhang (2015, pp. 196–198) in cities.

This is an institution that centralises and mediates governmental responses to changing conditions. It constitutes a unique form of governance and makes us re-think what a modern state, or a developmental state, or a nation-state may be.

We leave you with these two answers to 'yes' China is exceptional: self cultivation and governance through a huge Party, as food for further thought. They are just two of many issues that you can raise from the study of China in comparative perspective. This book is an exercise for finding your own answers.

Further Readings

Ames, R. 2011. *Confucian Role Ethics: A Vocabulary*. University of Hawai'i Press.

Birney, M. 2014. Decentralisation and veiled corruption under China's rule of mandates. *World Development*, **53**, pp. 55–67.

Feuchtwang, S., Morais P., and Hui, Z. 2015. The formation of governmental community and the closure of housing classes. In *China's Urban Century: Governance, Environment and Socio-economic imperatives*, Francois Gipouloux (ed.). London: Edward Elgar, pp. 195–212.

Pia, A. (forthcoming, 2017). "We follow reason, not the law": Disavowing the law in rural China. *Political and Legal Anthropology Review*.

Pieke, F. 2015. Cadre training and the party school system in contemporary China'. In *The EU-China Relationship: European Perspectives. A Manual for Policy Makers,* Brown, K. (ed.). London: Imperial College Press. pp. 82–87.

Steinmuller, H. 2013. *Communities of Complicity: Everyday Ethics in Rural China*. New York and Oxford, Berghahn Books.

Thireau, I., and Hua, L. 2002. Power beyond instituted power: Forms of mediation spaces in the Chinese countryside'. In *Politics in China: Moving Frontiers*, Mengin, F., and Rocca, J. (eds.). New York: Palgrave Macmillan

Yan, Yunxiang 2003. *Private Life under Socialism: Love, Intimacy, and Family Change in a Chinese Village 1949–1999.* Stanford, CA: Stanford University Press.

Index